D1520488

"This 'final word' from Australian liturgical theologian Graham Hughes is a distinctive and rich contribution to contemporary discussions about sacramentality. He ably demonstrates the need to balance disseminated sacramentality with a 'condensed' sacramentality, through which our awareness of the sacred is found in specific trusted material actions, our physicality is acknowledged and engaged in Christian worship, and our encounter with God is given physical form."

—E. Byron Anderson
    Styberg Professor of Worship
    Garrett-Evangelical Theological Seminary

"The Reformed tradition is in need of sacramental reform! This timely work comes to light in an era in which brain research makes clear that human knowing arises from sensory engagement with the material and social environment. This bold and provocative work by Hughes calls for a fundamental reconsideration of the role of embodiment in Reformed approaches to baptism and the Lord's Supper. Taking cues from a robust Christology that highlights Christ as the icon of God, Hughes provides a fresh way of thinking about the fusion of materiality and the sacred in the sacraments. Lösel's introductory essay provides illumination and context for the thought-provoking challenges offered here."

—Rev. Dr. Gordon S. Mikoski
    Princeton Theological Seminary

Reformed Sacramentality

Graham R. Hughes

Edited and Introduced by Steffen Lösel
Foreword by Gordon W. Lathrop

A PUEBLO BOOK

Liturgical Press   Collegeville, Minnesota

www.litpress.org

A Pueblo Book published by Liturgical Press

Cover design by Monica Bokinskie

1	2	3	4	5	6	7	8	9

Library of Congress Cataloging-in-Publication Data

Names: Hughes, Graham, 1937–2015, author. | Lösel, Steffen, editor.
Title: Reformed sacramentality / Graham Hughes ; edited by Steffen Lösel ;
    foreword by Gordon W. Lathrop.
Description: Collegeville, Minnesota : Liturgical Press, 2017. | Includes
    bibliographical references. | Description based on print version record
    and CIP data provided by publisher; resource not viewed.
Identifiers: LCCN 2017004824 (print) | LCCN 2017025455 (ebook) | ISBN
    9780814663790 (ebook) | ISBN 9780814663547
Subjects: LCSH: Sacramentals. | Liturgics. | Reformed Church—Doctrines.
Classification: LCC BV875 (ebook) | LCC BV875 .H84 2017 (print) | DDC
    264/.042—dc23
LC record available at https://lccn.loc.gov/2017004824

Contents

Foreword

When Graham Hughes died in February 2015 we lost an exceedingly important voice in worldwide ecumenical liturgical theology. That voice was known principally in his magisterial *Worship as Meaning: A Liturgical Theology for Late Modernity* (Cambridge: Cambridge University Press, 2003). But it also echoed in many articles and shorter books, in the memory of many of his students in Australia and New Zealand, in memorable conversations he had over the years undertaken with other scholars at Congresses of *Societas Liturgica*, and especially in the hearts of his colleagues and friends. Still, he had much more to say. The loss was thus the greater as many people came to know that Graham had been at work on yet another important book, this one on the issues involved in a Reformed Christian approach to sacramental meaning and practice, a book he did not live to finish.

But the loss has at least some mitigation. *Mirabile dictu*, this present volume is that book—or *nearly* that book. Graham did leave several articles which had been conceived as part of the total project, and he did leave two chapters of the projected manuscript. Through the kindness and skill of two people—William Emilsen, one of Graham's closest friends and colleagues, and Steffen Lösel, one of his most insightful interpreters—and through the willingness of Liturgical Press in Collegeville, those fragments toward a book have been assembled here into something very close to the book Graham intended. The book has been marvelously filled out by an interpretive introduction by Lösel and the record of a conversation

Emilsen had with Graham shortly before his death, a conversation which clearly articulates what Graham was doing with this work.

If you do not know Graham Hughes's work, let me urge you to begin with Lösel's introduction. There you will find not only an outline of the argument in the chapters to follow but also a lucid and inviting summary of the contents of *Worship as Meaning*. I have long said that *Worship as Meaning* is not only a hugely significant contribution to the field of liturgical theology but also the clearest and most helpful study I know of how "meaning" functions in our late-modern/"postmodern" times and why this concern is significant for Christian worship. Lösel's introduction is a worthy interpretation of that book—and a worthy invitation to this present new book—not least because of its own brilliant clarity.

And if you do not think that questions involved in *Reformed* sacramental theology concern you, let me urge you to think again. It is not only that healthy practice of baptism and the Lord's Supper in the worldwide Reformed churches matters to all Christians. It is also that many of the questions so well dealt with here are questions for anyone, Catholic, Protestant, or Orthodox, who thinks about Christian liturgy: the sacraments as images; the signifying work of the sacraments; the relationship of materiality and the divine as also of idolatry and faith; and counsel for all of us on how to avoid disappointing and trivializing sacramental practice that has the assembly—or at least those in the assembly who care about meaning—scrambling to do most of the interpretation in their own individual heads.

Hughes began *Worship as Meaning* with the image of a woman coming anew into a church. He continued his exploration into liturgical meaning with this arriving woman never far from mind. Indeed, she functioned as Hughes's "Mrs. Murphy"; and she returned in the summarizing epilogue to the book. But if that book could be said to be framed by a "subject entering a church unfamiliar to her" (*Worship as Meaning*, p. 300), then this present book moves well beyond that initial entrance. It is deeply concerned with the central matters at the heart of the meaning making and meaningful assembly.

In 1519, Martin Luther wrote a series of treatises or "sermons" on the sacraments, in which he sought to explore their significance, to urge people to practice them in such a way that the practice would be "a true and complete sign of the thing it signifies,"[1] and to invite people to trust God through them. *Sign, significance, faith*: such was his Augustinian pastoral hermeneutics. For Luther, the faithful sign needed to be immersion for baptism, communal eating and drinking for Eucharist, and the clear announcement of absolution for penance. In many ways it feels to me as if the chapters you are about to read are Graham Hughes's late-modern version of these treatises, his plea for strong sign, profound significance, and responding faith. Indeed, immersion—or, at least, more water!—and beautiful, communal eating and drinking are part of his argument for the sacraments as images. We would do well to pay attention.

Graham Hughes was a practicing Christian; he was a theologian who went to church and cared deeply about what going to church was like for anyone. Before he was a seminary professor, he was a parish pastor. And before he was either, he was a New Testament scholar and a baptized Christian. His New Testament connection was always fascinating to me; I too had done my doctoral studies in New Testament, though I had worked on Mark, while Graham wrote on Hebrews and hermeneutics.

I vividly recall my last face-to-face conversation with Graham. We were at the 2013 Congress of *Societas Liturgica* in Würzburg, Germany, and we were talking at length about sacraments. In classic Lutheran-Reformed mode—perhaps in classic Markan–Letter to the Hebrews mode—I was defending the paradox of *finitum capax infiniti* and the idea of the ubiquity of the "right hand of God." Graham was having none of it. But he was reinterpreting Calvin for current need in a beguiling and helpful way. It struck me at the time that Reformed ease with philosophy and Lutheran concern for existential meaning need each other, just as they both need Catholic materiality. I was to see more of that beguiling way and its importance as, after his return to Australia and in the year that followed our conversation, Graham sent me a first chapter of

---

1. Martin Luther, "The Blessed and Holy Sacrament of Baptism, 1519," 1, in *The Roots of Reform*, ed. Timothy J. Wengert, vol. 1 of *The Annotated Luther*, ed. Hans J. Hillerbrand, Kirsi I. Stjerna, and Timothy J. Wengert (Minneapolis: Fortress, 2015), 207.

his new book. You will find both that chapter and that inviting way in this volume.

It is clear from the final exchanges between Hughes and Emilsen, the exchanges that conclude this volume, that Graham ended the interview reluctantly, ambiguously even, as if he had more he really wanted to say but not at all the energy to say it. Emilsen: "Do you mind if we pause now?" Hughes: "I think so." Emilsen: "I think that would be good."

That would be good.

Graham Hughes ends reluctantly, and we reluctantly let him go. Surely he needs to rest.

But thanks to the work he did in the last years and months of his life, and thanks to William Emilsen and Steffen Lösel, this book is indeed very good.

Gordon W. Lathrop
Societas Liturgica
Past-President
All Saints Day 2016

Introduction

Steffen Lösel

1. Graham Hughes: A Short Introduction

When Graham Robert Hughes published his magisterial *Worship as Meaning: A Liturgical Theology for Late Modernity* with Cambridge University Press in 2003, he was already a well-known liturgical authority in Australia. Down Under, the book represented the pinnacle of his literary career. Worldwide, it established him as an authoritative voice in liturgics to be reckoned with. Of course, Graham's many friends at the international *Societas Liturgica* had known him well for a long time as an insightful thinker and beautiful writer. But *Worship as Meaning* broadened his scholarly prominence far beyond the inner circle of the liturgical world.

That Hughes would one day become one of the world's preeminent *liturgical* scholars had not always been clear. He grew up on a farm in rural New Zealand with parental expectations that eventually he would take over responsibility there. By the age of twenty-one, however, he experienced a call to the ministry through the preaching of one of his evangelical pastors, and he embarked on the journey toward ordained ministry in the church. Even though he had not enjoyed the privileges of a humanistic education in classical languages, which makes the study of theology so much easier, he not only acquired supreme command in Greek but also in theology. After his first two degrees at the University of Otago (bachelor of arts and master of arts in Classical Greek), he went on to do postgraduate studies in Cambridge, England, and eventually became a promising New Testament scholar whose dissertation on the Epistle to the Hebrews received scholarly acclaim.

After completing his dissertation, Hughes became a parish pastor in New Zealand for five years before he received a postdoctoral fellowship at the University of Otago, at the end of which, in 1977, he successfully applied for a position in New Testament Studies at United Theological College in Sydney, Australia. There, Graham's career developed over the course of three decades: first, as a New Testament scholar, or perhaps more precisely as a scholar of biblical theology, and later, since the mid-1980s, upon the prompting of his then-dean, as a professor in the fields of worship and preaching—a field which had not been taught before at his school and which finally assumed the name of Liturgical Studies. As Graham once remembered in an interview with his friend and colleague, William W. Emilsen, he had already moved toward an interest in biblical hermeneutics and the reception of the biblical texts by other communities of listeners. Therefore, the move over to the study of worship and preaching was well prepared for.

Since the early 1980s, then, Hughes taught preaching and worship at the United Theological College and in this capacity trained several generations of pastors and ministers in the church of Australia to appreciate what Emilsen and John T. Squires aptly named as Graham's passion for "doxological excellence."[1] As a minister and scholar in the Reformed tradition, Graham was not a natural liturgist. As he is quick to point out at several occasions in this new book, the Reformed tradition has since its inception de-emphasized the material aspects of the church's liturgy in favor of an almost exclusive emphasis on the spoken, seemingly nonmaterial word. And yet, Graham developed a zeal for liturgy born from an acute awareness of the inadequacies of much of Protestant worship. As he put it in 2002, "I was reaching for more aesthetic and satisfying forms of worship, forms based not just in words and on the sermon."[2] Naturally, as we would expect, introducing Protestant students into

---

1. *Prayer and Thanksgiving: Essays in Honour of Rev. Dr. Graham Hughes,* ed. William W. Emilsen and John T. Squires (Sydney: UTC Publications, 2003), v.
2. Ibid., 4.

more sacramental and materially rich forms of liturgy encountered significant opposition rooted in a long anti-Catholic tradition.[3]

Hughes's search for more material forms of signification drawn from the wells of the church's rich liturgical tradition has been the mark of his scholarship from the beginning. It expresses a deep conviction—rooted philosophically in the insights of late-modern thought—that the human person is an inseparable unity of body and spirit. Meaningful worship will therefore have to engage the totality of its human recipients with all of their senses. Similarly, liturgical leadership must emerge from the totality of a human being. It must, as Hughes put it in 2002, involve two aspects: "[O]ne is, as with a musical instrument, one must practise it so as to store it, so to speak, in one's 'muscle memory.' . . . The other is that a liturgical leader will actually show in her or his practice the prayer life that he or she exercises in private. One should not be a liturgical leader—lead public prayer—if one is not practising prayer in one's personal life."[4] In other words, liturgical leadership must emerge from the whole embodied human person. And it is not simply a task to be routinely performed, which one can separate from one's own personal existence.

This appreciation for the materiality of the human person and hence the materiality of all forms of human communication and signification has led Hughes to affirm, first, the importance of a eucharistic spirituality. Hughes recognizes in the Eucharist a strong communal element, which "draws people out of their individuality" and which "draws us into community."[5] He notes historically that an emphasis on sacramental worship has, at least in nineteenth-century Anglicanism, often been combined with an urge to social action and outreach into the community. For Hughes, this development might not have been accidental: "[I]t seems to me that a mission ideal which is organised around *personal conversion* tends to see people being saved out of their places of deprivation, whereas a mission which is organized [sic] on the basis of Eucharist and of *eucharistic community* tends to go and live in those places and,

3. See ibid., 6.
4. Ibid., 5.
5. Ibid., 7 and 8.

as it were, generate mission *in* rather than taking people *out* of their social situation."[6] Accordingly, Hughes's wish was to establish a strong eucharistic spirituality in his own Reformed tradition, which has lost both an appreciation of the Eucharist and often a sense of communal spirituality.

If Hughes emphasized the importance of sacramental and especially eucharistic forms of worship and spirituality, he was also invested in the rediscovery of rich semiotic forms of worship. For him, this emphasis on what his colleague and friend, Lutheran liturgical theologian Gordon Lathrop, aptly calls "strong and primary symbols" has to do primarily with the semiotic character of worship.[7] Worship is a communicative event. It constitutes primarily a sort of communication between God and the Christian congregation. But worship includes also communication between those who lead worship and those who actively participate in worship. As an event of communication, worship—or liturgy, as Hughes sometimes prefers to say—involves meaning, and meaning for its part is communicated through symbols: through words, actions, things, times, and spaces. This is where semiosis comes in: for the meaning of these symbols to be best understood, they have to be as strong as possible. The things of the liturgy need to be meaningful. That is, they need to be *full* of meaning. To express an act of washing, one needs to use a sufficient amount of water. To communicate the community of a shared meal, one best breaks a real loaf of bread and uses a handsome cup full of wine. The material things we use in worship matter, because they express meanings, and some do so more strongly than others.

2. Worship as Meaning

This recognition of worship as a communicative event necessitates a discussion of Hughes's *magnum opus*, *Worship as Meaning*. In this groundbreaking work, Hughes lays out a semiotic theory of worship as an event of communication, which involves the production and

---

6. Ibid., 9.

7. Gordon W. Lathrop, *Holy Things: A Liturgical Theology* (Minneapolis: Augsburg Fortress, 1993), 5.

reception of meaning. Hughes's guiding question is how meaning emerges in worship. How, to put it differently, can a participant in a worship service make sense of what happens in this communal event? Hughes avers that a proper understanding of how meaning develops in worship provides an important step to overcoming the crisis of Christianity in the late-modern age.

a) Charles S. Peirce and Semiosis

In order to answer this question of meaning, Hughes turns to American philosopher Charles S. Peirce's theory of semiosis. On the backdrop of a discussion of late modernity or postmodernity, Hughes applies Peirce's semiotic theory to the event of public worship. According to Peirce, whom Hughes follows closely, meaning is not simply a given in the world—something that just exists— but rather something that emerges from the interaction between its producers and its recipients.[8] Hence, meaning is not static but develops in an active process of communication, more specifically, in the exchange of signs, which involves respective responsibilities on all sides.[9]

In his theory of meaning, Peirce distinguishes three distinct factors: the producer, the recipient, and the interpramen or interpretative context, which allows for the production and reception of meaning in the first place.[10] Similarly, for Peirce, each sign as the carrier of meaning involves three factors: the signifier, the signified, and the interpretant, or else: the representamen, the object, and the interpretant.[11] Again, for the signifier or representamen to actually communicate the meaning of what is signified, that is, its object, a third factor must join the first two: the interpramen, which supplies possible interpretations to both the producer and the recipient of meaning.

8. Against, for example, the position of Karl-Heinz Menke, *Sakramentalität: Wesen und Wunde des Katholizismus*, 2nd ed. (Regensburg: Verlag Friedrich Pustet, 2012), 88. Menke argues rather too matter-of-factly that meaning is factual.

9. See Graham Hughes, *Worship as Meaning: A Liturgical Theology for Late Modernity* (Cambridge: Cambridge University Press, 2003), 41, 62, and 185. On the question of respective responsibilities, see ibid., 193–94.

10. See ibid., 62.

11. See ibid., 62, 122, and 184–85.

Peirce's theory of meaning is distinct in that it offers a triadic rather than simply a dyadic view of meaning. It distinguishes itself herein from that of Swiss linguist Ferdinand de Saussure (1857–1913). In his theory, Peirce puts the emphasis on the interpramen as the third factor of meaning making: a factor that mediates between the producer and the recipient of the sign. For meaning to occur, the interpramen or interpretant must join its producer to its recipient. As Hughes puts it, "Successful semiosis, a meaningful transaction of meaning . . . depends upon the ability of both producer and recipient to bring their respective interpretants sufficiently close for their mutual satisfaction."[12] Meaning, in other words, is not simply a given. Rather, it has to occur. Meaning is both made and found, both construction and discovery.[13] It "is made; but it is not made *ex nihilo*."[14] It is therefore neither arbitrary nor relativistic. It is a grasping together of identity and difference: not just of identity, as modernity had it, but neither simply of difference, as deconstruction insisted.[15] Although there are no absolute certainties, we can still give what Charles Taylor calls a "Best Account,"[16] an account that is—in Paul Ricoeur's term—followable.[17] And in this entire meaning making, it is something we do: an action.[18]

Since it cannot be assumed in an a priori fashion that the producer and the recipient of meaning share the same interpretants, meaning making is always a fragile endeavor, however. It consists of "identity and difference" and inevitably runs the risk of failure.[19] What one person means to say is never exactly identical with what another understands. In the extreme case, the recipient of a sign is incapable of understanding it altogether. Here, the producer and the

12. Ibid., 185.

13. See ibid., 63–65. Here, Hughes tries to avoid the one-sidedness of positivism, on the one hand, and phenomenology, on the other.

14. Ibid., 75.

15. See ibid., 82 and 83.

16. Ibid., 71, with reference to Charles Taylor, *Sources of the Self: The Making of the Modern Identity* (Cambridge: Cambridge University Press, 1989), 57.

17. See Hughes, *Worship as Meaning*, 72–73. Hughes points out that Ricoeur borrowed the term "followability" from Walter Bryce Gallie, *Philosophy and the Historical Understanding* (New York: Schocken Books, 1968).

18. See Hughes, *Worship as Meaning*, 66.

19. Ibid., 62. See also ibid., 81–98.

recipient of a sign do not share a world of meaning, which allows communication to take place. Communication simply fails.

Attention to the interpramen as the third, decisive factor of meaning making, therefore, requires attention to the world in which both producers and recipients of meanings live and to whom it provides their interpretants for meaning making. If I want to convey meaning successfully, I need to be aware of the world in which the recipient of my meaning-making signs live, because by providing the recipients of my signs with their interpretants, this world either helps or hinders an understanding of the signs I use to convey meaning.

b) Meaning and Christian Worship: Iconic, Indexical, and Symbolic Signs

All of this, Hughes avers, has important consequences for Christian worship. Just as all meaning, so also meaning in worship is produced and found, here in an interaction between the people who produce and lead the liturgy and those who receive it. While the former seek to convey meaning in and through the signs of the liturgy, the second actively participate in liturgical meaning making through their own construction of meaning from the signs they receive. Both the producers and the recipients of worship, then, participate in their own way in the liturgy's meaning.

This cooperation between the producers and the recipients of worship means that the construction of meaning on the part of the liturgy's recipients can fail. Much depends on their ability to interpret the signs appropriately.[20] In this process, the signs of the liturgy exercise a "critical jurisdiction" with regard to their reception.[21] The signs themselves present what Peirce calls " 'thirdness' in signification."[22] The same is true for their production. The leaders of worship can also miss their object.

In order to better understand this communication of meaning in worship through the use of signs, Hughes distinguishes with Peirce among three different sign types: "iconic, indexical and symbolic

---

20. See ibid., 103.
21. Ibid.
22. Ibid., 84. See also ibid., 180.

signs."[23] Iconic signs point to their object by virtue of a similarity between the sign-vehicle (representamen) and its object.[24] For many people in the West, icons on the computer are today perhaps the most common form of such iconic signs. Indexical signs, by contrast, point to their object through "contiguity between the sign-vehicle and the sign's object."[25] For example, smoke functions as an indexical sign of fire. Finally, symbolic signs point to their object solely by virtue of convention and thus of tradition.[26] For example, in many religious traditions, the smoke of burning incense symbolizes the rising of human prayers to God.

If meaning occurs in Christian worship in an act of communication, the signs of worship play a crucial role in the production and finding of meaning. In accordance with their nature, iconic signs must offer a similarity between what takes place in worship and how Christians imagine the transcendent world of God, which they seek to address.[27] In fact, the signs must themselves effect "the sense of transcendence."[28] Hughes maintains that this has momentous implications for many aspects of worship, including liturgical space and direction, worship's temporal progression, or the sense, which liturgy provides of the "vertiginous edge" at which human life takes place vis-à-vis the transcendent.[29] The success of iconic signs thus depends entirely on their ability to offer a likeness to the transcendent object to which they point.[30]

The indexicality of Christian liturgy, for its part, plays a role for Hughes with regard to the "truthfulness or authenticity" of the words and actions of worship. If iconicity carries weight for the *meaning* of worship, indexicality determines the *meaningfulness* of worship. Even the best iconic signs fail to convey meaning, if they are presented without authenticity. The indexicality of worship

23. Ibid., 125. Note that this distinction is never absolute or exclusive. See ibid., 139.

24. See ibid., 139.

25. Ibid., 140.

26. See ibid., 141.

27. See ibid., 148 and 151–52.

28. Ibid., 182.

29. Ibid., 159. See also ibid., 154–64.

30. See ibid., 169–70.

offers the participants a sense that its signs "are 'meant.'"[31] For Hughes, routinization (Max Weber) is perhaps the most common enemy of liturgical truthfulness, yet there are other examples of poor indexicality in Christian liturgy, such as the exercise of liturgical leadership in imitation of models from contemporary media culture or the politization of worship. Iconicity and indexicality must work together harmoniously if the desired meaning shall emerge from the liturgy.[32]

The symbolic dimension of the liturgy, finally, depends on its recipients being able to recognize it as Christian. The Christian tradition offers worship's participants a familiar context for what takes place. What makes a particular worship experience Christian is determined by how this religious community has worshiped throughout time: their ways, signs and symbols, recognizable patterns of worship. This liturgical tradition helps participants to identify a particular worship service as Christian. As Hughes puts it, "[T]he symbolic dimension of the signs . . . *interprets* and *disciplines* this experience [of the frontier behind the here and now and the transcendent realm of God] in the name of tradition."[33]

This does not mean necessarily that Christian worship is simply a repristination of the past without any meaningful connection to the present. Every Christian liturgy, Hughes maintains, "draws on, presupposes, [and] depends upon an incalculable depth of tradition in its construction of contemporary significations."[34] The tradition of the past is not repristinated for its own sake, but precisely in order to speak to the present. The tradition, however, calls the leaders of worship to accountability vis-à-vis the church of all ages. To be sure, this accountability, for Hughes, is not a one-way street, not an uncritical deference to tradition. If each lived liturgy is accountable to the tradition, the liturgical tradition itself must also be open for reasoned critical investigation. Liturgical tradition and present cultural moment find themselves in a dialectical relationship. The criteria for a theological critique of the liturgical tradition, however,

31. Ibid., 183.
32. See ibid., 173.
33. Ibid., 176.
34. Ibid., 148.

cannot be external ones. Rather, they must arise from the tradition itself. Picking up on the old axiom, *lex orandi lex credendi* (the law of praying is the law of believing), Hughes sides with those (mostly Protestant) scholars, such as Geoffrey Wainwright, who recognize a critical function of theology vis-à-vis liturgical practices.[35]

c) Christian Worship in Late-Modern Times

The dialectical tension between tradition and the present moment raises the larger question of why Christian liturgy finds itself in such a precarious situation in the late-modern era. Hughes contends that those principally responsible for the liturgy need to take into account the condition of the late-modern age when they plan and lead worship.[36] Because the epistemological conditions of late modernity supply people's interpramens for the signs and symbols of worship, these conditions largely determine people's ability or inability to interpret the "synthetic whole"[37] of Christian worship, including verbal utterances or nonverbal signs, such as actions, artifacts, or spatial arrangements. Without sufficient attention to late modernity, successful communication of meaning in worship becomes difficult.

What, then, are the characteristic marks of late modernity? Anthropologically, late-modern theorists reject the modern notion of a self-contained self, favoring instead an understanding of the self as social construction.[38] Epistemologically, they dismiss the idea that there are any kind of certainties, purities, and stable entities.[39] Meaning, for these thinkers, is always both found and constructed.[40] As such, any claim to knowledge can attempt to demonstrate at best that they are reasonable.[41] Hughes often refers to what contemporary sociologist Charles Taylor terms the "Best Account"–principle: all we can offer is a "best account" of the state of affairs as we see it.[42] We can never say with any certainty that things are this way or that.

35. See ibid., 181.
36. See ibid., 18–30, 300–301.
37. Ibid., 182.
38. See ibid., 47–48.
39. See ibid., 82–83.
40. See, e.g., ibid., 63–66 and 118.
41. See ibid., 31.
42. See above, n. 16.

Another defining mark of the late-modern condition is what Hughes calls the "repudiation of religious conviction as a source of meaning"[43]—a trait that goes back all the way to the modern "disenchantment" of the world.[44] As Hughes sees it, the situation of religion in Western societies is rather bleak today: late-modern people have lost the ability to represent the sacred, and many are no longer capable of making sense of the notion of God.[45] Institutional Christianity has lost its stronghold in society.[46] People construct their world in the absence of God.[47] In fact, late-modern meaning making is "inimical" to religious readings of the world.

Ironically, the modern disenchantment of the world gains its power from its emergence in and continuous relationship with Christianity.[48] Many late-modern people, however, are so immersed in these secularist assumptions that they are largely unaware of them. They simply take their own secularism for granted, not recognizing it for what it is, namely, the product of modernity in the Western world.

For Hughes, this situation creates a specific challenge for Christian worship, because it threatens the communication of the meaning of the liturgy's signs. In light of this risk, Hughes sees two basic options for Christian congregations, with a third being a kind of *via media* between these two.[49] First, churches can accommodate their message to their late-modern environment, by shaping the meanings of the liturgy accordingly. This often takes place in liberal or mainline Protestantism, where worship becomes near identical with fellowship and mission with social justice programs.[50] Second, congregations can take the opposite approach and offer an explicit alternative to their cultural environment. Fundamentalist churches

43. Ibid., 51.
44. Ibid., 53, with reference to Taylor, *Sources*, 149.
45. See Hughes, *Worship as Meaning*, 52 and 219.
46. See ibid., 53.
47. See ibid., 53, 54, and 220.
48. See ibid., 55.
49. See ibid., 53 and 222–52.
50. See ibid., 57.

often choose this approach, but at considerable cost. They opt for a premodern understanding of religious truth, but in so doing they risk bifurcation. Members of fundamentalist churches live with a double consciousness, in which a premodern religious worldview exists side by side with a secular one, though unmediated. Ironically, Hughes notes, fundamentalist churches are at once most opposed to modernity and at the same time most desacralized.[51] Finally, churches can simply trust in the inherent power of "the church's traditional liturgical formulations," hoping that these, "when joined with an appropriate performance of them, may confidently be relied upon to effect their own meanings."[52] Here, the liturgy simply is not in need of cultural mediation.

These three approaches mark not only contemporary churches but also today's Christian liturgical theology, albeit with some variations. Again, the question is how late-modern people find meaning in Christian worship in the midst of a secular world, which not only surrounds them but deeply marks their own understanding of reality.[53] Hughes finds three general approaches to answer this question among his colleagues.

First, some desire to do liturgical theology as "church theology."[54] The—mostly, although not exclusively—Roman Catholic representatives of this approach see theology emerging first and foremost in and from the celebration of worship itself.[55] Here, what happens in the liturgy constitutes first-order theology or *theologia prima*. In comparison to this theology proper, all subsequent theological reflection on the liturgy constitutes merely second-order theology or *theologia secunda*.[56] While all theologians who subscribe to this approach agree that the law of prayer is the law of believing (*lex orandi est lex credendi*), the Protestant representatives of this group (and some Roman Catholics) argue that this law is by no means a

---

51. See ibid., 57–58.
52. Ibid., 222.
53. See ibid., 221–22.
54. Ibid., 222. See also ibid., 225–33.
55. See ibid., 226.
56. For this distinction, see also Lathrop, *Holy Things*, 5–7. Lathrop speaks of primary and secondary liturgical theology and adds pastoral liturgical theology as a third version.

one-way street: while the liturgy informs our belief, critical theological reflection can and must have an impact on how Christians
worship.[57]

Nevertheless, for all of the theologians who subscribe to this
approach, the liturgy is self-explanatory, that is, it communicates
meaning to the participants of worship simply by being celebrated
together. Here, an explicit mediation to the surrounding secular
world is unnecessary. Modernity, therefore, is not an issue that needs
to be dealt with in the liturgy. Hughes detects in this approach an
"apparently unquestioned optimism in the theological efficacy of
the rites themselves."[58] For him, there is no recognition of the role,
which the recipients of the liturgy have as active "contributors" or
"agents" in liturgical meaning making. If one acknowledges this
active contribution of the participants in worship, he avers, one
cannot so easily ignore the effects of secular modernity. The latter
is not just a reality that surrounds Christians externally. It deeply
affects them, by shaping—consciously or unconsciously—their own
view of God, world, and humanity. Secular modernity has infiltrated
late-modern worshipers' thinking and has "undermined for vast
numbers of people in the western world . . . their confidence in a
theistic reading of reality."[59] Thus, modernity is inescapable in the
West and must not be ignored. This, however, means that liturgical
theologians cannot simply ignore the fact that there no longer is
"an unmediated reality." As Hughes puts it, "[S]ome element of
our own culturally shaped construction enters into any meaningful
apprehension of God."[60] Or else: "[T]here is no 'finding' purified of
our own constructive 'making.' "[61] With Ricoeur, Hughes contends
that we no longer have access to a first naiveté, "a naive (unreflec-
tive) assumption of a sacral world."[62] Moreover, "[T]he recovery of
such a world view could not be regained *simply by wishing it so*,

57. See ibid., 181 and 227–28.
58. Ibid., 228.
59. Ibid., 230–31.
60. Ibid., 232.
61. Ibid., 233.
62. Ibid.

but must pass through a chastened (eyes-wide-open) modernity to what [Ricoeur] called 'a second naiveté.' "[63]

Hughes attributes the second approach to modernity to evangelicalism.[64] Although there is quite a great historical variety of Christian traditions that fit under this umbrella, they all share certain main characteristics, most important, their opposition to modernity, their biblicism, and their "clarity of conviction, of self-awareness, the sense of spiritual completeness and deliverance from uncertainty."[65] Evangelicals explicitly reject modernity; yet they live in a cultural contradiction insofar as they—paradoxically—make heavy use of contemporary styles in their worship services. This becomes all the more pronounced due to the evangelical rejection of the liturgical tradition and what Hughes calls a "nearly singular dependence on language as their medium" to connote transcendence.[66]

Hughes finds this evangelical approach even more problematic than that of the "church" theologians. He points to its brittleness due to its "comparatively high degree of construction or interpretation."[67] Fundamentalist beliefs require the development of ever more complicated secondary doctrines, which render such beliefs quite tenuous. For example, the doctrine of scriptural inerrancy required those of verbal inspiration and the accommodation of the Holy Spirit to the language and worldviews of the various biblical writers—two secondary doctrines, which historically ended up reinforcing the problem they were supposed to solve, namely, by first opening up an understanding of the historical contingency of the scriptural writings.[68] Other problems include, for Hughes, evangelicalism's "casuistic style of rationality" and its "high esteem for truth [which] was being formed at just the time that 'truth' meant *correspondence* between verbal utterance and facts in the world."[69]

63. Ibid.
64. See ibid., 233–44.
65. Ibid., 239.
66. Ibid., 244.
67. Ibid., 239. See also ibid., 240.
68. See Wolfhart Pannenberg, *Systematic Theology*, vol. 1 (Grand Rapids, MI: William B. Eerdmans Publishing Company, 1991), 189–258.
69. Hughes, *Worship as Meaning*, 240 and 241.

Most important, evangelicalism, just like all modern forms of fundamentalism, falls prey, for Hughes, to a "bifurcation between faith and culture."[70] This fact expresses itself well in the evangelical approach to history. On the one hand, evangelicals share the original Protestant conviction that ordinary life rather than a separate sacred realm is the place where humans encounter God. On the other hand, they separate a special salvation history as the stage of God's self-manifestation from the rest of world history. (It almost goes without saying that evangelicals reject studying this separate history of divine self-manifestation with the methods of secular historiography.) Again, evangelicals paradoxically both dismiss and embrace modernity: they oppose many of the modern philosophical assumptions, while making pragmatic use of modernity's achievements. As Hughes observes, "[T]he media, styles, [and] forms of engagement [in evangelical worship] are all directly continuous with prevalent cultural patterns."[71] Form and content, however, cannot easily be separated.

Hughes identifies a similar bifurcation between the semiosis of evangelical worship and the demands of evangelical discipleship. On the one hand, evangelical worship "attests a God who is immediately accessible."[72] On the other hand, "[t]he 'separatist' dimension of evangelicalism . . . requires an actual, or distinguishable, conversion *from* ordinariness *to* discipleship."[73] There is a paradoxical bifurcation, then, between the assertion that God meets us in ordinary life and the demand to exit this ordinary life if one desires to be a true Christian.

Evangelical worship's semiosis of an immediately accessible God is problematic for Hughes also in another way. Although Scripture testifies that God has made God's self immediately accessible both in the incarnation and in the sending of the Holy Spirit, it balances God's immanence with God's transcendence and alterity. Hughes finds this balance painfully missing in evangelical worship. As he puts it, here "signs of God's unequivocal 'difference', an actual semiosis of alterity," are often missing, because evangelicals "[draw]

70. Ibid., 241.
71. Ibid., 242–43.
72. Ibid., 243.
73. Ibid.

cultural norms such as informality and immediacy as deeply into
worship practices as they have."[74] By rejecting all liturgical forms
and language and elevating what can appear as a Starbucks-inspired
informality, evangelicals present God as an intimately close friend
with whom one shares a cup of coffee on the couch in a sanctuary that refuses to be a sanctuary. The always-greater difference
between God and creation and the awe-inspiring quality of what
Rudolf Otto called the *mysterium tremendum et fascinans* seems
painfully missing.[75] Hughes doubts that the evangelical approach
to Christian worship therefore possesses "a long term viability."[76]

The situation looks similarly bleak for the third approach to
modernity, mainline Protestantism's, albeit for the opposite reasons.[77] In contrast to evangelicalism's rejection of modernity, mainline Protestantism fully embraces the consequences of modernity as
indisputable facts. Its "espousal" of modern culture expresses itself
in attempts of assimilation, an emphasis on God's immanent working in creation, and a progressivism, which sees the kingdom of God
increasingly asserting itself in human history. Theologically, this third
approach to modernity can take different forms, from Dietrich Bonhoeffer's "religionless Christianity," to the death-of-God theology of
the 1960s, all the way to contemporary contextual theologies of lib-
eration, including feminist, postcolonial, and ecological theologies.[78]
What marks all of these different approaches, for Hughes, though,
is their "insistence on the secular as the arena of religion," their
corresponding "traditional Protestant predilection for the everyday
world," and their identification of God with God's immanence.[79]

The dangers Hughes detects in this assimilationist approach are
great. Most important, it mistakes ordinariness for God and God
for ordinariness. Hughes insists, however, that God manifests God's
self not only in the midst of ordinariness but also at its "edge."[80]

74. Ibid., 243–44.
75. Similarly, Lathrop insists that God is not our buddy but rather to be
feared. See Lathrop, *Holy Things*, 130.
76. Hughes, *Worship as Meaning*, 243.
77. See ibid., 245–52.
78. See ibid., 247–48.
79. Ibid., 247 and 248. See also ibid., 249.
80. Ibid., 252.

Similarly problematic, Hughes claims, is liberal Protestantism's "apotheosis of our ordinary condition," be it in the identification of "God's presence . . . (without remainder) with acts of human benevolence, especially for disenfranchised members of society," or in the "prerogative importance on 'knowing one another'" in so-called "caring communities."[81] Many mainline Protestant churches have developed a culture of intimacy for its own sake, so much so that intimacy has become "a primary liturgical value."[82] As Hughes points out,

> Intimacy, or even community, however, is *not* the point and purpose of an assembly ostensibly gathered for the worship of God. By all means it may be a hoped-for byproduct of corporate worship, but when the priorities are reversed, the one becomes the other's sublimate.[83]

To be sure, all of these tendencies are well rooted in the original Protestant opposition to a separation between a profane and a sacred realm and thus are not completely new. Today, however, believers when sent into the world as the place to encounter God are faced with a thoroughly secularized world: a world, that is, which has excluded God from its daily life. Today, therefore, the consequences of the Protestant rejection of a specifically sacred dimension of reality are significantly more radical than at the time of the Reformation.[84]

None of the three approaches to modernity, for Hughes then, successfully navigates the dangerous waters for the church. First, it does not help to just ignore modernity, as the "church" theology does, because modernity is not just an external reality. Rather, it has long invaded the church from the inside in the individual consciousness of the believers. The dangers are even greater if one rejects modernity, as evangelicalism is prone to do. Because such rejection is never complete, as the lived reality of evangelical worship amply demonstrates, it leads to a bifurcation of reality, which—due to its

81. Ibid., 250–51.
82. Ibid., 251.
83. Ibid.
84. See ibid., 252.

high level of construction of meaning and its internal inconsistencies—is doomed to fail sooner rather than later. Mainline Protestantism's embrace of secular modernity without remainder finally runs the risk of the church's self-annihilation. When people detect God only in ordinary life and ordinary life no longer needs a theistic foundation, the church itself becomes superfluous.

In light of this dire situation, Hughes advocates for a new and different approach to modernity. Against "church" theologians and evangelicals, he argues that this approach can neither ignore nor reject modern insights. We cannot go back to a "first naiveté" and we cannot separate reality into two realms: one in which modern reason applies and one in which the logic of faith reigns. Rather, a self-consciously late-modern liturgical theology must acknowledge modernity, as "we can only construct our meanings from those available to us."[85] This, however, does not mean that one constructs meanings simply "by submersing oneself in the modern paradigm."[86] What is required is "a theorization which is recognizable from within present-day presuppositions while not remaining ensconced therein; which is clear-eyed about our dependence on late-modern cultural forms and *at the same time* works towards the relativization of these in the name of a theistic reading of reality."[87] In other words, Hughes desires to overcome the either-or approach, which ironically unites mainline Protestantism with evangelicalism and the "church" theology, despite all of their differences. Late-modern Christians cannot choose between being Christians and being modern; they can be Christians only as late-modern persons. Neither simple identification with nor mere differentiation from modernity will do, because neither one of these two options takes its surrounding culture seriously. As Hughes puts it, "[A]n absence of genuine engagement with its other—modern culture for the [church theology and evangelicalism]; God's alterity for [mainline Protestantism]—renders doubtful for the recipients of liturgical significations their capacity to complete the semiosis."[88] What Hughes desires from the church

85. Ibid., 253.
86. Ibid., 254.
87. Ibid.
88. Ibid., 257.

and from liturgical theology is both a critical and a constructive engagement with modernity. Rather than refuse engagement of modernity, church and theology must advocate for the Christian proclamation of God "from within" late modernity and with the help of the late-modern cultural forms, while also showing "the *relativity* of those cultural assumptions."[89] This includes that over against either modernity's identity and postmodern deconstruction's emphasis on difference, one opts for "a dialectic of identity (recognizability) and difference (alterity)."[90]

But how does one do that? Following Langdon Gilkey, Hughes suggests that "[l]iturgical meaning is effected at the extremity of what we can manage or comprehend as human beings."[91] All human beings know limit or boundary experiences in their lives, either advertent, that is, sought after, or inadvertent, that is, encountered involuntarily.[92] Such limit experiences provide liturgical theology with an opportunity to connect to people even in a secular environment, because limit experiences—as Hughes puts it—offer an "intensification of otherwise familiar matters," "yield what are perceptibly religious—at the very least quasi-religious—effects," and "serve to reveal a quality of vulnerability."[93] Liturgical theology, Hughes contends, must first explain, then, how "religious sensitivities" emerge, before we attend to the ways in which our religious traditions "bring to symbolic expression, this basic religious susceptibility."[94] If "[w]orship is a journey 'to the edge of chaos,'" as Hughes formulates with Roman Catholic liturgical theologian Aidan Kavanagh, liturgical theology must first attend "to the *inalienable alterity* by which we are confronted" in our everyday lives.[95]

Alterity, Hughes notes, meets us in our daily life in different degrees. Because it is threatening to us, we constantly try to keep our distance from it or try to bring it under our control. Ordinariness itself, as Hughes observes, is a way to keep "the *alterity* of 'the edge' "

89. Ibid., 255.
90. Ibid.
91. Ibid., 257.
92. See ibid., 257–60 and 260–76.
93. Ibid., 264.
94. Ibid., 257.
95. Ibid.

at bay.[96] The problem is a universal human one, but it is also a particularly modern one. As Emmanuel Levinas remarks, the Western philosophy of consciousness is a large-scale attempt to suppress alterity. Or, as Hughes puts it with Jürgen Habermas, "An unprecedented modernity . . . can *only fashion its criteria out of itself.*"[97]

For Hughes, worship functions as an antidote to this modern tendency to keep alterity at bay. Worship's "*vocative dimension*" opposes "modernity's strident advocacy of the 'return to the self'" and "the near mesmeric power of immanentism for late modern theology."[98] This vocative dimension distinguishes worship from all other limit experiences, be they advertent or inadvertent. As Hughes points out, one cannot call on a landscape, a piece of art, or a last-minute winning goal in a soccer match—even though all of these may well constitute limit experiences.[99] In worship, the congregation not only encounters "the edge of chaos" but also calls on and communicates with the ultimate "Other." This openness to the alterity of God includes an orientation to the otherness of human persons, if—as Levinas insists—God's alterity is indissolubly related to that of other human beings. In biblical terms, the love of God is inseparable from the love of neighbor. "[O]*therness* or *difference*," then, are foundational dimensions of worship.[100] Worship orients the congregation away from itself. Note here that the vocative dimension of worship is not "unidirectional."[101] In the encounter with the divine Other a "claim [is] made upon the self in its encounters with another."[102] This claim can be answered in different degrees, all the way to an explicit religious conversion.

96. Ibid., 277.

97. Jürgen Habermas, *The Philosophical Discourse of Modernity: Twelve Lectures*, trans. Frederick G. Lawrence (Cambridge, MA: MIT Press, 1995), 41 (Hughes's emphasis), quoted in Hughes, *Worship as Meaning*, 278.

98. Hughes, *Worship as Meaning*, 280–81. Hughes borrowed the notion of the "vocative dimension" from philosopher of religion Ninian Smart, *The Concept of Worship* (London: Macmillan Press, 1972), 10. See Hughes, *Worship as Meaning*, 282.

99. See Hughes, *Worship as Meaning*, 282.

100. Ibid., 281.

101. Ibid., 283.

102. Ibid.

If worship is in principle and in its very conception oriented to the divine Other, the daily reality of much Christian worship shows quite another picture. As Hughes puts it: "The reality . . . is one thing, . . . but the *gesture* is another."[103] Christian worship is never a pure thing. Here as elsewhere, people's self-interests play an important role and can easily overshadow the orientation toward God with a return to the self. This raises the question for Hughes how worship can truly be vocative.[104] Taking his cue from late-modern critiques of modernity, Hughes maintains that all human images, even those of the liturgy, are humanly constructed and therefore call with necessity for an iconoclastic critique.[105] Otherwise, these images only serve as another form of return to the self, of looking into a liturgical mirror.

The question of images in worship classically divides not only iconoclasts from iconodules in the patristic era but also Calvinists from Lutherans. As is well known, John Calvin's claim that "*finitum non est capax infiniti* (the finite cannot contain the infinite)" severely limits the use of images in Christian worship.[106] By contrast, for Martin Luther, as Hughes puts it, we can perceive the inward only through the outward.[107] For Hughes, who follows Ricoeur on this point, there can be no return with the images of the liturgy to a first naiveté. Liturgical signs do not offer immediate access to a religious universe. Late-modern persons, as Ricoeur suggests, have lost the capability to access the transcendent in an unmediated way. And yet, for Hughes as for Ricoeur, the old religious symbols are not without worth, as modernity suggested, substituting them through an overly optimistic confidence in the exercise of reason. With Ricoeur, Hughes suggests that in the late-modern age, one can profit from ancient religious symbols by approaching them with a second naiveté—an approach that Hughes characterizes as "a process of thought in which a modern person first critically examines the effects of her or his own cultural conditioning *as*

103. Ibid., 285.
104. See ibid., 285–86.
105. See ibid., 289.
106. Quoted in ibid., 286.
107. See ibid.

modern . . . so as then to be free to ponder the ancient symbolic formulations."[108] Hughes suggests that Christians would do well to apply Ricoeur's notion of a second naiveté to Christian worship.[109] In fact, for Hughes, late-modern Christians cannot do otherwise, for they are inescapably shaped by modernity, and to ignore that fact would mean "disowning some essential aspect of [their] identity."[110] For late-modern Christians, a second naiveté can express itself in a number of ways. First, they need to recognize that worship is nothing anyone can ever master. As Hughes formulates, worship has about it a "fundamental unsophistication . . . [as] the product of worship's in-built iconoclasm."[111] Furthermore, if one can never master worship, if one—in other words—can never be an expert at worshiping, this needs to lead one to acknowledge that the most basic response to the God encountered in worship is adoration. As Hughes puts it *tout court*, "only doxology will do."[112] Third, the built-in iconoclasm of worship needs to translate into the recognition that all of our images, including those used in Christian liturgy, are in fact "constructed," are "imaginative constructions."[113] This does not mean that they do not make truth claims, but such truth claims need to be made "more lightly and experimentally."[114] In fact, a self-aware late-modern person's faith itself has to be understood as "more daring, more experimental, more nearly a 'wager.' "[115]

Note that Hughes does not propose that late-modern believers make a choice between "myth" and "reality," as if one really had such a choice, which would amount to one of being a late-modern person or not. All any Christian can offer is, in Taylor's term, a "Best Account." The liturgical theologian must acknowledge the epistemological limitations of this "Best Account." One may be tempted to present the content of faith with a pretended first naiveté as an

108. Ibid., 287–88.
109. See ibid.
110. Ibid., 289.
111. Ibid., 288. On this point, see also Lathrop, *Holy Things*, 119–28.
112. Hughes, *Worship as Meaning*, 289.
113. Ibid.
114. Ibid., 291.
115. Ibid.

unmediated reality. The mere claim, however, does not make it so. One still offers just a "Best Account," acknowledged or not.

What Hughes does want to defend as "real" is the universal human limit experience, which underlies all particular religious constructions of it in different religious traditions. This limit experience, for Hughes, "places firm restraint on the constructive aspects of theology. . . . The worshipper who turns away from the phenomenal world to address the Other whom Christians name as the God and Father of our Lord Jesus Christ is not indulging in sheer speculation. To repeat: there is an objective (discovered) dimension of belief fused in and with the constructed one."[116] Still, the church, like all religions, only has "as if" words to describe what we experience at this limit or boundary. In other words, the church makes "proposals, invitations, mythic constructions."[117] Such are our only modality of God-talk.[118] We do not really have a choice here. The question, rather, is if one self-consciously accepts the epistemological limitations of one's own faith or if one chooses to ignore them at the price of either disowning part of one's own identity as a late-modern person or of living a bifurcated life.

With this proviso, Hughes believes that worship needs to translate the characteristics of universal human boundary experiences into meaningful signs and symbols. Just like other limit experiences, it must do so by intensifying our quotidian human experiences. Furthermore, it must lift up the inherently religious character of all limit experiences. And finally, Christian worship must uncover the experience of alterity or otherness, which is so regularly obscured in daily life.[119]

Let us look at the first of these strategies in more detail. What Christians do in worship is commonplace: they read, they speak, they eat and drink together, they bathe. But in worship Christians do so not in the same way humans ordinarily do. In the liturgy, these ordinary actions are intensified, because "we subject them to what

116. Ibid., 294.
117. Ibid.
118. See ibid., 292.
119. See ibid., 299.

have been called 'ritualizing strategies.'"[120] Hughes uses the example of music in worship. He points out that in their communication with God Christians have used not ordinary language but versified prose. Furthermore, they have patterned their speaking according to rhythm and sound. By singing rather than speaking, they have employed a greater tonal range, and they have often employed instruments to augment the character of their singing. All of these strategies represent forms of ritualization.

Singing in worship offers a good example for an *expansive* form of ritual intensification, that is, a form which intensifies a common human experience by heightening the way it is enacted. Other expansive forms of ritual intensification include the architectural shape and arrangement of the worship space and the use of special vestments, of (colored) light, of liturgical time, and of accompanying rituals, such as incense. Ritual intensifications in worship can also be *contractive*, however, such as the act of administering communion—an act which encapsulates the encounter with God in the shortest and most intense moment.[121]

If general human limit experiences can be either advertent or inadvertent, Hughes contends that Christian worship resembles both. On the one hand, all of what Christians do in worship is intentional and thus advertent. On the other hand, the limit experiences worship evokes are more similar to inadvertent boundary experiences. As Hughes puts it, "[T]here is here . . . the sense of being wholly overwhelmed, of powerlessness and awe, of wonder and joy, of thankful self-giving and rich benefaction."[122] The goal of those who plan and lead worship, then, must be to use strategies and signs, which lead to the experience of God's radical alterity over against the world and the meanings it proposes. Worship must offer its participants, as Hughes puts it with Lathrop, a "sanctuary of meaning."[123]

If worship is indeed a cooperative endeavor between its producers and its recipients, it can only offer such a sanctuary of meaning

---

120. Ibid., 295.
121. See ibid., 297.
122. Ibid., 298.
123. Lathrop, *Holy Things*, 217, quoted in Hughes, *Worship as Meaning*, 299.

successfully if both parties are capable of assuming their respective responsibilities. The producers of worship need to be aware that worship transcends the ordinary experience of the quotidian, that worship "*is* a 'boundary' or 'liminal' (threshold) event . . . [which] takes place at a kind of virtual 'edge' of what we can manage conceptually and emotionally."[124] Worship must not fall victim therefore to "domesticity" or "routinization."[125] In order to achieve this goal, leaders of worship need to allow the three dimensions of liturgical signification to do their work: They must employ the iconic signs in such a way that they truly point to the transcendent realm and "signal the 'boundary' nature of the entire event."[126] They must honor the indexical dimension of worship, by ensuring that their work is authentic. Therefore, they must not misuse the liturgy as a means to achieve another aim but the communication with God. Neither must they offer a routine or a performance. Finally, liturgical leaders must bring out the symbolic dimension of Christian worship, namely, by signaling to the participants of the liturgy that what happens here and now is rooted in the larger Christian tradition, "is something not made up on the spur of the moment, but forged from millennia-deep sources of wisdom and knowledge."[127]

If liturgy must be accountable to the Christian tradition, it must also be "followable" (Ricoeur) for its present participants. For this to happen, ministers must be aware, Hughes insists, that modernity has deeply entered into the consciousness of contemporary worshipers. Ministers must therefore translate a second naiveté about faith claims into their manner of communication. As Hughes puts it, "[C]onvictions need to be held on an open palm rather than in clenched grip; our work must be undertaken in a seriously experimental way, as a wager for meaning rather than senselessness, and for the *particular* wager suggested by the liturgical signs themselves."[128]

124. Hughes, *Worship as Meaning*, 301.
125. Ibid.
126. Ibid.
127. Ibid., 302.
128. Ibid.

Worship leaders must respect that contemporary worshipers need to be included actively in Christian meaning making, that meaning can no longer be passed on simply on authority, that modern persons "think it quite unlikely that there will be finally definitive meanings."[129] The leaders of worship need to understand that the signs of the liturgy are just that: signs, symbols, "pictures of reality; not final, definitive ones, but pictures which allow us to grasp into some sort of whole the 'making' and the 'discovery' aspects of our project of meaning."[130] This, Hughes avers, is no reason to succumb to "despair," no embrace of relativism: "[A] 'Best Account' [will be enough] for us to get along on a day-to-day basis."[131]

The recipients of the liturgy, for their part, must be both attentive to the signs of the liturgy and actively complete the meaning proposed in the liturgy.[132] They must do so from where they find themselves at home in the world. They must "*reach* for the meanings being suggested to see where, how, or perhaps whether, these can 'make sense' in terms of a recognizable world."[133] Finally, they must willingly take up the wager for meaning, for faith. In their daily life, a whole number of myths compete with each other as explanations of reality. As Hughes observes, the proposals for meaning, which contemporary culture offers late-modern persons, "are as mythic in their claims as anything that recognizable religion has to offer, though on infinitely slighter grounds."[134] The contemporary worshiper, then, must actively engage this competition for meaning and trust the meaning suggested by the liturgy.

3. In Search for a Reformed Sacramentality

If Hughes's book, *Worship as Meaning*, offers—as its subtitle suggests—a liturgical theology for late-modern times, his projected new book on Reformed sacramentality develops some of its central

129. Ibid., 300.
130. Ibid., 301.
131. Ibid., 300.
132. See ibid., 196, 201–3, 300.
133. Ibid., 302.
134. Ibid.

themes—the significance of semiosis in worship, of God's alterity, and of difference, to name just a few—further and in a distinctly confessional direction. It also draws out the implications of these themes with regard to the church's liturgical practices. Here, Hughes shows himself interested in how the church concretely constructs the communication between God and the believers. For this purpose, Hughes investigates the role of materiality or physicality in this event of communication between God and the congregation. What difference, Hughes asks, does materiality make in the development of meaning in worship? In order to answer this question, Hughes seeks to develop a distinctly Reformed perspective on sacramentality.

As Hughes explains in his last interview with Emilsen (included at the end of this book in chapter 6), the idea for his new book on Reformed sacramentality originally grew out of his insights on how meaning develops in worship. Recall that in a Peircean perspective meaning emerges in cooperation between those who plan and lead worship, on the one hand, and those who participate in worship, on the other hand, with the signs of worship playing the third major role. In this model of liturgical meaning making, the responsibility of worship leaders for the communication of meaning in the liturgy is of crucial importance. Hughes therefore wanted to investigate the theological significance of the act of ordination and its implied call to represent alternately either God or the assembled congregation in worship. As Hughes puts it, "If the role of the ordained person is as important to the implementation of this meaning project as seems to be implied in the *Meaning* book, then what do we have to say about ordination and its meaning? . . . Differently put, what do we think we are doing when we ordain a person, set someone aside as a person who facilitates this meaning project?"[135] After Hughes developed his initial idea to investigate the meaning of ordination, he soon became aware, however, that he could not look at the question of ordination in an isolated manner. As he suggests in the interview, "[T]he question is to be conceived much more comprehensively. . . . [It] began to open up into the question of our

135. See below, chap. 6, "The Last Interview," 177.

Reformed sacramentality."[136] Ordained persons are just one instance of God's presence in the created order. Other examples include Christian practices, such as baptism and Holy Communion, or a Christian understanding of particular spaces and times of worship. For Hughes, all of these examples raised the same questions: How is God present in the world? And are there perhaps different modes of divine presence in the world? Ordination is just one example of the much more comprehensive issue of sacramentality per se, and in particular of the possibility of material or physical bearers of holiness—what Hughes calls "condensed" or "compressed" symbols or "sedimentations" of the Christian faith.

As Hughes soon realized, both the question of ordination and this larger issue of sacramentality could only be answered from a distinctively confessional perspective. Different ecclesial traditions— from the Eastern Orthodox and the Roman Catholic on the one end of the ecumenical spectrum to the Reformed churches on the other end—vary significantly in their theological evaluation of sacramentality. Hughes thus wanted to develop a theological concept of sacramentality specifically from within his own Reformed tradition, based on Calvin's foundational theological rule, *finitum non est capax infiniti* (the finite cannot contain the infinite). For Hughes, this meant that "Reformed sacramentality . . . can never allow that physical forms can be carriers of divine presence."[137] Sacraments can at best be pointers to such presence. Hughes showed himself convinced that the Reformed concern about "reification"—that is, about the "apotheosis" of material carriers of divine presence—was as relevant today as it had been in Calvin's time and that it must therefore set the framework of any Reformed reappreciation of sacramentality.[138]

There could be no doubt for Hughes, however, that such a re-appreciation of material sacramentality was desperately needed in his own Reformed tradition, which shows itself today particularly vulnerable of a "cultural colonization" by modernity. In fact, the

136. Ibid., 179.

137. Chap. 4, "The Embodied Word: In Search of a Reformed Sacramentality," 151–52.

138. Ibid., 141 and again 146.

Reformed tradition's longstanding tendency to secularity has created a close proximity with modernity from the very beginning. While this proximity might have presented a particular strength of the Reformed tradition in the past—for example, when it laid the theological foundation in Geneva for the leveling of all social hierarchies in modernity—today, it creates a major liability. As Hughes points out, it has become increasingly difficult to tell what is particularly Christian about the Reformed faith.

Often, Reformed Christians are unable themselves "to say what is distinctively *Christian* about the Reformed style."[139] "[W]ithout such a [sacramental] dimension," Hughes contends, "Christianity becomes either a society of like-minded people with a more-or-less religious bent or an agency directed (admittedly, with religious motivation) to social improvement."[140] In other words, Reformed spirituality boils down for many Reformed Christians either to mere community or to a social action program. The result is worrisome: "[R]eally quite anxious-making consequences flow from this in terms of the future of the church's life in the face of modern and, in some places, militant secularism."[141] Hughes contends that "the Reformed churches [seem] to have been especially prone to invasion by assumptions that are not at all Christian ones."[142] Other traditions, such as the Eastern Orthodox churches with their much more robust liturgical practices, seem to be much less vulnerable to the invasion of modernity.

In this new book, Hughes offers a bold proposal to remedy the ensuing malaise of Reformed Christianity in the late-modern age. He suggests that only a rediscovery of "condensed" or "compressed" sacramentality will help overcome the present predicament of secular colonization by modernity. To be sure, Hughes does not reject the classical Reformed appreciation for "disseminated" sacramentality per se, that is, the theological recognition of God's omnipresence in the world as God's creation and in human beings

139. Chap. 3, "The Uncertain Place of Materiality in the Reformed Tradition," 104.
140. Chap. 4, "The Embodied Word," 115.
141. Chap. 6, "The Last Interview," 182.
142. Ibid.

particularly, by virtue of their quality as images of God (*imago Dei*). Rather, Hughes suggests that Reformed theology needs to amplify this appreciation for disseminated sacramentality with an equally robust reappropriation of condensed sacramentality. Hughes favors an integrated approach, a dialectic of both sacramental traditions, in which the condensed sedimentations of faith function as the center to the periphery of a disseminated sacramentality.[143]

Hughes's approach in this book is threefold: First, he deftly analyzes the historical reasons for the Reformed tradition's rejection of physicality as a carrier of divine presence and the ecclesial and cultural consequences of this theological rejection. Second, Hughes reevaluates the Reformed antimaterialist tradition from an explicitly late-modern vantage point and advocates for physicality as an aspect of difference and alterity. Third, Hughes offers a constructive case for a Reformed sacramentality, which employs condensed symbols of faith both as a lever against modern solipsism and as iconic pointers to God's radical otherness.

Let us look at these three steps in more detail. Historically, Hughes identifies the strong influence of the Western philosophical tradition, from Plato to Descartes, on Calvin's theology as the main culprit for the Reformed tradition's antimateriality. In Hughes's view, this Western philosophical heritage has led Calvin to identify materiality prematurely with idolatry. As a consequence of this distrust of materiality, the Reformed tradition has rejected condensed sacramentality, that is, the affirmation of God's special presence in particular material signs. Instead, this tradition has developed the concept of a disseminated sacramentality—an affirmation of God's universal presence in the world as a whole and in human beings as images of God, in particular. Such disseminated sacramentality has become the hallmark of "low church" traditions and is highly influential today across the spectrum of Protestant churches in the widespread desire for so-called contemporary worship.

In his critical reevaluation of the Reformed liturgical tradition, Hughes identifies the problem with such disseminated sacramentality, especially where it remains the dominant or even only form of sacramentality, as the inadvertent takeover of Christianity by mo-

---

143. See chap. 1, "Disseminated and Condensed Sacramentality."

dernity's immanentism. As Hughes puts it, "Reformed Christianity's predilection for the diffused sacramental type leaves it dangerously exposed to a 'cultural colonization' by modernity. . . . Reformed Christianity, and most especially its present-day contemporary-worship mutation, is now insufficiently in touch with its tradition to be able to summon the necessary critical acumen in face of the modernist threat."[144]

Over against such invasion, Hughes advocates for a rediscovery of physicality as a vehicle of divine-human communication. He uses insights of contemporary anthropology with its much higher appreciation for bodiliness and its corresponding understanding of the human person as an embodied being to demonstrate the deficiencies of Reformed worship with its restriction to oral/aural forms of communication between God and humankind. Hughes turns to late-modern thinkers, such as philosopher Levinas and theologian Jean-Luc Marion, to show that the interiority and high degree of imagination required by Reformed worship dangerously exposes it to becoming simply a mirror of the self, which reflects but the image of the spectator's gaze. Hughes subjects both late-modern Reformed spirituality and contemporary worship to a devastating critique when he analyzes the concrete forms such solipsism takes in today's forms of Protestant worship.

Hughes looks to the condensed symbols of faith as help against modern solipsism. Their physicality, he argues, presents a safeguard against endless self-referentiality, because they confront us with alterity and therefore serve as pointers to God's ultimate alterity. To be sure, Hughes rejects any identification of such material sedimentations of faith with God's presence, thus hoping to avoid what he perceives as the trap of reification. He is well aware that iconicity and idolatry are closely connected, and yet he insists that materiality is not identical with idolatry. Idolatry, he insists, is a problem of the human heart, which can assert itself in a whole different range of ways.

A Reformed sacramentality, then, builds on three presuppositions. First, sacraments must be semiotically capable of transcendent signification. The material signs and symbols used in worship

144. Ibid., 30. See also ibid., 25.

must have the ability to point beyond themselves to the divine. Second, such signs must be invested with transcendent meaning, because they do not carry such signification per se. Meaning, we recall, is always both a finding and a making. Investing the material signs and symbols of faith with transcendent meaning, then, truly changes their status. Given his Reformed sensibilities about reification, Hughes rejects the notion of transubstantiation. With Edward Schillebeeckx, he suggests that one rather speaks of transsignification. In any case, the meaning of these condensed symbols of faith truly changes. Third, in order to be able to function as material symbols of faith, sacraments require "some order of canonicity."[145] Individuals cannot just determine subjectively what carries transcendent meaning for them personally. Rather, sacraments require to be recognized by the religious tradition as sedimentations of faith with objective symbolic significance. There must be, then, a canonical agreement of the community of faith on the meaning of the sacraments. That baptism is a dying and rising with Christ or that in the eucharistic celebration the faithful truly have communion with the risen Christ is not a momentary intuition of the pious soul or a clever idea by an entrepreneurial minister; rather, it rests on a long liturgical tradition.[146]

Let us look in some more detail at the first of these three requirements, namely, the necessity that material sedimentations of the faith must be semiotically capable of transcendent signification. For Hughes, much of the current malaise of the Reformed tradition lies in the fact that its actual sacramental practices have a severely diminished semiotic power. In his interview with Emilsen, Hughes speaks of a "low level of semiosis" due to "the serious inadequacy . . . from the material side of the sacrament."[147]

What Hughes refers to, for example, is the all too common practice of sprinkling baptismal candidates with a few drops of water rather than baptizing them by full submersion. Similarly inadequate,

---

145. Chap. 3, "The Uncertain Place of Materiality," 110.

146. See, for example, chap. 2, "What Is a Sacrament? What Is Sacramentality?," 88–89; chap. 3, "The Uncertain Place of Materiality," 110–11; and Hughes, *Worship as Meaning*, 302.

147. Chap. 6, "The Last Interview," 183 and 181. See also ibid., 182.

from a semiotic point of view, are—in Hughes's view—many of the practices regarding Holy Communion, even though some progress has been achieved here in recent years. Hughes refers rather disparagingly to the poor semiosis of "little glasses of grape juice," whose power to signify, "both in taste and actually in sight," can hardly "compare with a handsome silver cup of port wine."[148] Again, this is not primarily an aesthetic problem but rather one of semiosis. For Hughes, "there is a great deal still to be done in bringing the physicality, the actual taste of the element into coherence, into some kind of semiotic conformity with what we are saying is the meaning of this sign, and similarly with the fragment of bread."[149]

How can this semiosis succeed? Hughes explains a successful sacramental semiosis as one in which the "prototype" and the "ectype" of the sacramental action have a sufficiently close relationship with one another to express the symbolic meaning of the action. The signified reality must be well recognizable in the sacramental action. With regard to Holy Communion, Hughes asks the church: "[H]ow closely can we bring the actual experience, the semiosis of the sacramental action of the celebration of the sacrament . . . in its now ritual form, to the kinds of immediacy between actual and metaphorical that were experienced in Jesus' own ministry. And then he left to the church the ritual forms, the sacramental forms, in which we receive his presence. We receive Christ's presence in and with and behind . . . these sacramental forms."[150] Both Christian sacraments are multivalent; that is to say, they represent more than just one meaning: biblically, baptism represents both a (one-time) ritual washing, on the one hand, and a symbolic death, burial, and resurrection with the risen Lord, on the other. Similarly, Holy Communion represents both a farewell meal with Jesus and the anticipation of the eschatological festal banquet with the risen Lord. Hence, the church must bring to expression in its liturgical practices all of these symbolic meanings both through the material elements and in the manner of the liturgical celebration itself.

148. Ibid., 186.
149. Ibid.
150. Ibid., 185.

Here is where the church's actual liturgical practices show themselves semiotically so inadequate. Sprinkling with a few drops of water simply does not express well either of the two symbolic meanings, which the New Testament ascribes to baptism, namely, that of a ritual washing and that of dying and rising with Christ. Similarly, offering people a tiny wafer and a small plastic shot glass of grape juice hardly represents "the eschatological joining of Christ with his church in festal banquet."[151] *Tout court*, inadequate semiotic practices do not successfully convey transcendent meaning. Their power to point to what lies beyond our direct perception is too severely compromised.

Here, both the quality and the quantity of the material elements play a crucial role. Successful washing requires a sufficient amount of water to be recognizable. Similarly, the symbolic representation of a death, burial, and resurrection demands submersion to be recognizable as such. Submersion simply represents death far better than sprinkling. And reemerging from underneath the water suggests resurrection far better than . . . — actually what is the common baptismal practice? The same holds true for Holy Communion: wafers and plastic shot glasses of grape juice hardly make for a farewell meal and even less for the eschatological festal banquet. What material elements the church uses, then, and how it uses them, is of quintessential semiotic importance.[152]

Hughes is well aware that the sacraments, even when practiced in their usual form in the Reformed churches, are not completely devoid of meaning and can constitute an important experience in the life of those who receive them. The problem, however, is that, due to the severely diminished power of the semiosis in the sacramental practice, all the work of meaning construction has to take place in the imagination of the faithful. As Hughes puts it, "[B]oth in baptism and in the celebration of the Eucharist . . . people actually have to do 90 percent of the work in their heads. They have to imagine that

---

151. Ibid., 183.

152. Here, one might add that the common Catholic practice of distributing to the faithful hosts retrieved from the tabernacle at Holy Eucharist rather than those consecrated during the Mass itself raises similar semiotic problems, as Catholic liturgical theologians have long noticed.

here I am participating in Christ's festal banquet or that I have here communion with Jesus and the forgiveness of my sins. All of that has to be a kind of emotional response, an intellectual response. We have to imagine, as Calvin wanted to put it, that we are lifted up out of this earthly life and that we eat and drink of Christ."[153] In other words, the commonly used sacramental practices in the Reformed tradition reduce the process of liturgical semiosis to an intellectual or imaginative exercise, which takes place mostly if not almost exclusively in the participants' heads rather than in the interaction between the community, the signs, and their recipients. If meaning is always both making and finding, in the diminished practices of the Reformed (and many other Protestant) traditions, there is incomparably much more making than finding. This, however, poses two problems.

First, such diminished practices put a heavy burden on the faithful in an increasingly secularized cultural environment. Due to the larger culture's inability to make sense of religious meanings, the culture no longer provides the imaginative tools for such meaning construction on the part of the faithful. After all, the secularism of late-modern culture is not just something that surrounds the church. Rather, it has deeply penetrated the faithful, even where they are not consciously aware of it. As a result, it is increasingly difficult for the faithful to complete the production of meaning, which is required of them in their participation in the sacraments.

Add a second problem: If the faithful have to construct most of the sacraments' meanings in their imagination, this burden makes them especially prone to the modern danger of solipsism. Louis-Marie Chauvet speaks of the power of the imaginary to erase difference.[154] Similarly, Marion argues that in the imagination the icon all too easily becomes an idol, which serves merely as the mirror of the self's gaze.[155] Hence, celebrating the sacraments with an extremely diminished level of semiosis makes them more vulnerable to misinterpretation. Low-level semiotic practices rob the sacraments of their regulative function, namely, to point us to the Other, the

153. Ibid., 186.
154. See chap. 1, "Disseminated and Condensed Sacramentality," 18–19.
155. See chap. 2, "What Is a Sacrament?," 74–75.

living Christ—the face of redemption turned visibly toward us, as Hughes puts it with Schillebeeckx—and thus, as Marion is prone to say, "to render visible the invisible as such."[156]

Note here again that for Hughes, semiotic signification is all a sacrament can do. As he conceives of it, it is nothing more than "a metaphor, saying that it both is and is not the thing that it is pointing to."[157] In the absence of divine real presence in the sacraments, all these can do is to *point* to the divine. As Hughes formulates, though, "[T]he pointing to is of great importance, because we in this post-Easter church . . . have no real possibility of the direct apprehension of Christ. We apprehend Christ always through or via this sacramental meal."[158]

For Hughes, sacramental representations of the divine in concrete material realities are needed desperately, even in a world where everything is permeated by the divine, as the Reformed tradition's concept of disseminated sacramentality has it. Where everything equally points to the divine, nothing in the end does. In fact, the sacramental character of the world itself becomes obvious only in light of the condensed sacraments. In other words, distributed sacramentality needs condensed sacramentality in order to be recognized in the first place. As Hughes puts it, the two sacraments "give us a kind of canonicity," "a kind of canon of what sacramentality is," "a kind of canonical standard in very similar ways to the ways in which the church had to figure out which would be its canonical writings," or else, a "some kind of sacramental center, some kind of sacramental reference point that we can say: Well yes, this is a sacramental appropriation of God's presence in this world and this is just suiting myself."[159] Only because we learn of God's sacramental presence in baptism and Holy Communion can we actually speak of God's sacramental presence in God's creation more generally and in every human being created in the image of God.

156. Jean-Luc Marion, "The Idol and the Icon," in *God without Being*, trans. Thomas A. Carlson, with a foreword by David Tracy (Chicago and London: University of Chicago Press, 1991), 18, quoted in chap. 2, "What Is a Sacrament?," 75. See ibid., 88, for the reference to Schillebeeckx.

157. Chap. 6, "The Last Interview," 184.

158. Ibid.

159. Ibid., 188–89.

To be sure, Hughes recognizes that God's sacramental presence in the world takes its primordial form not even in baptism and Holy Communion but rather in Jesus Christ himself: "It is Christ, in the vastness and in the vagueness of God's presence in the universe, which actually allows us to say who God is and even to say who is God for us."[160] With many other theologians of the last century, Hughes speaks of Jesus Christ as the primordial sacrament. After his resurrection, however, we no longer encounter Christ directly but rather in the symbolic representations of baptism and Holy Communion. As Hughes puts it, "[W]ithout those two sacraments we could not speak with any kind of confidence about that," namely, Christ's continuing presence in the world.[161] Therefore, a renewal of material sacramentality based on semiotically strong signs and symbols is quintessential for the church's future.

In conclusion, let us take a look at the five chapters, which together compose this book. The first two chapters are those that Hughes completed for this book. The last three chapters consist of preliminary studies, which Hughes had originally published in advance of his book. They serve well to sketch the direction the book would have taken had Hughes been able to complete it. The book concludes with an interview Hughes's colleague and close friend Emilsen recorded with him shortly before his death, which I edited for the purposes of publication.

In the first chapter, which I have titled "Disseminated and Condensed Sacramentality," Hughes makes the case for the "strategic priority" of a condensed sacramentality, as it emerged historically in conjunction with developments regularly referred to as early Catholicism, that is, the emergence of doctrinal standards for orthodoxy, of ecclesial standards of organization, of a hierarchical leadership in the church, and of the scriptural canon. Hughes argues here that recognizing a strategic priority for condensed sacramentality does not imply a rejection of disseminated sacramentality per se. Rather, Hughes sees both sacramentalities as dialectically related to one other, with the one serving as the center and the other as the periphery.

160. Ibid., 189.
161. Ibid.

In a further step of the argument, Hughes analyzes the double nature of the sacraments: on the one hand, they are physical fabrications that direct us beyond themselves to the Invisible; on the other hand, they are human constructions that as such can never contain the divine. Nonetheless, in this double constitution, they save us from the ever-present danger of our own imagination's "erasing of the difference."[162] They thus protect us from ourselves and make room for God's alterity.

Finally, Hughes argues that the distance of material sacramentality helps the church to avoid the cultural colonization, which is the inherent danger in upholding only a disseminated sacramentality. Often, churches confront the choice between traditionalism and the "unwitting identification with the enveloping culture."[163] Over against this choice between Scylla and Charybdis, Hughes propagates "a *critical reception* of both," the tradition and the cultural moment.[164] Arguably, in the Reformed churches of today, the second alternative exercises the greatest attraction: contemporary worship seems to offer salvation for all problems with worship attendance. Here, Hughes raises his critical voice: the obsession with novelty in contemporary worship presents itself to him as a mirror image of modernity's immanentism. The fact that the arguments in favor of contemporary worship are almost always drawn exclusively from the pervasive culture rather than from the church's own tradition demonstrate for him furthermore the danger of modernity's influence on the church itself. Here, Hughes sees the material symbols of faith as a desperately needed corrective as a standard of reference.

In the second chapter, titled "What Is a Sacrament? What Is Sacramentality?," Hughes offers an at once theological and anthropological foundation for a renewed Reformed sacramentality. Anthropologically, Hughes bases his sacramental approach on the inescapable psychosomatic unity of the human person, which does not allow for antitheses or dualisms. Theologically, Hughes draws

---

162. Louis-Marie Chauvet, *The Sacraments: The Word of God at the Mercy of the Body* (Collegeville, MN: Liturgical Press, 2001), 15, quoted in chap. 1, "Disseminated and Condensed Sacramentality," 18.

163. Chap. 1, "Disseminated and Condensed Sacramentality," 26.

164. Ibid., 29–30.

on Daniel Hardy's distinction of God's extensity and God's intensity in the world to explain the difference of God's presence in condensed and distributed sacramentality. In the condensed sacraments, God is not present more, Hughes contends, but rather differently.[165]

In order to counter Calvin's fear that material sacramentality leads inevitably to idolatry, Hughes offers a sustained reflection on iconicity and idolatry, and here especially on the notion of the *imago Dei*. The image of God offers us, Hughes avers, a bridge between God's extensity and God's intensity in the world. While all human beings are created in the image of God, only Jesus Christ is the definitive image of God, as already Irenaeus of Lyon noted. Nonetheless, for Hughes, the doctrine of the image of God makes the crucial point that my neighbor functions for me as a sacrament of God. Hughes engages insights by Jewish philosopher Levinas to make his point: Insofar as another person is endlessly other to me, he or she becomes a parable of God's radical alterity, which helps counteract the "endemic human preoccupation with the self."[166] The encounter with my neighbor's alterity exposes me to God's infinity. Similarly, Hughes draws on Marion's thesis that icons can serve as pointers to infinity. In contrast to the idol, which—according to Marion—acts only as a mirror that reflects the gaze's image, the icon directs the person beyond itself to the divine.

In the third chapter, titled "The Uncertain Place of Materiality in the Reformed Tradition," Hughes analyzes the current problems of the churches in the Reformed tradition. In his view, the Reformed tradition's rejection of condensed sacramentality has led to a close connection between Reformed Christianity and modernity, which today makes this brand of Christianity most susceptible to secularization. Hughes detects the root cause for this development in the Reformed tradition's rejection of materiality. Therefore, he argues, the problem can only be solved by a reappreciation of materiality and condensed sacramentality, yet not in the way some

---

165. This explanation is similar to that of Thomas Aquinas, who distinguished between different forms of causality (material, formal, etc.) to explain the difference of God's presence in the sacraments from God's difference elsewhere in creation.

166. Chap. 2, "What Is a Sacrament?," 68.

post-Christian thinkers develop it in abstraction from a religious tradition. If we want to see God as active in all of life, we can only do so if we detect among us "*particular* bearers of holiness."[167] As Hughes warns us, "[W]hen everything is sacred, nothing is any longer sacred."[168]

In the fourth chapter, titled "The Embodied Word: In Search of a Reformed Sacramentality," Hughes argues once more that "the attenuated sacramental life" of the mainline churches contributes to their "present plight."[169] He contends accordingly that only a re-evaluation of the sacraments and of sacramentality in general will help the churches resolve their ecclesiological crisis and avoid the danger of their own dissipation in the enveloping culture. As Hughes puts it, without sacramentality there is no authentic Christian life. As background to his thesis, Hughes introduces the different ecclesial traditions, with the low church including the Reformed tradition, on the one hand, and the high church, on the other. Hughes analyzes the theological reasons behind the emergence of the low church tradition, going back to Calvin's fear of idolatry in material representations of the divine. In response to Calvin's concerns, Hughes argues against an identification of physicality and idolatry and asks why God cannot accommodate God's self to other sentient forms if God can indeed do so with human linguistic forms, as Calvin admits.

Finally, Hughes offers an evaluation of traditional Reformed sacramentality from the perspective of the contemporary situation. He detects in his ecclesial tradition a curtailment of bodily sensation, problems with God's alterity, and disheartening proximities of a desacralized religion with secular modernity or, in other words, a secular colonization of the church by the surrounding culture. As a remedy against the dangers of unbridled interior speculation, the absence of alterity, and cultural assimilation, Hughes proposes a reformulation of Reformed sacramentality on the basis of Levinas's notion of an encounter, which Hughes develops in a threefold form:

---

167. Chap. 3, "The Uncertain Place of Materiality," 109.
168. Ibid., 107.
169. Chap. 4, "The Embodied Word," 114.

encounter, encounter with God, and encounter with God in Christ by way of embodied experience.

In the fifth chapter, titled "Faith's Materiality, and Some Implications for Worship and Theology," Hughes draws out the consequences of his view on sacramentality, especially with regard to contemporary worship practices. Hughes here once more analyzes the historical reasons for the church's assumption that faith is immaterial—reasons that he finds both in the Bible and in the influence of Hellenism on the early development of Christian theology. Hughes then contrasts this development with postmodern insights into the absence of purities and develops, through a reflection on Romans 6:1-14, two insights into faith's materiality, namely, the nature of Christian praxis and the material conditions within which faith is lived. Hughes concludes that faith is always embodied in human life and that liturgy encompasses both ideas and concrete material practices.

Again, Hughes draws on Levinas to argue that what we need today more than anything else is a strong sense of God's alterity. Both the dialogical structure and the physicality of worship deliver us from solipsism, that is, from finding only ourselves in worship. Materiality, Hughes suggests, is of quintessential importance in what happens in worship, both on the side of the presider and of the faithful. Thus, the presider's actions and attitudes are just as important as the physical structure of the building, in which worship takes place, or the temporal progression of worship itself. Hughes concludes with a clarion call for the Reformed churches to recognize the importance of the material, the physical, and the visible as signs and symbols for the Invisible.

Chapter One

Disseminated and Condensed Sacramentality

It is not strictly true that Reformed Christianity has had little interest in sacramentality. What is true is that—at least in comparison with other Christian confessions—Reformed sacramentality has not focused so directly on the church's major sacraments, baptism and the Lord's Supper. Rather, it has taken overwhelmingly a form that I will call "distributed" or "disseminated" or "diffused" sacramentality (which descriptions I shall treat as synonymous and use indiscriminately). This is a style of Christian awareness that locates God, or the sacred, in everyday experience. A recent survey of members of the Uniting Church in Australia,[1] for instance, found that something like 94 percent of those questioned sensed God's presence most vividly through the natural environment.[2] Another example

---

1. The Uniting Church in Australia derives from the union (in 1977) of Presbyterian, Methodist, and Congregational churches. It may be asked whether the Methodist presence in this union qualifies or modifies the Reformed character of the resultant denomination. Methodist influences are certainly to be identified. I venture the judgment, however, that the UCA shows most of the marks which I shall henceforth call "Reformed."

2. William W. Emilsen, ed., *An Informed Faith: The Uniting Church at the Beginning of the Twenty-First Century* (Melbourne: Morning Star Publishing, 2014).

is to be seen in this remark as reported in a local newspaper: "The discussions followed on from Abraham Kuyper [the widely influential nineteenth-century Dutch Reformed theologian], that all of our life is religion, all is worship, whether I'm washing the dishes or writing a poem or cleaning out the rubbish bin or feeding the dog, it's all done in the service of God."[3]

As an idea, sacramentality encompasses a considerable spectrum. There are two constants: in all cases there is a material signifier and, also in each case, some sense of transcendent reference is said to be apprehended through or within the signifier. There are also, however, wide differences across the spectrum. Both the *nature or texture of the material signifier* and *the means by which the transcendent referent is apprehended* vary greatly.

At one end of the spectrum, sometimes called "aniconic" or more conventionally "low church," it is the world of everyday sense experience, as we have just heard, which is reckoned to be the locus of divine disclosure. Bernard Cooke, for example, though a Roman Catholic, holds that "[i]t is the ordinary sequence of experiences that provides the context of consciousness in which awareness of divine self-giving and therefore the presence of a saving God occurs."[4] Or the Reformed theologian Hans Boersma writes: "The purpose of all matter . . . is to lead us into God's heavenly presence, to bring about communion with God, participation in the divine life."[5]

At the other end of the spectrum ("iconic" or "high church") is a view of sacramentality that centers on what Mary Douglas called "condensed symbols."[6] This, in Douglas's description, holds "the

---

3. *Sydney Morning Herald*, "Good Weekend" (December 18–20, 2009): 12.

4. Bernard J. Cooke, *The Distancing of God: The Ambiguity of Symbol in History and Theology* (Minneapolis: Fortress Press, 1990), 359. Cooke argues that the tendency, from early in the church's history, to locate divine presence in special times, places, rites, and persons has resulted in what he calls "the distancing of God" (hence his title). See further below, p. 7.

5. Hans Boersma, *Heavenly Participation: The Weaving of a Sacramental Tapestry* (Grand Rapids, MI, and Cambridge, UK: William B. Eerdmans Publishing Company, 2011), 9. It is important to observe that later in his book Boersma gives extended attention to the Word as sacrament and to the Eucharist.

6. Mary Douglas, *Natural Symbols: Explorations in Cosmology* (New York: Penguin Books, 1978), 29, 41, 54, 69, etc.

deity [to be] located in a specific object, place and time and under control of a specific formula."[7] Otherwise expressed, this kind of sacramentality is seen as deriving from, or depending on, "saturated" or "dense" or "intentional" sentient signification: elaborate ritual actions, authorized officiants, enriched aesthetic experiences, and so on. Here the transcendent reference is understood to derive precisely from the *non*-ordinariness of the material vehicle; encounter with the divine is facilitated exactly through the extraordinary nature or texture of the physical sign.

I have cast the two conceptions as points on a spectrum. That implies, their differences notwithstanding, that they are not wholly separable. According to Herbert Vorgrimler then: "[Paul Tillich] was convinced that human beings can encounter the sacramental everywhere. The Church's sacraments he regarded as places in which the sacramental, which can be encountered everywhere, is especially concentrated."[8] And David Power describes the relationship as it comes to expression in eucharistic celebration: "This sensible presence is *both* the presence of the whole world of creation through objects such as bread, wine, oil and water *and* the presence of God who is present in these things through the creative act of self-communication."[9] But insofar as they are indeed points on a spectrum they differ, in some respects seemingly diametrically. It is arguable that precisely the divergent ways of understanding sacramental presence constitute the cleft, which has divided Western churches for roughly five centuries.

There can be no doubting the appeal, especially in our times, of the "aniconic" end of the spectrum. Its great strength is its democratic, "secular" nature: It is open to everyone. It depends on no

7. Ibid., 69.

8. Herbert Vorgrimler, *Sacramental Theology*, trans. Linda M. Maloney (Collegeville, MN: Liturgical Press, 1992), 72–73.

9. David N. Power, *Sacrament: The Language of God's Giving* (New York: Crossroad, 1999), 56 (my emphases) and see similarly, ibid., 91, 120. Or Gordon Lathrop asks (rhetorically): "What if that 'taste and see' [the congregation gathered in eucharistic celebration] and that 'holy ground' [the world in which Christians find themselves in daily living] really do go together?"; Gordon W. Lathrop, *Holy Ground: A Liturgical Cosmology* (Minneapolis: Augsburg Fortress, 2003), 4. See, further, n. 99 below.

"special" times, places, rituals, or persons. It locates God in a familiar world, the world, as we heard above, of everyday routines. God's self then seems more familiar, not shrouded in arcane mystery. It means a great deal to people to sense God as present in each moment of their day and accessible in every circumstance.

It was from the beginning the hallmark style of Reformed churches and has empowered Reformed Christianity through now nearly five centuries and across the entire Western world. In its modern guise—so-called contemporary worship—it threatens to undermine and overtake many, even most, of the so-called mainline churches in its appeal.[10]

But questions arise. It will be my contention in this book that in the absence of a much more specific sacramentality—that is, an acceptance of ideas which it has historically tended to disparage as "catholic" or "high church"—deep and serious questions of Christian identity lie before Reformed Christianity as it is presently constituted.

In the next several paragraphs I will attempt to delineate some of these deficits and liabilities as I see them.

A Periphery without a Center?

Advocates of a disseminated sacramentality point with justification to the largely "desacralized" character of Christian faith as depicted in the New Testament. Already in Jesus' ministry, in sharpest distinction to the prevailing customs, the boundaries of "who God is and where God is to be found"[11] are redrawn. He "was not preoccupied with matters of ritual purity after the fashion of the priests, Pharisees and Qumran sectaries"; his mission, rather, "was dominated by . . . the coming of God in mercy and justice."[12] The critical

---

10. See, e.g., Alister McGrath, *Evangelicalism and the Future of Christianity* (Downers Grove, IL: Intervarsity, 1996), 184–86.

11. Stephen C. Barton, "Dislocating and Relocating Holiness: A New Testament Study," in *Holiness Past and Present*, ed. Stephen C. Barton (London and New York: T&T Clark, 2003), 195.

12. Ibid., 198. See also James D. G. Dunn, "Jesus and Holiness: The Challenge of Purity," in *Holiness Past and Present*, ed. Stephen C. Barton (London and New York: T&T Clark, 2003), 168–92.

difference between Jesus and his contemporaries is exactly the difference between, on one hand, dependence on outward, formal, or ritualistic means of marking (or demarcating) God's presence in the world and, on the other, an encounter in wonder and praise with God's mercy and acceptance in the weft and woof of daily life. We might even risk the idea: "justification by faith" (cf. Luke 18:14). What we have in Jesus' proclamation is pretty much the paradigm of "disseminated sacramentality."[13]

The impetus did not cease with Jesus. Through his astonishing encounter with the risen Christ, the apostle Paul's understanding of "who God is and where God is to be found" was also revolutionized (see, notably, Phil 3:4-9). Here, of course, we can more assuredly speak of "justification by faith": namely, the refusal to find favor with God through what Paul liked to call "works of the law,"[14] the elaborate edifices of ritual purity (e.g., Gal 4:10). It is thus not at all coincidental that, in Paul's diction, traditionally cultic terminology has been "secularized." God's "temple" now consists in Christian believers themselves (1 Cor 3:16). Of the famous injunction to the Romans that they are to "present [their] bodies as a living sacrifice" (Rom 12:1), the great exegete Ernst Käsemann writes: "What was previously cultic is now extended to the secularity of our earthly life as a whole" and "at issue is a fundamentally different understanding of true worship. Here the *temenos* [a temple's sacred enclosure] of antiquity is shattered."[15] Or, finally, the liturgical theologian and New Testament scholar Gordon Lathrop writes of Paul's "priestly service" (Rom 15:16): "Paul sees his nonsacrificial, noncultic *announcement of the gospel* of Jesus Christ as his 'priestly service' and

---

13. It is probably important also to recall, however, that "neither did [Jesus] dispense with the Sabbath or attendance at Temple or synagogue" (Dunn, "Jesus and Holiness," 191). Dunn goes on: "We should also note that Jesus worked within the rules and conventions of the day in recognizing a link between uncleanness and sin, and in requiring the leprous man to show himself to the priest and to offer for his cleansing what Moses commanded (Mark 1:44)." Such qualifications tend to be overlooked by exponents of "disseminated sacramentality."

14. Rom 3:27-28; Gal 3:2; and often.

15. Ernst Käsemann, *Commentary on Romans*, trans. Geoffrey William Bromiley (London: SCM Press, 1980), 327–28.

the responding faith in God, awakened throughout the world, as the only 'pure offering' of the nations."[16] It is then no coincidence that churches in which "justification by faith" has been strongly affirmed tend also to aniconic forms of faith and/or worship.

The sense of "charismatic endowment"[17] was not sustained, however, at least not uniformly.[18] It was largely supplanted by what is now sometimes called "early Catholicism," namely, a view of "the church as [an] institution of salvation, [with] ordained church officers, apostolic succession, sacramental priesthood, authoritative interpretation of Scripture, [and the] linking of the Spirit to the institution."[19] In the New Testament and the immediate sub-apostolic writings these features are still embryonic. They are nonetheless significant. They represent the transition to a more structured and manageable church than the earlier models had envisaged or allowed. Views of "truth" and "falsity," for example, have become or are becoming standardized: so-called right doctrine (literally, "healthy teaching") is much in evidence;[20] the church has become "the pillar and bulwark of the truth";[21] and "faith" is becoming "*the* faith."[22] Second (not necessarily in importance; all the elements hang together and mutually reinforce one another) is the emergence of a permanent leadership structure: "overseers,"[23]

16. Gordon W. Lathrop, *The Four Gospels on Sunday: The New Testament and the Reform of Christian Worship* (Minneapolis: Augsburg Fortress, 2012), 19 (my emphases). See also Louis-Marie Chauvet, *The Sacraments: The Word of God at the Mercy of the Body* (Collegeville, MN: Liturgical Press, 2001), 61–63.

17. Barton, "Dislocating and Relocating Holiness," 199.

18. Though appearing relatively late among the New Testament documents, the Johannine writings also insist on "the Church's newness in its final and most radical form" (Eduard Schweizer, *Church Order in the New Testament* [London: SCM Press, 1961], 124).

19. Werner Georg Kümmel, *Introduction to the New Testament,* trans. Howard Clark Kee, revised and updated translation of *Einleitung in das Neue Testament* by P. Feine and J. Behm (London: SCM Press, 1975), 146.

20. 1 Tim 1:10; 6:3; 2 Tim 1:13; 4:3; Titus 1:9, 13; 2:1, 2.

21. 1 Tim 3:15.

22. 1 Tim 4:1, 6; Titus 1:13.

23. 1 Tim 3:1-7; Titus 1:7; and especially prominent in the letters of Ignatius of Antioch, for example, Eph 1:3; 2:1-2; 3:2; and often.

"elders,"[24] and "deacons."[25] Of critical importance in this is that such leaders are recognized not because of some charismatic gift (as in Paul) but on the basis of their orthodoxy[26] and their moral integrity.[27] There is increasingly a sense of rank in these offices.[28] Some sort of official authorization ("ordination") is visible,[29] as are set forms for prayer.[30] What is at stake in these developments is the ability to identify *particular physical forms and structures* as trusted and trustworthy *carriers of the divine.* They represent a kind of canonicity—indeed the canonization of Scripture will be a central element in the process.[31]

The transition is variously interpreted. I have already noted that advocates of aniconic forms of belief read it, predictably, wholly negatively, as lamentable devolution. To cite Cooke again, then:

> [T]he shift in early Christianity to ritual that was distanced from ordinary life was quick and largely uncontested, because it appeared so traditional and religious. In a matter of only a few generations the revolutionary proximity of the divine to the human which had characterized the career of Jesus himself and much of earliest Christianity had been replaced by religion. Whereas sacrality attached to ordinariness of human experience in the first few decades of the church, and designations of places or times or persons as sacred was eschewed, the attribute of special sacrality very early became associated with "removed" places and actions and persons, and belief

---

24. Titus 1:5; Jas 5:14; 1 Pet 5:1; and especially prominent in 1 Clement, for example, 44:5; 47:6; 54:2; 57:1.

25. 1 Tim 3:8-10, 11-13.

26. 1 Tim 5:17; 2 Tim 2:2; Titus 1:9.

27. 1 Tim 3:2-7, 8-10, 12-13; Titus 1:6-7; Didache 15:1.

28. 2 Tim 2:20-21; 1 Clement 42:1-2, 4-5; Ignatius to the Trallians 3:1; etc.

29. 1 Tim 4:14; 5:22; 2 Tim 1:6.

30. Didache 9:10.

31. See, for example, Lee M. McDonald, *The Formation of the Christian Biblical Canon* (Peabody, MA: Hendrickson Publishers, 1995), 138–42 (esp. 141n19), 178 (on the way in which the *regula fidei*, the canon of faith, would eventually become a scriptural canon), 190.

grew that divine saving presence was to be encountered through involvement with these sacred realities.[32]

This is not the only possible reading of the facts, however. It is important to recognize, first, that the movement was occasioned by explicit and concrete circumstances, namely, the emergence of, and threat created by, gnostic and other forms of Christian heterodoxy. It is not particularly helpful to see it, the transition, simply as natural attrition, what Max Weber called "the routinization of charismatic authority"[33] (as is implicit in Cooke's view). The advent of "early Catholicism" implies then, second, that the charismatic openness of the earliest stages of the Christian movement proved to be less than adequate in the face of emergent challenges. No one denies, of course, that as the process advanced, eventually producing "the church as an institution of salvation" (at the cost, that is, of its early charismatic spontaneity), immense losses were incurred. Nor is it correct or helpful to valorize "charisma" over "office"; both turned out to be necessary in the ongoing history of Christianity, and each is the corrective of the other. Eduard Schweizer, then, in his classic study of church order in New Testament times, writes:

> When, in face of the menace of gnostic fanaticism, there was a danger that the gospel would disintegrate into something time-less and unhistorical, and the Church into a sum total of religious individualists, the Church's historicity, tradition, and order had to be stressed. . . . But with the threat of an institutional Church, in which a monarchical bishop wanted to rule everything, the self-sufficiency of the Church as it stood under the living activity of the Holy Spirit had to be stressed.[34]

32. Cooke, *The Distancing of God*, 263.

33. Max Weber, *Economy and Society: An Outline of Interpretive Sociology*, ed. Guenther Roth and Klaus Wittich, trans. Ephraim Fischoff and others (Berkeley: University of California Press, 1978), 439–42, 1121–48.

34. Schweizer, *Church Order*, 168; see, similarly, ibid., 104: "[W]e have to ask whether the looseness of this order [in the Pauline churches], which entrusts so much to the working of God's Spirit, can be maintained in a period when Paul's personal influence has ceased. Or is it inevitable that the Church does not sustain this freedom . . . and that it either develops . . . one-sidedly into

Spirit and form ("charisma" and "office") are thus equally necessary and mutually complementary; to resume my earlier form of expression, each is a marker on a continuum. Theologically speaking, we will say there is no priority of importance between them.

There is, however, an argument to be made for a *strategic* ordering of them. This, I say again, has nothing to do with the intrinsic worth of each—their importance from God's point of view if we may put it like this. It has everything to do with human necessities. And is not the less important for that. There are two aspects of the "early Catholic" developments which give them their strategic priority. These are, first, their materiality and, second, their human constitution.

Matters of spirit turn out to be elusive, difficult to track, hard to account for. Substantial forms, on the contrary, both allow and demand accountability. Precisely herein lay the value of the "early Catholic" elements in the emerging church. They gave a visible profile. They were identifiable markers. They could not so easily be mistaken, distorted, or manipulated. They provided some possibility of drawing boundaries, of saying what was, and what was not, acceptable. They were publicly accessible. In short, they constituted a measure of objectivity. So that—in a context in which personal charisma could be, and was being, exploited either for personal advancement or fissiparous individualism—such possibility of an appeal to an established tradition, to agreed truths, to publicly approved and tested leaders, and to established understandings of what "church" means was crucial. The possibility lay in the physicality of these things: they could be pointed to and pointed out, they could be summoned in argumentation, and they were public artifacts. This remains true even of the elements, which might at first seem less than substantial such as "the tradition"; here too, however, there are such things as historical evidences and language itself is not without its material dimension.[35]

They were also human constructs. They came into play because of the human condition—by which is meant both our human

<hr>

a Church with an organized hierarchy, or just as one-sidedly turns the momentum of freedom into a system, till it dissolves itself in gnostic individualism?"
35. See further.

constriction within time and space but also human proclivities for error and/or perversity. The human factor is clear in the case of officials elected on the basis of orthodoxy and orthopraxis. It might seem less applicable to the content of the tradition, which is still recognized in the literature we are considering as given of God ("the divine economy,"[36] or "the gospel of the glory of the blessed God,"[37] and so on). Yet the very construal of such content as "sound doctrine" (with its implied value judgment about alternative versions) is humanly contrived and is directed to the same ends of objectivity and identifiability. The point is that it is *as human beings* that we require touchstones, consolidated meanings, and defining artifacts (symbols, we may say).

All of this, I am arguing, has a direct bearing on the kinds of sacramentality experienced by Christians.

I have already touched on the attraction a distributed or disseminated sacramentality holds for large numbers of believing people in our time. It offers a clear sense of God's presence in the midst of daily life. It permits a personal relationship with God, not bound by times and seasons or official regulation. It thus enables a sense of freedom, of spontaneity, and self-possession. But further, it locates the divine presence in a familiar world—through cultural styles and idioms we have learned to take for granted and in a landscape and climate we have known since childhood, what Thomas Troeger once called "the landscape of the heart."[38] Disseminated sacra-

---

36. 1 Tim 1:4.

37. 1 Tim 1:11.

38. On 15 August 1995, Thomas H. Troeger presented a lecture at United Theological College, Sydney, titled "The Landscape of the Heart: The Function of the Conventional Imagination in Worship" (to the best of my knowledge the lecture has never been published). The lecture included *inter alia*: "[O]ur version of the world is shaped and limited by the culture and environment in which we have been raised. These stories [Troeger had earlier offered two or three anecdotes] remind us that each of us has a landscape of the heart, a world of memories, visions, values, dreams, beliefs." Troeger acknowledged the Australian poet James McAuley as the inspiration of his title; it comes from McCauley's poem, "An Art of Poetry"; see James McAuley, *Collected Poems 1936–1970* (Sydney: Angus and Robertson Publishers, 1971), 70.

mentality thus draws into itself reflections on "enculturation"[39] and "contextualization."[40] We can take it yet further: this kind of sacramentality ascribes the highest possible worth to the created order; nature itself becomes the means or medium through which transcendence makes itself apparent.

These important values duly affirmed, a disseminated sacramentality also carries certain liabilities, liabilities not dissimilar to those which, in its time, "early Catholicism" found it necessary to meet.

The overwhelming problem with so-called disseminated sacramentality lies in its lack of definition. It generates a sense of wonder, of mystery even. But in itself this may be, often is, quite unrelated to the God of Christian faith.[41] Second, it relies heavily on intuition,

39. See, particularly, Gerard Moore, "Sacramentality: An Australian Perspective," in *Christian Worship in Australia: Inculturating the Liturgical Tradition*, ed. Stephen Burns and Anita Monro (Strathfield: St Pauls Publications, 2009), 139–53. Reference might also be made to Carmel Pilcher, "Poinsettia: Christmas or Pentecost—Celebrating Liturgy in the Great South Land that is Australia," *Worship* 81, no. 6 (November 2007): 508–20, though Pilcher here deals with the worship of gathered congregations, which I will consider more nearly under the idea of "condensed" sacramentality.

40. Daniel Hardy reminds us that "context" means an "interweaving"—in this case the "braiding" (also Hardy's word) of local knowledge and transcendent reference; see Daniel W. Hardy, *God's Ways with the World: Thinking and Practising Christian Faith* (Edinburgh: T&T Clark, 1996), 32, 68.

41. Jürgen Habermas, for example, recognized that "ordinary life, now fully profane, by no means becomes immune to the shattering and subversive intrusion of extraordinary events [*das Außeralltägliche*]." Cited by Peter Dews, *The Limits of Disenchantment: Essays on Contemporary European Philosophy* (London and New York: Verso, 1995), 10–11.

Reference might also be made to what is sometimes called "post-secularism," the view that in the vacuum created by the collapse of conventional religious observance a new sense of the sacred has made itself apparent, one which has emphatically nothing to do with Christian belief but acknowledges unexpected epiphanic moments, such as glimpses of the uncanny, of wonder, and of the mysterious; see, e.g., Mukarand Paranjape, ed., *Sacred Australia: Post-secular Considerations* (Melbourne: Clouds of Magellan, 2009).

Finally, John Rogerson's thesis could be noted: "Holiness [for which we might as easily write 'the sacred'] is a word in the English language whose meaning depends on the contexts in which it is used and the interests of those who use it" (the ensuing essay is then the thesis's defense); John Rogerson,

on a "sense" of otherworldliness, an "intimation" of immortality.[42] Of course, it is true that what I am calling the condensed sacraments (and sacramentality) of the Christian church also depend on what I shall call "indirection" and are thus something less than direct embodiments of the divine (so-called "real presence"). In comparison with the sacramentality of which we are here speaking, however, their material constitution and their "canonicity" achieves a vastly higher clarity of definition. Third, the diffused sacramentality here in view is seriously liable to "projection"—that is, the reading into the sign of the desired or supposed signification. Again, "projection" is by no means restricted to this kind of sacramentality.[43] But, also, again in comparison with the condensed symbols of the church, the risk is proportionately much higher.[44]

It is from this point of view that I am claiming for condensed forms of sacramentality a strategic priority over these more loosely textured styles. (I mention again that the notion of "condensed sacramentality" is after Douglas; see notes 6 and 7 above.) The two established sacraments (for Protestants), baptism and the Lord's Supper, unquestionably stand at the heart of this. But the category extends more widely.[45] A broader demographic thus reaches to mat-

---

"What Is Holiness?," in *Holiness Past and Present*, ed. Stephen C. Barton (London and New York: T&T Clark, 2003), 3–21.

42. To borrow William Wordsworth's famous title: "Ode: Intimations of Immortality from Recollections of Early Childhood," in *The Poetical Works of William Wordsworth* (London and Edinburgh: William P. Nimmo, 1878), 300–304.

43. See Robert Banks, *And Man Created God: Is God a Human Invention?* (Oxford: Lion Hudson plc, 2011), 133–47.

44. In his essay to which I have already referred, Moore writes of the transience of place-names: "In a sense these names ['Australia', etc.] do not denote anything of their original content. Rather, terms such as 'New South Wales' or 'Australia' have *the meanings that the inhabitants give* in light of their experience of living there" ("Sacramentality: An Australian Perspective," 142, my emphases). In a way somewhat analogously, people are able to "import" their sense of transcendental encounter into the phenomena.

45. We may recall that for many centuries, which of the church's sacramental actions and how many of them should formally be named as sacraments remained inconclusive. See, for example, James F. White, *The Sacraments in Protestant Practice and Faith* (Nashville: Abingdon Press, 1999), 23–27, 119–39, esp. 120.

ters such as designated time, appointed spaces and their architecture, officially recognized ministers, perhaps the music of worship, and, again unquestionably, gathered congregations and the events that transpire within them (and neither is this list necessarily exclusive).

The importance of this order of sacramentality lies in the first place in its physicality or—better perhaps—its *particular* physicality. Another way of saying this is that in this case the degree of semiotic transference between the material condition and its purported transcendent referent is markedly higher than in the more discursive sacramental styles (which is why, in the latter, so much more depends on intuition or imagination). It is precisely this considerably higher level of semiosis that achieves for condensed sacramentality its much sharper definitions.

Liturgical or sacramental space will come in for extended treatment later in my discussion but it may serve us here—in an anticipatory way—as an example of how this comes about. The Catholic sacramental theologian Louis-Marie Chauvet writes of liturgical space:

> Space is something other than simple extent. It is a place which has been constructed culturally and has psychological connotations. As liturgical space, it is a place which is "informed" . . . by the tradition and collective memory of Christians. . . . Thus liturgical space constitutes as it were a quasi-sacramental crystallization of the whole of the value system specific to Christianity. The whole ecclesial tradition is presented here.[46]

The relevance of this to our present discussion is that such judgments ("a place informed by the tradition and collective memory of Christians" and "the whole ecclesial tradition is presented here") arise from, depend on, the semiotic values embedded within the actual artifacts over which such judgments are made. Of course, people's fond attachment, encapsulating personal memories and associations, is not absent from such evaluations.[47] But, more fundamental, it is the form

46. Louis-Marie Chauvet, "The Liturgy in Its Symbolic Space," in *Concilium*, vol. 3: *Liturgy and the Body*, ed. Louis-Marie Chauvet and François Kabasele Lumbala (London: SCM Press, 1995), 29, 30.

47. Recalling Tom Troeger's story of the red horsehair couch; Thomas H. Troeger, *The Parable of Ten Preachers* (Nashville: Abingdon Press, 1992), 21.

of the space (its height and length and breadth), its lighting, the arrangement (proxemics) of furnishings and articles within it, the kinds of furnishings and their design, its textiles and the combination of colors, which together and *inter alia* become the carriers of this meaning (and none of this is less so when the space is filled with people at worship who bring to the overall effect their own semiosis). It is *just this physicality* that marks off, distinguishes, this space from other spaces so as to achieve Chauvet's "quasi-sacramental crystallization of the whole value system specific to Christianity." Of course, Christians can and do gather for worship in spaces not so intentionally designed (increasingly, one senses, on the part of Reformed congregations): schools, public halls, abandoned warehouses, and so on (in other words, tending strongly in the direction of a diffused sacramentality). There may be good and extraneous reasons for this and my remarks are not intended (well, not overly I hope) to criticize the integrity of such worship. They, the remarks, are, however, most certainly intended to emphasize the greatly heightened level of imagination thus required in order to construe such space as "worship" space. To resume: It is its particular physicality that defines, distinguishes, *this* space as a space for worship. The same may be extrapolated for the other sacramental forms, which I have mentioned and which encourages one to think of them as "condensed" sacramental forms.

I said above that it was not only their physicality but also their human constitution that helped the "early Catholic" developments give definition over against the unpredictability of the charismata. Following on then from these few observations on liturgical space, it is easy to show that the semiosis, which helps to define the space as liturgical, does so insofar as it *bears upon the senses*. In a word, signification is a matter of physical (human!) sensations: it is as *embodied* beings that we are able to distinguish one space—along with its intentional and unintentional references—over against another.

Spirit is much less dependent on the senses; as I have said now a couple of times, it *intuits* a transcendent reference in distributed sacramentality. In comparison, condensed sacramentality invests much more heavily in sentient signification: it expects to "read" the signs much more directly.

This leads to the consideration that, markers though they are on a continuum, we need for each sacramental order a different spatial imagery. For dispersed sacramental presence, that is, one reckons oneself never not to be in God's presence, therein is the point: "Seven whole days, not one in seven, I will praise thee."[48] One does not then here speak of coming "into" divine presence; as said just now, one is never apart from such presence. When all is said and done, *God* is *omni*present. As embodied creatures, contrariwise, *we* are anchored in times and spaces. For us *not* all space and time is equal. For the more condensed forms of sacramentality it is therefore appropriate to speak of "entering" God's holy presence. To reiterate: this has nothing to do with where God may be; it has everything to do with human limitations:

> It could be inferred . . . that the Protestant interpretation of nature would attribute sacramental qualities to everything. No finite object or event would be excluded. . . . This is true in principle, but not in our actual existence. Our existence is determined not only by the omnipresence of the divine but also by our separation from it. If we could see the holy in every reality, we should be in the Kingdom of God. But this is not the case. The holy appears only in special places, in special contexts. The concentration of the sacramental in special places, in special rites, is the expression of man's ambiguous situation.[49]

But now this "coming into" becomes heavily dependent on the physical signs of which I have spoken—not absolutely, that is certain, for, as I have yet to say, these signs have to be filled with spirit, the spirit of those entering and the spirit of the ministers who gather and greet them in God's name, and, we will unquestionably say,

48. George Herbert, "Praise (II)," from *The Temple* (1633), in *The Complete English Poems*, ed. John Tobin (New York: Penguin Books, 1991), 138.

49. Paul Tillich, *The Protestant Era*, abridged edition, trans. James Luther Adams (Chicago: University of Chicago Press, 1957), 110–11. See, similarly, Donald Macpherson Baillie, *The Theology of the Sacraments and Other Papers* (London: Faber and Faber, 1957), 51; and Michael A. Horton, "Participation and Covenant," in *Radical Orthodoxy and the Reformed Tradition: Creation, Covenant and Participation*, ed. James K. A. Smith and James H. Olthuis (Grand Rapids, MI: Baker Academic, 2005), 120: "Although, ontologically speaking, God is omnipresent, the real question is, Where is God *for us*?" (his italics).

the Spirit of God, the Holy Spirit. Still, physicality is of paramount importance. People have to *apprehend* that they have entered a *different* presence,[50] that they have *encountered* the Holy One.[51]

The condensed symbols of faith thus carry a critical and strategic priority of importance; it is these that interpret and give definition to our more elusive intimations of God in diurnal experience. It is as if they constitute a center of which the glancing indicators all around us form a periphery.[52]

It is a *strategic* priority; we have said that theologically each is the necessary complement of the other. We have seen this well enough in the long history of the church—the sterility, that is, of an institution bereft of spirit, formality lacking spontaneity, a cloistered credence cut off from the world. Spirit is to form as music to the libretto, breath to the body.

And yet neither are they exactly the same things. That is why we have the weekly rhythm between, on one hand, gathered worship and, on the other, what Karl Rahner called "the liturgy of the world,"[53] a dialectic of distributed sacramentality and of the con-

---

50. That we "enter" God's presence is an idea at least as biblical as that of God's ubiquity: Psalms 5:7; 15:1; 27:8; 95:2; 100:2; Isaiah 55:6-7; Hebrews 12:22; Revelation 15:4, for example, and perhaps also Matthew 6:6.

51. Sacramentality as "encounter" has been widely popularized through Edward Schillebeeckx's work; see his *Christ the Sacrament of the Encounter with God*, trans. Paul Barrett and N. D. Smith, English text revised by Mark Schoof and Laurence Bright (Kansas City, MO: Sheed and Ward, 1963).

52. The notion of "center" and "periphery" has some affinity with, and also some differences from, Gordon Lathrop's constant call for "a strong center and an open door" in public worship; typical, then, of dozens of such statements is this from his *Holy People*: "an intense symbolic center but with a wide open door," or again, "The assembly . . . should have its strong and cherished center in the things in which the community participates . . . [and] . . . an open door, a permeable outer boundary" (Gordon W. Lathrop, *Holy People: A Liturgical Ecclesiology* [Minneapolis: Augsburg Fortress, 1999], 12, 23). On some differences between Lathrop's and my conception, see n. 100 below.

53. Karl Rahner, "Considerations on the Active Role of the Person in the Sacramental Event," in *Theological Investigations*, vol. 14, trans. David Bourke (London: Darton, Longman and Todd, 1976), 161–84, esp. 169–76; and idem, "On the Theology of Worship," in *Theological Investigations*, vol. 19, trans.

densed symbols of faith. But then we have to say that, because as human beings we need to know where we stand, what we believe, to whom we pray, *we need definitions*. And it is the condensed representations of faith, I have tried to say, which furnish these for our everyday life as Christians.

The Question of Alterity

Alterity (an other's "otherness") is, we may presume, as old as human apperception. To become aware of oneself *as* self is, *ipso facto*, to apprehend the otherness of that other than oneself. Primordial and fundamental as it doubtless is, such awareness was largely lost sight of in the period we call "modernity"—in short: "in the West's obsession with identity, singleness, and purity, with its belief that only unified, homogenous entities . . . can act effectively."[54] It has been postmodernity's discovery that difference (Jacques Derrida's famous or infamous *différance*[55]) plays a fundamental role in human cognition that has brought to prominence, as a direct corollary, the otherness of the other, alterity.

God's otherness, needless to say, has always been a central conviction of Christian faith and perhaps nowhere more so than in Reformed theology. Calvin's thunder reverberates down the centuries: "God's nature [as] immeasurable and spiritual . . . forbids our imagining anything earthly or carnal of him";[56] *finitum non*

Edward Quinn (New York: Crossroad Publishing Company, 1983), 141–49. I shall take up Rahner's "liturgy of the world" in greater detail in chap. 3, below.

54. John McGowan, *Postmodernism and Its Critics* (Ithaca, NY, and London: Cornell University Press, 1991), 20.

55. See perhaps Derrida's famous "non-definition" of *différance*: Jacques Derrida, *Margins of Philosophy*, trans., with notes, by Alan Bass (Chicago: University of Chicago Press, 1982), 26. Most theorists now agree that in fact it is the play of identity *and* difference which yields recognition and meaning. See the discussion in my *Worship as Meaning: A Liturgical Theology for Late Modernity* (Cambridge: Cambridge University Press, 2003), 81–98.

56. John Calvin, *Institutes of the Christian Religion*, ed. John T. McNeill, trans. Ford Lewis Battles (Philadelphia: Westminster Press, 1960), 1.13.1.

capax infiniti.[57] Curiously—ironically we might better say—it is now precisely this deepest conviction of Calvinism that is (at least in its present-day avatar, so-called contemporary worship) placed in question.

I want to approach this matter also (as I did that of sacramental space, above) from the point of view of the Catholic theologian Chauvet:

> [W]hereas the symbolic places the real at a distance by representing it and thus enabling it to be integrated into a culturally significant and coherent whole, the imaginary tends to erase this distance in order to regain the immediate contact with things. As a consequence, things are only the mirror into which the subject projects itself and where it attempts to find (of course unconsciously) its own "image," only embellished. This is an erasing of the difference or otherness in order to find again the "image of what is the same." Everything always returns to the "same," that is, to the subject itself, unavoidably idealized.[58]

Chauvet sets in counterpoint, in juxtaposition, "the symbolic" and "the imaginary." Of the latter he says essentially two things: that it *erases distance* and that it works a *mirror effect*, "an erasing of distance to find again the image of the same." "The symbolic," oppositely, actually *affects distance* by way of representation.

I want to apply these theses to prevalent assumptions (and practices) in current Reformed worship.

First, *"the imaginary" tends to erase distance*. I have already drawn attention to the high level of intuition—imagination we may say or, now following Chauvet, "the imaginary"—invested in aniconic sacramentality. Intuition or imagination gains its importance in this form of encounter with transcendence insofar as the semiotic

---

57. "The finite cannot encompass the infinite," a phrase regularly used in Reformed theology to express the wholly otherness of God; see, e.g., Daniel W. Hardy, "Calvinism and the Visual Arts: A Theological Introduction," in *Seeing Beyond the Word: Visual Arts and the Calvinist Tradition*, ed. Paul Corby Finney (Grand Rapids, MI, and Cambridge: William B. Eerdmans Publishing Company, 1999), 4.

58. Chauvet, *The Sacraments*, 15, drawing on the writings of Jacques Lacan.

markers are as restricted as they are (one has to *deduce* the hand of God in the uncanny coincidence or *sense* the Spirit's leading in an impetuous decision).

We now learn from Chauvet that this intuitive apprehension is an "erasing of distance." Imagination is not particularly beholden to an objective world. It dreams, it contemplates what it will—and constantly does so, sometimes setting before itself the worst possible (worst imaginable!) scenario, but equally often concocting hopelessly unrealistic ones. It is the cold dose of reality, the sharp intrusion of an outside world, which, as we sometimes say, "brings someone to their senses" or "brings us down to earth." But this is to *confront* the imagination. This sets over against it an "other": a world alternative to the speculative one summoned up in imagination; it posits a "distance" with which the imaginary is forced to come to terms. And, often as not, this "distance," which is the real, is not exactly welcome to the imaginary, for it is just such externality, which inhibits its freedom—its freedom, that is, to imagine what it will. That is why it "tends to erase the distance." Alterity is not particularly welcome to spirit in its solitary independence.

Which is why Chauvet goes on to speak of "immediacy": "in order to gain immediate contact with things," he says. The word "things" here is ambiguous. At the very least these "things" are to be distinguished from the "reality" with which "the symbolic" deals. Further, in a moment it will turn out that these "things" through which, or within which, the imagination so hankers for immediacy are not other than mirror images, ephemera, simply reflecting to the imaginer her or his own desired image. The emphasis here, then, is not on the solidity of things but on the *imaginative desire for immediacy*. We understand how this is so: it follows directly from what we said a moment ago about the resistance of spirit to the confrontation with alterity. Unfettered spirit lives in and for immediacy: the immediacy of its own phantasmagoria, the immediacy of kindred spirits, the immediacy of its own aspirations, its hopes, its dreams.

Perhaps the single most striking thing about so-called contemporary worship is its insistence on an immediate continuity between the event, which is gathered worship and the people's everyday experience. The pertinacity shows itself at every turn (examples are scarcely necessary): The clothing and manner of leaders is that of weekday relaxation; the forms of greeting could be those of any club or friendship group: "Good morning, everybody, and welcome. What have we to celebrate this week? Someone has had a birthday? Or some especially good news?" So is the tone set for the entire time together. Another way of construing this is to say that what purports to be a *condensed* symbol (a gathered congregation) is in fact constituted in terms of *disseminated* sacramentality; the people have assembled but do not sacramentally (symbolically) "enter" God's presence; it, the congregation, is—were such an idea thinkable—an aniconic icon. If, then, we allow ourselves to follow Chauvet, we are pressed to draw these threads together: first, the high level of intuition or imagination inherent in all dispersed sacramentality; second, the refusal to contemplate any kind of "break" ("distance") between the event of worship and everyday life; and, third, that all this plays out in the interests of "immediacy." These Christians remain very much "at home" in their worship.

The first thing about "the imaginary," then, is that it "erases distance." The second thing is that for the imagining subject *things become a mirror*, reflecting surfaces wherein the subject "attempts to find (of course unconsciously) [his or her] own image, only embellished." In this sentence we apprehend, if we had not already, the depth of seriousness resident in the worship styles we are considering: things become a mirror reflecting to the viewer her or his own image, though embellished; and all this remains unconscious.

Needless to say, there are "things" in worship: people assemble, that means a *place* of assembly, *words* are said, *actions* are undertaken, prayers are offered, songs are sung, Scriptures are read, and images are projected. All of these things are said and done unquestionably in good faith and with the best of intentions. Can it be that they are simply reflecting those who do and say them the image of themselves? That must seem a harsh judgment. But some things will give us pause. In the first place, we have already noted that the entire setting for the prayers is continuous with people's everyday experience, a disseminated sacramentality, we called it. So is what now happens simply the reflection of the everyday, excepting that the people have gathered in one place? But now, second, we see that the prayers themselves evince the same "weekday" immediacy.

Prayer here appears no formidable thing. The one who prays seems well able to slip in and out of divine presence without preamble and apparently on the best of terms. One recalls, in fact, Annie Dillard's line about worshipers who "seem to saunter through the liturgy like Mohawks along a strand of scaffolding who have long since forgotten their danger."[59] But now a third factor comes to mind. Along with the alignment of gathered worship and everyday experience we are bound to notice the equally determined proscription of any and every form of "ritual"—forms of language, that is, or patterns of action deriving from another time. Of course, the tendency is deeply embedded in the Reformed genetic code.[60] In this day and age, however it may have been seen in the past, the disposition now clearly shares in and contributes to the modern fixation of an "endless return to the same."[61] In fact, this is exactly Chauvet's judgment: "Everything always returns to the 'same', that is, to the subject itself, unavoidably idealized." "Contemporary" here thus means not just "appropriate to our times"; it means "*our* forms of expression, what *we* think worship is and how it should be undertaken." It means:

59. Annie Dillard, *Holy the Firm* (New York: Bantam Books, 1979), 60.

60. Calvin was already scoffing at "the ceremonial pomp . . . the tricks . . . the trifling follies" of Roman Catholic worship (Calvin, *Institutes*, 4.10.12). Puritans within the Church of England complained bitterly about "singing, pyping, surplesse and cope wearyng" (E. Brooks Holifield, *The Covenant Sealed: The Development of Puritan Sacramental Theology in Old and New England 1570–1720* [New Haven, CT: Yale University Press, 1974], 34) or of "groaning as under a common burden of human rites and ceremonies" (White, *The Sacraments in Protestant Practice and Faith*, 43). In American Puritanism, "ministers regarded the capacity to frame their own conceived or extemporary prayers as one of the gifts of the ascended Christ to his Church" (Horton Davies, *The Worship of the American Puritans, 1629–1730* [New York: Peter Lang Publishing, 1990], 134). There is, then, a veritable legacy!

61. Levinas frequently compares the homeward voyage of Ulysses as a "return to the same" with Abraham's "departure with no return"; see, for example, Emmanuel Levinas, "The Trace of the Other," in *Deconstruction in Context: Literature and Philosophy*, ed. Mark C. Taylor (Chicago: University of Chicago Press, 1986), 346, 348; or Emmanuel Levinas, "Meaning and Sense," in *Emmanuel Levinas: Basic Philosophical Writings*, ed. Adriaan T. Peperzak, Simon Critchley, and Robert Bernasconi (Bloomington: Indiana University Press, 1996), 48.

"We need not to be told, we need nothing from another age, need not hear how our forebears in faith might have prayed and sung." In practice, it means that the order of service itself and then everything within it will be created anew every Sunday morning. Consciousness of Christianity is for these believers wholly punctiliar; it is as if the Christian church consists solely in this group of people meeting now and here; it is as though the word "catholic" had been deleted from these Christians' creed, as if, we might dare to say, their worship is simply the reflection of themselves.

Lathrop, himself deeply interested in the "things" of worship, trenchantly said: "We have little grounds for hope if all we have are mirrors of ourselves, even if the mirrors are big ones";[62] and Dietrich Bonhoeffer's suspicion that all too easily "have [we] been confessing our sins to ourselves and also granting ourselves absolution" serves to haunt us all our days.[63]

Over against "the imaginary" Chauvet sets in sharp juxtaposition "the symbolic." Whereas "the imaginary" works for the erasure of distance and reflects those so imagining their own image, "the symbolic"—or, in the terminology I have been using, the condensed symbols of faith—"places the real at a distance by representing it."

Representation necessitates distantiation. Disseminated sacramentality, the sacramental encounter of everyday, I wanted to say, seems to confer immediacy. ("Seems" here is important because in fact *all* encounter with the divine is mediated—in this case in or through the epiphanic moment or sudden inspiration. Yet these do give a sense of immediacy in that they are matters of moment, highly personal, and not stylized in conventional imagery.) Condensed sacramental forms, contrariwise, are deliberately representational; their meaning is seen as residing *in* their design, texture, appearance, and/or sound. As such, they explicitly intend to represent otherness, alterity—whether this takes form as sedimentations of Christian

---

62. Gordon W. Lathrop, *Holy Things: A Liturgical Theology* (Minneapolis: Augsburg Fortress, 1993), 100.

63. Dietrich Bonhoeffer, *Life Together*, trans. and intro. by John W. Doberstein (London: SCM Press, 1954), 90. Cf. also Nathan Mitchell's question "whether . . . we have really encountered *God* or merely heard ourselves talking" (Nathan D. Mitchell, *Meeting Mystery: Liturgy, Worship, Sacraments* [Maryknoll, NY: Orbis Books, 2006], 137 [his emphasis]).

faith from another age or representation here and now of the divine presence. The very fact of their condensation (materiality), the fact that they *are* sedimentations and representations, means that their transcendent referent is *mediated*, distanced, effected in and through the particular material constitution of the space, artifact, person, or utterance, which is the condensed symbol.

I said—when speaking of the "early Catholic" developments—that the value of such sedimentations rests in two factors: they are physical and they are human fabrications. In the first case, as substantial forms, the condensed symbols discharge semiotic values—meanings, we can say—and therein distinguish themselves from other physical forms; we are able to decipher what they are and what they stand for by reason of, or through, their particular configurations. "This" is not so easily mistaken for "that." And, second, they are humanly arranged.

It is at just this point, then, that my earlier note about the distinctive spatial imagery attaching to the two orders of sacramentality reenters our discussion—the difference between "being in" and "entering." In the first place, the formulation "to enter God's presence" can only bespeak human action, human intention. God occupies no particular space, or better, I suppose, God fills *all* space and time. It is we who live in defined times and spaces. So that to encounter God's presence in or through these consolidated symbols means, *ipso facto*, coming *to* them wherever they are (or *into* them if we are talking about sacramental space or time) and *at* a specified time. "Coming into" God's presence, then, is the marker of human limitations, not of God's (ubiquitous) presence. But now, second, any such experience of "entrance" depends on, derives from, the sentient significations given out by that space (its physical lineaments as I mentioned earlier); and, we may now say, not least from the human enunciation(s) signaling such entrance. "We are gathered in the name of the Father, of the Son, and of the Holy Spirit . . ." accompanied with the sign of the cross *means* (signifies) something wholly other than "Good morning." Of course, materiality here means not just the utterance of the words: tone of voice and the bearing of the speaker are just as much a part of the meaning conveyed as the words' simple semantic sense.[64]

64. See Hughes, *Worship as Meaning*, 37–38, 117.

Such sedimentation "places the real at a distance." We may specu-
late that it is exactly this which alienates so deeply the exponents
of so-called contemporary worship. We have seen that for them
"distance" is their horror, so indefeasibly committed are they to
similarity and continuity. Ironically, it is precisely distantiation—the
objective physicality of the condensed symbols—which smashes the
mirror effect of the signs and allows us actually through them to
encounter the holy. Catherine Bell, a foremost exponent of ritual
studies, thus writes:

> [R]itualization is a way of acting that is designed and orchestrated
> to distinguish and privilege what is being done in comparison to
> other, usually more quotidian, activities. As such, ritualization is
> a matter of various culturally specific strategies for setting some
> activities off from others, for creating and privileging a qualitative
> distinction between the "sacred" and the "profane," and for ascrib-
> ing such distinctions to realities thought to transcend the power
> of human actors.

Or, again: "Ritualization is the production of . . . differentiation."[65]
In a subsequent book she writes: "[R]itualization is a way of acting
that tends to promote the authority of forces deemed to derive from
beyond the immediate situation."[66]

What is here affirmed of ritual ("ritualization" is Bell's preferred
term), namely, "a strategy for setting some activities off from others," for "creating a qualitative distinction between the 'sacred'
and the 'profane,'" is easily extrapolated to all the material forms
of worship: space, time, utterance, music, etc. All this is to achieve
distance. But (*pace* for Cooke and others) it is *exactly this distance
which saves us*. It saves us from ourselves. It permits (should we
better say: it creates) the distance, which allows the genuine otherness of God. As creatures habituated to the comfort of the same
("Similarity [is] a desired quality . . . we tend to see [others] as

65. Catherine Bell, *Ritual Theory, Ritual Practice* (New York: Oxford University Press, 1992), 74 and 90.
66. Catherine Bell, *Ritual: Perspectives and Dimensions* (New York: Oxford
University Press, 1997), 82.

reflections of ourselves"[67]), God's radical alterity will come as a shock.[68] The strange thing, then, is the warmth and felicity that Levinas can ascribe to alterity when it is allowed its presence. David Ford quotes him:

> This extraterritoriality has a positive side. It is produced in the gentleness or warmth of intimacy, which is not a subjective state of mind, but an event in the oecumenia of being—a delightful "lapse" of the ontological order. By virtue of its intentional structure gentleness comes to the separated being from the Other. The Other precisely *reveals* himself in his alterity not in a shock negating the I, but as the primordial phenomenon of gentleness. . . . The welcoming of the face is peaceable from the first, for it answers to the unquenchable Desire for Infinity.[69]

Here is the paradox: coming "into" the presence of God works distance, but it is just this distance that achieves "presence."

Cultural Colonization?

The interface between Christian belief and its enveloping culture is a matter for perennial reflection. On the one hand, Christians know they belong to a tradition that distinguishes itself from the cultural goals and values by which they are surrounded: "in the world but not of the world" (John 17:15-16) and "having here no continuing city" (Heb 13:14) are classic expressions of this. And, on the other hand, they are always and inevitably immersed in a particular culture: only in the language into which they have been born, only in the ways in which the world is construed, only in the fundamental

67. Ronald J. Allen, "Preaching and the Other," *Worship* 76, no. 3 (May 2002): 212; and see, similarly, Allen's monograph, *Preaching and the Other: Studies of Postmodern Insights* (St. Louis, MO: Chalice Press, 2009), 28–32.

68. John D. Caputo, *The Tears and Prayers of Jacques Derrida: Religion without Religion* (Bloomington: Indiana State University, 1997), 18.

69. David F. Ford, *Self and Salvation: Being Transformed* (Cambridge: Cambridge University Press, 1999), 40–41, citing Emmanuel Levinas, *Totality and Infinity: An Essay of Exteriority*, trans. Alphonso Lingis (Pittsburgh: Duquesne University Press, 1969), 150 (his emphasis).

structures of thought, which they receive from the culture of which they are part, can they make any sense of themselves, of God, and indeed of the believing tradition within which they stand: "Culture is thus not merely the inevitable context within which Christians celebrate the liturgy; it is the indispensable means by which they recognize and respond to God's action among them."[70] This means there is always a dialectic that must be held up to, or for, conscious reflection. Not so to reflect is to fall into one or another of the two dialectical elements: either a ghetto-like tradition*ism* or (which is perhaps more usual) an unwitting identification with the enveloping culture at the expense of fidelity to the tradition.

That Reformed Christianity was born into the humanist re-naissance, which—depending on how one draws the boundary lines[71]—was already the dawn of the modern era, is probably to be adjudged both a blessing and a bane. To take the above remarks seriously about dependence on the prevalent culture in making sense of anything, and then to reach back to what I had earlier observed about "the landscape of the heart" (p. 10 above), we may suppose that it was this alignment of constellations—Reformation belief and the emergence of modernity—which would give Calvinism traction through the next five centuries and in a majority of North Atlantic societies (and then their antipodean offshoots). At any rate, Charles Taylor, in his compendious account of modern secularity, has no hesitation in identifying Calvin as a prime mover in the disenchant-ment of the world:

> The Reformation . . . is central to the story I want to tell—that of the abolition of the enchanted cosmos, and the eventual creation of a humanist alternative to faith. . . . First, disenchantment. We can see the immense energy behind the denial of the sacred if we look at Calvin. . . .
>
> The energy of disenchantment is double. First negative, we must reject everything which smacks of idolatry. We combat the enchanted world, without quarter. . . . [T]he second energy was

70. Mitchell, *Meeting Mystery*, 3; Mitchell's entire first chapter attends to this matter.

71. See Stephen Toulmin, *Cosmopolis: The Hidden Agenda of Modernity* (Chicago: University of Chicago Press, 1992), 5–13.

positive. We feel a new freedom in a world shorn of the sacred, and the limits it set for us, to reorder things as seems best. We take the crucial stance, for faith and glory of God. . . . We are not deterred by the older tabus, or supposedly sacred orderings. So we can rationalise the world, expel the mystery from it (because it is all concentrated in the will of God). A great energy is released to re-order affairs in secular time.[72]

Here *in nuce* is all I have tried to say about the homing instinct of Reformed Christians for a disseminated sacramentality. It has been there from the beginning!

But I am also arguing that when this is at the expense of the condensed sacramental forms of faith, then something utterly crucial has been misplaced. From this point of view, the proximities of Reformed faith and the modern cultural paradigm must be seen at least as hazardous if not as an actual liability.

Rather obviously, this precariousness lies within two of the emblematic marks of contemporary worship we have identified: the near direct continuity it draws between gathered worship and everyday experience (the surrounding culture, that is say), and the paucity of its Christianly defining symbols. And I will come to these. But it may first be instructive to consider the coercive, not to say seductive, power that the modern cultural paradigm carries within itself.

It can be presumed that every cultural force has its coercive strategies. Where modernity perhaps differs is that its compulsions are not overt, as were those, for example, of the Roman Empire[73] or the British or, I suppose, any empire, but are covert, concealed. If in any sense modernity is a threat to institutional Christianity, then one might say it is "the enemy within." It seduces rather than coerces. Stephen Toulmin, in his personal account of how he became disillusioned with the "received wisdom" about modernity, writes: "Those of us who grew up in England in the 1930s and '40s had

---

72. Charles Taylor, *A Secular Age* (Cambridge, MA: Belknap Press of Harvard University Press, 2007), 77, 80.

73. See Wes Howard-Brook and Anthony Gwyther, *Unveiling Empire: Reading Revelation Then and Now* (Maryknoll, NY: Orbis Books, 1999), 87–119; also Lathrop, *The Four Gospels*, 16–32.

little doubt what Modernity was, and we were clear about its merits. . . . For us Modernity was unquestionably 'a Good Thing'; and we only hoped that, for the sake of the rest of humanity, the whole world would soon become as 'modern' as us."[74]

Perhaps modernity's most conducive property is its offer of autonomy. We have already heard from Charles Taylor about "freedom in a world shorn of the sacred . . . the older tabus." But this goes far beyond religious dependencies. *All* received opinions were now open to interrogation. Toulmin thus speaks of Descartes "turning a flamethrower on all inherited ideas";[75] and Joseph Glanville celebrates the newfound independence of thought: "'tis better to own a Judgement . . . then [than] a *memory*, like a Sepulchre, furnished with a load of broken and discarnate bones."[76] So have we all learned from our earliest moments the premium value attaching to "thinking for oneself," "not believing everything one reads," and so on. Then of course the sheer momentum, the seeming invincibility, of the modern success story has its own coercive power. Susan White, in her account of the relationship between worship and technology, writes of the latter's mesmeric fascination: "For many, technology's ability to increase human freedom and autonomy, to maximize choice, and improve the quality of life gives it a quasi-religious status," and goes on to speak of the "mysterious" quality of many technological systems, and the power of the scientific "high priesthood."[77]

One of the upshots of this enchanting power of "disenchantment"[78] is to nurture "forgetfulness"—an asphyxiation of alternative cultural possibilities. Paul Ricoeur thus roundly asserts: "[M]odernity

74. Toulmin, *Cosmopolis*, 13.

75. Ibid., 82.

76. Joseph Glanville, as cited by Basil Willey, *The Seventeenth Century Background* (Harmondsworth: Penguin Books, 1962), 166 (his italics).

77. Susan J. White, *Christian Worship and Technological Change* (Nashville: Abingdon Press, 1994), 110.

78. "Disenchantment" (*Entzauberung*) was Weber's term for the modern epoch; see, e.g., his essays "Science as a Vocation" and "Religious Rejections of the World and Their Directions," in *From Max Weber: Essays in Sociology*, ed. Hans H. Gerth and C. Wright Mills (London: Routledge and Kegan Paul, 1974), 139, 155, 350–51, 357.

is defined by forgetting";[79] and Daniel Hardy can also speak of our "forgetfulness" of ancient wisdom.[80] Modernity tends to work its own soporific.

Which for Christian believers is not salutary. For reasons already given. Modernity (when all has properly been said about its benefits) is the glorification of human autonomy. Jürgen Habermas observes, "[M]odernity . . . has to create its normativity out of itself,"[81] and goes on to cite Heidegger: "That period we call modern . . . is defined by the fact that man becomes the center and measure of all beings. Man is the *subjectum*, that which lies at the bottom of all beings, that is, in modern terms, at the bottom of all objectification and representation."[82] Ricoeur, then, is not in doubt:

> [S]ometimes I think that the idealistic concept of consciousness is by construction an atheistic concept. When placed in contrast to the assertion of radical autonomy, dependence is perhaps the only possible truth of religion, an avowal of an element of passivity in my existence, an avowal that in some ways I receive existence. As soon as I put autonomy at the top of the philosophical system, as soon as I promote to such an extent this Promethean dimension of autonomy, then *surely autonomy becomes godlike itself.*[83]

I began this section of the essay by remarking on the unavoidable dialectic between the received confession within which Christians stand and the cultural milieu in which they are equally embedded. The circumstance requires, equally unavoidably, a *critical reception*

---

79. Paul Ricoeur, "The Symbol: Food for Thought," *Philosophy Today* 4, nos. 3–4 (Fall 1960): 197, 203; see also his *The Conflict of Interpretations: Essays in Hermeneutics* (Evanston, IL: Northwestern University Press, 1974), 288, where he speaks of "certain traits of our 'modernity' . . . forgetting hierophanies, forgetting the signs of the Sacred, losing hold of [oneself] as belonging to the Sacred"; also ibid., 298.

80. Hardy, *God's Ways with the World*, 43.

81. Jürgen Habermas, *The Philosophical Discourse of Modernity: Twelve Lectures*, trans. Frederick G. Lawrence (Cambridge, MA: MIT Press, 1995), 7 (emphasis removed).

82. Ibid., 133.

83. Paul Ricoeur, *Lectures on Ideology and Utopia*, ed. George H. Taylor (New York: Columbia University Press, 1986), 32 (my emphases).

of both: an interrogation of the tradition in order to be able to say how it may be understood in the present age and, at least as stringently, a critique of the cultural moment in order to say in which ways this offers faith a *Lebensraum* (habitat) and, otherwise, in which ways it threatens as a competitive, alternative ideology. Lathrop observes from a historical perspective: "The New Testament itself evidences an awareness that the cultural treasures of the nations are to be both welcomed *and criticized* in the life of the church."[84]

My contention is that Reformed Christianity's predilection for the diffused sacramental type leaves it dangerously exposed to a "cultural colonization" by modernity (or, in fact, by postmodernity; in this case the "post-" prefix either makes little difference or perhaps only amplifies the vulnerability).[85] Otherwise expressed, this is suggesting that Reformed Christianity, and most especially its present-day contemporary-worship mutation, is now insufficiently in touch with its tradition to be able to summon the necessary critical acumen in face of the modernist threat.[86]

The difficulty lies in the confluence of two forces: modernity's immanence and Reformed secularity.

84. Lathrop, *Holy People*, 183 (my emphases); see, by way of exposition of the sentence, chapters 7, 8, and 9 of this work.

85. I owe the term "cultural colonization" to an important essay by Gary Deverell, "Uniting in Worship? Proposals toward a Liturgical Ecumenics," *Uniting Church Studies* 11, no. 1 (March 2005): 21–36; see esp. p. 35 of this article. I suspect that Deverell may himself have had in mind Habermas's phrase, "the colonization of the lifeworld." The idea occurs several times toward the end of his *The Theory of Communicative Action*, meaning the over-rationalization ("juridification" and "administration") of areas of communal life which ought, in Habermas's opinion, be better regulated along the lines of the theory of communicative action: Jürgen Habermas, *The Theory of Communicative Action*, vol. 2, *Lifeworld and System: A Critique of Functionalist Reason*, trans. Thomas McCarthy (Cambridge: Polity Press, 1987), esp. 367–73 and 391–96.

86. One of its own exponents writes: "There is a real need for evangelicals to consider carefully whether they are in danger of being overwhelmed by the world, precisely because they have chosen to imitate its methods and norms as they attempt to confront it" (McGrath, *Evangelicalism and the Future of Christianity*, 170).

To take up the first of these, it is impossible to overlook modernity's immanentism. To cite Taylor again:

> The great invention of the West was that of the immanent order in Nature, whose working could be systematically understood and explained on its own. . . . This notion of the "immanent" involved denying—or at least isolating and problematizing—any form of interpenetration between the things of Nature, on the one hand, and "the supernatural" on the other.[87]

So have we become accustomed to the often-remarked "relocation of the holy" in the modern era.[88] Among other manifestations are: the advent of "civil religion" (the honoring of soldiers fallen in battle ["they gave their lives for us"] has grown exponentially in Australia in recent decades); secularized rites of passage (the "celebration of a life" is now practically normal, even among practicing [Protestant] Christians); art galleries as "the cathedrals of modernity"; and sporting events experienced as ecstatic outpourings of spirit. And Protestant Christianity shares the instinct. William Hutchison, in beginning his account of Protestant modernism in America, names three defining characteristics of the early twentieth century: "first and most visibly . . . the conscious, intended adaptation of religious ideas to modern culture"; second, "the idea that God is immanent in human cultural development and revealed through it"; and, third, "a belief that human society is moving toward realization . . . of the Kingdom of God."[89] Subsequent events, the Great Depression and, desperately more so, two horrendous world wars, sufficed to extinguish the "progressive" element of this vision. But the immanentist zeal survived. By the 1970s we were reading of the Every

---

87. Taylor, *A Secular Age*, 15; and see his entire chapter 15, "The Immanent Frame," ibid., 539–93.

88. See, notably, Willem Frijhoff, "Witnesses to the Other: Incarnate Longings—Saints and Heroes, Idols and Models," *Studia Liturgica* 34, no. 1 (2004): 1–25.

89. William R. Hutchison, *The Modernist Impulse in American Protestantism* (Oxford: Oxford University Press, 1976), 2.

Day God,[90] the Secular City,[91] and Religionless Christianity.[92] The anecdotes at the head of this chapter, about finding God in Nature and in putting out the rubbish as a religious act, bear testimony enough to the robust presence of immanentism in Reformed styles of Christianity in the twenty-first century.

I said previously that the risk for this version of Christianity lies in the confluence of immanentism (from the side of circumjacent culture) and secularity (from the confessional side). Perhaps the point has already been made in accenting the Reformed proclivities for immanentism. But perhaps the point can be further reinforced by hearing Tillich on Protestant secularity: "Protestantism, by its very nature, demands a secular reality. It demands a concrete protest against the sacred sphere and against ecclesiastical pride, a protest that is incorporated in secularism. Protestant secularism is a necessary element of Protestant realization."[93] This seems a radical judgment though it does cohere with points of view we have already met. More pertinently, it underlies the entire burden of Tillich's book (written, we may recall, in mid-twentieth century): "[T]he Protestant principle is not the Protestant reality and the question had to be asked as to how they are related. . . . And, in every answer suggested, the need for a profound transformation of religious and cultural Protestantism is indicated."[94] The nature of this transformation comes later in the book: "No other question in Protestantism has from the beginning offered so much difficulty as has the question of the sacraments, and no other has received such uncertain answers. . . . A complete disappearance of the sacramental element . . . would lead to the disappearance of the cultus, and,

---

90. John Gordon Davies, *Every Day God: Encountering the Holy in World and Worship* (London: SCM Press, 1973).

91. Harvey Cox, *The Secular City: Secularization and Urbanization in Theological Perspective* (London: SCM Press, 1965).

92. See, for example, John Bowker, "Religionless Christianity," in *The Concise Oxford Dictionary of World Religions* (Oxford: Oxford University Press, 2000), 482.

93. Tillich, *The Protestant Era*, 213–14.

94. Ibid., xviii.

finally, to the dissolution of the visible church itself."[95] "No church can survive without a sacramental element."[96]

The risks, which have so far been depicted somewhat abstractly, can be shown more concretely in two current practices. One I have already referred to in passing, namely, the obsession in these worship styles for *novelty*; the other is the *form of arguments*, which are adduced in justification of the preferred styles.

"Modernity . . . rested on [the myth of] . . . the clean slate."[97] It is impossible to overestimate the degree to which this stamp of modernity has entered the contemporary Protestant mentality. I suppose the installation of data projectors, with their accompanying screens and banks of computers, is now *de rigueur* for all places of worship, mainline Protestant and Catholic alike. And, in itself, this is not just the question of technological innovation; as a born Presbyterian, I am old enough to have heard the stories of bitter resistance on the part of Kirk members to organs in churches: "tha' kist o' whistles!" Still, neither is it insignificant that the contemporary worship styles that I have in mind were energetically in the vanguard of such developments (projectors and so on); not for nothing do they name themselves "contemporary." There is here, barely concealed, an *ideology* of novelty; newness, we could almost say, as prized for its own sake. One should not miss, that is, the sense of superiority inherent in being people "on the cusp," "up to the minute," people who are "with it," and so on; and then on the other side the definite dismissiveness of those seen as "traditionalists," "conservative," "old-fashioned"—or just "old"! Nor is it possible to oversee here the ardor for immediacy to which I have already referred. The "myth of the clean slate" asserts the uselessness—actually, the impediment—of forms of language or musical idioms, of ritual movements or the ordering of events (the *ordo*, see note 99 below) for a sense of God's immediacy; everything is reduced to the *im*mediate moment, actually *our* moment. This was/ is pure modernity.

95. Ibid., 94.
96. Ibid., 109.
97. Toulmin, *Cosmopolis*, 179.

Second, the arguments offered for the favored style are, without exception, drawn not from within the tradition but from the pervasive culture. "Multipurpose worship space," for example, will be defended in terms of "it simply makes no sense to have millions (of dollars) tied up in a building used for an hour or so once a week"; or, "it's part of our mission of hospitality to allow other groups to use our space." Against the "practicality," "sensibleness," and "economic" arguments, a question such as "What is a community like that has no place of sanctuary?" hardly cuts the ice. Or, with reference to sacramental persons, the argument is: "Surely anyone can say the words and perform the actions of Holy Communion!" Again, the idea that every religious community needs at its heart an authorized interpreter of its tradition and a mystagogue will barely get a hearing.[98]

These, as it seems to me, are indices of the depth and degree to which the culture of modernity and now postmodernity has entered, surreptitiously, the very interstices of Reformed thinking in our times.

I have spoken of the demand laid on confessing Christians both to examine critically the tradition that has formed them and, no less, to interrogate the surrounding cultural mores and values of which they are equally the products. But in order to undertake this latter assignment, such a community needs some Archimedean point, some standard of reference, a touchstone *by which* to assess their inherited culture. My contention in this essay is that it is precisely what I am calling the "condensed symbols" of Christian faith that afford this standing place. Such symbols certainly include such deliberately formed places as we heard described by Chauvet as "crystallization[s] of the whole value system specific to Christianity." But they also include less tangible manifestations of the tradition, including ancient prayers and hymns, inherited ritual patterns and the well-established structures of worship.[99] But beyond

---

98. See, perhaps, Val Webb, "Is It Permissible to Ask Why We Ordain at All?," *Uniting Church Studies* 3, no. 1 (March 1997): 13–38; and see also, perhaps, my "Limping Priests: Ministry and Ordination," *Uniting Church Studies* 8, no. 1 (March 2002): 1–13.

99. See especially Lathrop, *Holy Things*, 33–83, but particularly 33–53.

all these, and even more important, it requires an *understanding*, a *way of ordering our thoughts*, that recognizes, in these physical artifacts and forms of expression, encapsulations of Christian faith and representations of the (mediate) presence of God. Without such recognition, without this grateful reception of gifts from beyond itself, a believing community is dangerously exposed to modernity's invasive colonization.

Postscript

The chapter seems to have been unrelievedly critical of what I have been calling "disseminated sacramentality" and the style of worship it engenders. So I am now constrained to say that the critique has been as sustained as it has been, not at all because I am critical of this order of sacramentality *per se*, but because it seems to me to be, or to have become, the dominant type of present-day Reformed thought and doxology—largely, I think, through the infiltration of secular modernity. I am therefore anxious to recuperate what I said on two or three occasions earlier about the continuities that run between the two sacramental models. *They belong together!*

As a matter of fact, this continuity finds clear expression at one point in the service of worship, namely, that moment variously called blessing/word-of-mission/dismissal. Exactly here the *condensed sacramentality* (which has been the gathered worship) is fused with a *dispersed sacramentality* (the week before them into which the worshipers are going forward).[100] The two sacramentalities are not two entirely different genuses; to pursue the metaphor we might say there is one genus (sacramentality) with two species. At the same time, it has been my concern to urge that people cannot "come out" if they had never "entered." And, more pointed perhaps, it is the one sacramental type that empowers and enables

100. Lathrop thus describes his "Liturgical Cosmology": "The assertion of this book is that the renewed Christian liturgy . . . is full of lines that run out to the world, full of a communal orientation that is also a personal ethical formation" (Lathrop, *Holy Ground*, 59). In large measure, Lathrop's book consists in an exposition of the *fusion* of what (in my language) are the two sacramentalities.

the other: it is the condensed form that actually enables the pursuit of a disseminated sacramentality through the week.

The second corrective point to make is that *within* the condensed symbol, which is gathered worship, the people's contemporaneity can hardly be denied—a person is not bifurcate: a worshiping person in one moment and a secular one in the next. This is to say, not only is there room within the worship service for twenty-first-century idioms (of music, language, imagery, etc.); such can hardly be avoided. The critical point is *not* contemporaneity of expression in itself but that such expressive forms should be *held within* the basic symbolism of "entering, being in, and coming out from" the particular presence of God. And for this, we have seen, there will need to have been a rich collocation of symbols: by all means some from the past, assuredly some from beyond the worshipers' immediate world, but also some which are familiar, recognizable. In this way, too, the two sacramentalities meet and embrace.

Chapter Two

What Is a Sacrament?
What Is Sacramentality?

Sacramentality is the fusion of spirit and physical form. As not infrequently in such matters, we catch this most clearly in its negation. Much sacramental expression (public worship, that is) disappoints because forms are followed from which spirit (whether we are thinking of the human spirit—presence, engagement, intention—or of the divine Spirit) seems quite to be missing; or alternatively there is an abundance of spirit ("enthusiasm" we sometimes say) in which embodiment, physicality, materiality has been severely discounted. Hence the thesis: sacramentality is the marriage of spirit and form.

This thesis suggests that sacramentality arises from, or is grounded in, our most basic humanity, because nowhere more clearly is this entwinement of psychical and physical energies to be seen than in the human person. From time immemorial we—human beings—have pondered this doubled dimension of our existence. We have been fascinated by our apparent ability—in imagination, ratiocination, or feelings—to fly free of bodily constraints. But of course neither have we been able to lose sight of our animality, our fixity in time and space, our restricted physical energies, proneness to sickness and death.

For most of this time, at any rate within the tradition that we in the West have inherited, the two dispositions have been seen as opposed, each contesting the other: spirit or thought striving ever to transcend its anchorage in embodiment but constantly frustrated by the body's weightedness, its susceptibility to error, and its ultimate mortality.

Such long-held presumptions are now, however, in disesteem. We have come to understand, pretty confidently, that the human person is a psychosomatic unit. We now recognize, for example, that all thought is contextual—i.e., arising from, dependent on, local perspectives and personal histories. We have learned that there is no immediate (untheorized) apprehension of the world; there is no meaning (signification) apart from its material signifier; that "facts" are in some important degree "constructed." And so on: the postmodern condition. More simply put, perhaps, we have recognized in recent times that "mind" is "embodied" and that the human body is "enspirited"—in other words, that every human person is an entanglement of noetic, imaginative, volitional energies, on the one hand, and physical embodiment, on the other.[1]

To say again, then: sacramentality, understood as the fusion of spirit and form, finds its primary manifestation in our most fundamental human constitution.

Sacramentality and the Human Condition

It is perhaps worth noticing that this is by no means an unusual view among sacramental theologians. We might refer, for example, to what Geradus van der Leeuw was inclined to call "sacramental phenomenology."[2] In speaking of the church's sacraments, he insisted:

> [I]t is necessary that we first alert ourselves to the place of the sacraments in the world; that is, in the material world and in human thought and intention. . . . Everywhere around the entire globe

1. See, notably, Nancey Murphy, *Bodies and Souls, or Spirited Bodies?* (Cambridge: Cambridge University Press, 2006); also, F. LeRon Shults, *Reforming Theological Anthropology: After the Philosophical Turn to Relationality* (Grand Rapids, MI: William B. Eerdmans Publishing Company, 2003), 163–88.

2. Geradus van der Leeuw, *Sakramentales Denken: Erscheinungsformen und Wesen der außerchristlichen und christlichen Sakramente* (Kassel: Johannes Stauda Verlag, 1959), 109–71.

people undertake actions, the purposes of which outrun the actions themselves. . . . Before we come to the theology of the sacraments [then] we must concern ourselves with their anthropology. . . . Whoever desires to grasp such theological matters must from the outset take account of the total earthly reality in which he finds his place.[3]

On this basis, van der Leeuw proceeds to detailed history-of-religions studies, first, of the place of eating and drinking as "something which, through a material component, transcends conventional suppositions . . . bring[ing] to light possibilities which either lay within the material component or which can be appended to it."[4] He speaks, for instance, of the act of "inviting someone to have a drink," which gesture—by common understanding—invariably implies a great deal more than simply the satisfaction of thirst.[5] He goes on to make similar phenomenological and sociological analyses of the act of eating together,[6] of other basic human actions such as washing,[7] human utterance,[8] sexual intercourse,[9] and numerous other forms of social engagement.[10] Of particular interest to us, as exemplifying sacramentality as a fusion of spirit and form, is van der Leeuw's by-no-means wholly whimsical example of getting dressed in the morning "in order that I shall successfully accomplish through the day those things which lie before me."[11] I *contemplate*, that is, how I shall present *my physical person* to the world!

We might also consider in this respect Rahner's provocative notion of "the liturgy of the world."[12] Rahner was concerned to say

3. Ibid., 109.
4. Ibid., 112.
5. Ibid., 116.
6. See notably, ibid., 115–34.
7. Ibid., 135–43.
8. Ibid., 144–50.
9. Ibid., 151–57.
10. Ibid., 158–71.
11. Ibid., 111.
12. Rahner's ideas on the "the liturgy of the world" and "the liturgy of the church" are found essentially in the two essays: Karl Rahner, "Considerations on the Active Role of the Person in the Sacramental Event," in *Theological Investigations*, vol. 14, trans. David Bourke (London: Darton, Longman and Todd, 1976), 161–84; and "On the Theology of Worship," in *Theological*

how the church's rituals might make sense to modern, secularized people for whom the sacraments, generally speaking, "make the same impression . . . as the sacrificial ceremony of a Vedic priest who feeds the gods and believes that by his actions he is keeping the world in harmony with them."[13] Rahner believed that the problem lay, or lies, in the cleft which exists for large numbers of people—worshipers included—between the ordinariness of everyday life and the act of public worship, a model in which the worshiper "passes to and fro from [his or her] secular world into a sacral sphere, a 'fanum' or 'temple.' "[14] He proposed, alternatively, what he called "A New Model: Using the Whole of Life to Bring the Sacrament to its Fullness."[15] Rahner's proposal "starts out from the assumption that the secular world from the outset is always encompassed and permeated with the grace of the divine self-communication":[16]

> [O]ne point must be emphasized about this grace precisely to the extent that it proceeds from the innermost heart and centre of the world and of man: it takes place not as a special phenomenon, as one particular process *apart from* the rest of human life. Rather it is quite simply the ultimate depths and the radical dimension of all that which the spiritual creature experiences, achieves and suffers in all those areas in which it achieves its own fullness, and so in its laughter and its tears, in its taking of responsibility, in its loving, living and dying, whenever man keeps faith with the truth, breaks through his own egoism in his relationships with his fellows, whenever he hopes against all hope, whenever he smiles and refuses to be disquieted or embittered by the folly of everyday pursuits, whenever he is able to be silent . . . whenever, in a word, life is lived as man would seek to live it, in such a way as to overcome his own egoism and the despair of the heart which constantly assails

Investigations, vol. 19, trans. Edward Quinn (New York: Crossroad Publishing Company, 1983), 141–49. A good overview and analysis of Rahner's proposal is given by Michael Skelley, "The Liturgy of the World and the Liturgy of the Church: Karl Rahner's Idea of Worship," *Worship* 63, no. 2 (March 1989): 112–32.

13. Rahner, "Considerations on the Active Role of the Person," 173.
14. Ibid., 162.
15. Ibid., 166ff.
16. Rahner, "On the Theology of Worship," 142.

him. *There* grace has the force of an event, because all this of its very nature . . . no longer has any limits or any end but . . . loses itself in the silent infinitude of God.[17]

It is this everyday encounter with God's "disseminated" grace (my term), which Rahner called "the liturgy of the world." This "liturgy" is indeed "different"[18] from the church's ritual actions, but the two are by no means to be seen as standing in opposition or antithesis. On the contrary, the latter must be regarded as the confirmation, the "symbolic manifestation,"[19] of the former: "The sacraments accordingly are . . . really to be understood as . . . 'outbursts' (if we can express it in this way) of the innermost, ever present gracious endowment of the world with God himself into history," says Rahner.[20] Or again:

> [I]n the light of this second conceptual model the Church's worship is not the installation of a primarily sacramental sphere in a profane, secular world, it is not an event otherwise without roots in reality, but the explicit and reflex, symbolic presentation of the salvation event which is occurring always and everywhere in the world; the liturgy of the Church is the symbolic presentation of the liturgy of the world.[21]

A third writer whom we might consider is the contemporary Reformed theologian and philosopher James K. A. Smith. In his study of how Christian formation may be undertaken in a secular, consumerist society, Smith develops the idea of "secular liturgies."[22] His point of departure, in some strong sense following Augustine,[23]

17. Rahner, "Considerations on the Active Role of the Person," 167–68 (his emphases).
18. Rahner, "On the Theology of Worship," 141.
19. Rahner, "Considerations on the Active Role of the Person," 169.
20. Rahner, "On the Theology of Worship," 143.
21. Ibid., 146.
22. James K. A. Smith, *Desiring the Kingdom: Worship, Worldview, and Cultural Formation* (Grand Rapids, MI: Baker Academic, 2009); see also James K. A. Smith, *Imagining the Kingdom: How Worship Works*, Cultural Liturgies Series, vol. 2 (Grand Rapids, MI: Baker Academic, 2013).
23. Smith, *Desiring*, 50.

is that we—human beings—are creatures of desire: "we are what we love." Smith says:

> To be a human is to love, and it is what we love that defines who we are. . . . [W]e are talking about *ultimate* loves—that to which we are fundamentally oriented, what ultimately governs our vision of the good life, what shapes and molds our being-in-the-world—in other words, what we desire above all else, the ultimate desire that shapes and positions and makes sense of all our penultimate desires and actions. . . . [O]ur ultimate love is what we *worship*.[24]

The questions are: *what* shall we love, and *how* are such "ultimate desires" formed in us? Smith holds that "liturgy" (the liturgical life of the church in the first instance) is essentially a formative practice.[25] He then has little difficulty in extending the term beyond its ecclesial usage to describe *all* the formative strategies brought to bear on residents of modern (and postmodern) industrialized societies—hence "secular" liturgies:

> *Liturgy* is the shorthand term for those rituals which are loaded with a Story about who and whose we are, inscribing in us a *habitus* by marshalling our aesthetic nature. Liturgies are "cunning" pedagogies that extort what is essential while seeming to demand

---

24. Ibid., 51 (his emphases).

25. A persistent worry for some readers of Smith must be whether he regards worship not as an end in itself but as a *means to* a further end, namely, the liturgical or Christian formation of the worshipers. There is one point (but just the one, I think) where Smith does recognize worship's ultimate goal: "[W]e do well to remember that even [the formative power of worship] is a by-product of the fundamental aim of worship, which is praise and adoration of the triune God" (Smith, *Desiring*, 150). But the single sentence is an exception to his more compelling agenda, and even here is almost immediately overtaken: "My concern is that [in making worship 'contemporary'] we *lose the key aspects* of formation and discipleship" (ibid., 153 [my emphases]). The tendency is a deeply embedded Reformed one. For example, on William Ames's (1627) "instrumental" conception of worship, William Dyrness states: "The goal [of worship] is to be manifest through the week" (William A. Dyrness, *Reformed Theology and Visual Culture: The Protestant Imagination from Calvin to Edwards* [New York: Cambridge University Press, 2004], 161–62).

the insignificant precisely because they are stories that are told by—and told upon—our bodies, thereby embedding themselves in our imagination, becoming part of the background that determines how we see the world.[26]

Smith is of course clear that these so-called secular liturgies have vastly different objectives—are dedicated to the inculcation of utterly different desires, we shall say—than the Christian liturgy. Indeed, they are properly to be called "idolatrous."[27] Notwithstanding, insofar as they are dedicated to the production and shaping of human desire, they may equally properly be called "religious."[28] Smith thus gives detailed attention to the energies invested by modern marketing and consumerism,[29] civic religion,[30] and the universities,[31] in advancing, by way of their "secular liturgies," their alternative visions of the desirable life. He is able to demonstrate some striking similarities between the "secular" liturgies and their Christian counterparts. His analysis does not follow exactly the line, which I myself am pursuing, namely, that as an inextricable admixture of spirit and embodiment the human person is a sort of prototypical sacrament. His work is all the same helpful in that it grounds sacramentality in our general human condition: "We are sacramental animals."[32]

26. Smith, *Imagining*, 139 (his emphasis). Similar statements may be found in Smith's *Desiring*: "[T]hese affective icons of the good life get into our bones and our hearts and thus shape our character by aiming our desire to a particular end" (59). Or again: "[L]iturgies [are] rituals of ultimate concern: rituals that are formative for identity, that inculcate visions of the good life, and do so in a way that means to trump other ritual formation" (86).

27. Smith, *Desiring*, 121–26.

28. "By *religious*, I mean that they are institutions that command our allegiance, that vie for our passion, and that aim to capture our heart with a particular vision of the good life" (ibid., 90).

29. Ibid., 19–23, 93–103.

30. Ibid., 103–12.

31. Ibid., 112–21.

32. Smith, *Imagining*, 101. Before leaving these considerations of a general sacramentality, it should not be overlooked that Reformed theology has had its exponents of such views. Donald Baillie, for example, was able to begin his *Theology of the Sacraments* with a section on "A Sacramental Universe," in

God's Extensity, Intensity

To begin one's reflection on sacramentality in our most basic humanity throws up at least two consequences. The first, rather obviously,
is the question of how one is to draw the relationship between this
large, vague, and thoroughly generalized view of sacramentality
and the well-defined symbols and actions that the church names as
its sacraments, which are held to be the clearest manifestations we
have of the divine presence among us. The second is not so much
a matter for investigation as a working principle deriving from the
paradigmatic sacramentality of the human person—namely, that
there can be here no dualisms, no dichotomies, no sharp-edged
antitheses. The human person is a *unit* of spirit and form!

To take the latter point first: there must seem a universe of difference between the seeming godless pursuits of men and women in
their daily preoccupations, hopes, affections, bloody-mindedness,
their egoistic ambitions, and so on, on the one side, and the disclosure and claim represented in the sacraments, on the other. We
have already met the description "idolatry" in reviewing some of
the "secular liturgies." The drawing of sharp oppositions seems irresistible. The grounding of sacramentality in our general human
condition urges us, however, to resist the temptation. To say again,
the human person is a fusion, a unity, impossible to anatomize, so
as to say: here is spirit and there is physical form. To extrapolate,
worshiping Christians are themselves this admixture of iconicity
and idolatry. If the point seems difficult to accept, it perhaps suffices
to note that when Christians gather in public worship, their nearly
first action is one of confession and contrition. In a word, these
iconic worshipers are quickly bound to confront their *idolatry*.[33]
(St. Matthew caught it in his parable of the weeds in the wheat field:
the kingdom of heaven itself, in the meantime, is an entanglement

---

which he cited Calvin himself, and which concludes: "[T]his is a sacramental
universe, because God created all things visible and invisible" (Donald M.
Baillie, *The Theology of the Sacraments and Other Papers* [London: Faber
and Faber, 1957], 42–47).

33. As Daniel Hardy has it: "The forms of alienation appear in the forms
of worship themselves" (Daniel W. Hardy, "Worship as the Orientation of Life
to God," *Ex Auditu* 8 [1992]: 61).

of good and base—no dichotomies! See Matt 13:24-30). Of course, there is, necessarily, one great division, that between the worshipers and the One who is worshiped, between creatures and Creator. But even here we shall have to ask whether the difference is *absolute*—as it is sometimes put, *wholly* other—which would seem to suggest that the worshipers could have no idea of whom it is they worship.[34] At any rate, in terms of sacramental theory, there will be no dichotomies.

Which, to return to the earlier question above, is not to say there is only continuity, uniformity, absence of differences between the kinds or versions of sacramentality. We can and do sense the clear differences between spirit and body even if we are unable to disentangle them.[35] So that to attempt to draw the line from humanity at large to the church's sacraments is to traverse an immense range—in kind and in degree—of sacramental expression. To begin with, we shall unquestionably be required to explore the differences between spirit and form and to say, as well as we may be able, just how they are fused so as to be, or become, a sacrament. Then we shall have to notice that though always linked the two are by no means always equally distributed: I noticed much earlier that not a little sacramental expression (worship, that is) disappoints because forms are followed from which spirit is largely missing, or *vice versa*, there is an abundance of spirit but in which embodiment, physicality, materiality has been severely discounted. Further, without falling back into dualism, we will also be bound to attend the complicated interface of iconicity and idolatry. The sacramental impulse can be steered in very different directions! Another important difference, on which I shall draw pretty heavily and to which I shall thus give detailed attention, is that between what I call "disseminated" sacramentality and its "condensed" form. And we shall need to notice

---

34. See Michael A. Horton, "Participation and Covenant," in *Radical Orthodoxy and the Reformed Tradition: Creation, Covenant and Participation*, ed. James K. A. Smith and James H. Olthuis (Grand Rapids, MI: Baker Academic, 2005), 122.

35. "[Contemporary neurobiological] sciences still allow for a weak sense of duality, i.e., a distinction between biological and mental events, but not for dual*ism*" (Shults, *Reforming Theological Anthropology*, 180 [his emphasis]).

religious (perhaps quasireligious) discoveries being made in this so-called postsecular age. These, and perhaps there will be others.

In seeking to comprehend this great trajectory from, on the one side, the beauty and banality of ordinary humanity and, on the other, the clearly defined forms of the church's established sacraments— we are afforded great conceptual help through the deliberations of the eminent Anglican theologian Daniel W. Hardy. For Hardy, it is axiomatic that no aspect of the created order can be beyond its Creator's care and attention. "God's graceful work is *in the same world* which we call 'natural' or 'social.'"[36] And again, "[I]f the God who is affirmed is seen as Creator, there can be no final division in the truth: there is a basic unity to which everything . . . must be referred."[37] But, no less obviously, this presence to the creation (natural and social) is not everywhere and equally apparent. Hardy thus develops his notion of God's *extensity* and *intensity*. Though the terms are not yet present, we see the basic conception in this relatively early piece:

> When human beings in the world are given the "space" and "time" by which to be themselves, they do so through the various "modalities" of human life in the world—those of environment, geography and demography, biology, sociality, polity, economy, culture and ideology—as they are ramified in historical time. But these modalities, in each of which there are wide possibilities of difference and consistency in any one time and through time, are also the conditions through which human beings in the world are both from and with God. . . .
>
> That is why these modalities appear in worship and are so construed there as to place the worshiper in a new relation to God. Through place and buildings, the environment is itself drawn into the worshiper's awareness of—or movement toward—God.[38]

36. Daniel W. Hardy, *Finding the Church: The Dynamic Truth of Anglicanism* (London: SCM Press, 2001), 84 (my emphases). See similar ideas in Kenan B. Osborne, *Christian Sacraments in a Postmodern World: A Theology for the Third Millennium* (New York: Paulist Press, 1999), 140–43.

37. Daniel W. Hardy and David Ford, *Jubilate: Theology in Praise* (London: Darton, Longman & Todd, 1984), 115.

38. Hardy, "Worship as the Orientation of Life to God," 57.

God is then not *more* and *less* present in the church and in the world at large but is present to each *differently*—as intensity and extensity:

> God's life at its fullest is an engagement with the *extensity and mani-foldness of the world* for the sake of bringing it to the perfection appropriate to it in the purposes of God, and [the] churches—indi-vidually and together—are an effective sign of the *intensity* of God's life and purposes engaging with this extensity and manifoldness.[39]

Or again:

> Those whose lives are so fully shaped by Scripture find the *intensity* of God's life and purposes in the sweep of biblical understanding as it shapes them. . . . Those [on the other hand] who place their experience as human beings uppermost, making all the dilemmas of understanding and life today normative, are preoccupied with the *extensity* of life in the world. . . . The sadness is that these two . . . tend to deplore each other.[40]

To ask, then, about the relationship of the sacramentality of human life to the sacraments of the church is to see the latter as crystal-lizing, in some sense objectifying, giving visibility and form, to the former. In Hardy's succinct sentence: Sacramentality is "the tak-ing up of any aspect of the material universe into being a sign or symbol of its Creator."[41] Yet there remains a critical question about *directionality* within the span (i.e., between extensity and intensity). I have so far assumed a beginning point in the extensity of God's presence through the entire created order and particularly in com-mon human experience. Hardy's sentence perhaps corroborates such an approach. This might seem to suggest that the intensity of God's presence in church and sacrament amounts to little more than a kind of incremental increase of this otherwise extensive presence. So to think would be a most serious error—one to which Hardy is in no sense disposed and against which I too must take guard. In terms of *method* it has suited me to begin in generalities;

39. Hardy, *Finding the Church*, 159 (some emphases deleted, others added).
40. Ibid., 234 (his emphases).
41. Hardy and Ford, *Jubilate*, 17.

but *theologically* we must ask: How is this extensive sacramentality identifiable in the first place? What is it that enables us to speak of God's extensive presence in the world? So that from this vantage point we must be clear that it is the brilliant, finally impenetrable intensity of God's presence in Jesus Christ—the man of Nazareth and God's eternal *Logos*, both flesh and Word, the "image of the invisible God" (Col 1:15), "the exact imprint of God's very being" (Heb 1:3) we are told—*which enables us to speak of sacramentality at all*. Though we shall continue to proceed from signs of God's extensity in the world, this in no wise may conceal from us that it is the *goal* and destination of this pursuit, Jesus Christ as sacramental presence, which throughout both enables and directs the pursuit.

The Image as Extruded Thought

Our first task must be to give an account, as well as we are able, of *how* spirit can infuse materiality. I noted at the outset of this chapter that for quite the greatest extent of our tradition (that is, for over two and a half millennia) the two had been seen as irreconcilable. Gotthold Lessing's vision of a "great ugly ditch" (between transcendent truths and empirical reality) has often been taken as epitomizing the opposition.[42] Or as a more contemporary philosopher has it: "[T]he problem . . . is the problem of how words 'hook onto' the world."[43] But I also said there that this view, its huge traditional impetus notwithstanding, has in recent decades been abandoned. It has indeed become possible to speak of spirit inhering flesh. There are doubtless multiple reasons for this seemingly sudden reversal, and, equally certainly, numerous and diverse ways of undertaking

---

42. Gotthold Ephraim Lessing: "That . . . is the ugly great ditch which I cannot cross, however often and however earnestly I have tried" (Gotthold Ephraim Lessing, "On the Proof of the Spirit and of Power," in *Lessing: Philosophical and Theological Writings*, ed. Hugh Barr Nisbet [Cambridge: Cambridge University Press, 2005], 87).

43. Hilary Putnam, *Realism with a Human Face* (Cambridge, MA: Harvard University Press, 1990), 43 (his emphasis) and again 105.

the new explanatory possibilities.[44] One of the more prominent of these has been the exploration and application of the philosophical tradition called phenomenology, originating from Edmund Husserl, whose working life spanned the late nineteenth and early twentieth centuries (1859–1938). My own attempt will be more nearly against the background of phenomenology rather than directly dependent on it. But it may not be out of place to say a word or two about Husserl and the ongoing effects of his philosophy.[45]

Husserl was driven by his conviction that our ordinary apprehensions of the world are riven with uncertainty and instability—this, and his dismay at the proliferating specialist domains of inquiry, the falsely called "sciences," thought Husserl. In true Cartesian

---

44. J. Wentzel van Huyssteen, for example, has given detailed attention to recent developments in "evolutionary epistemology," for which the claim is made that human intelligence has emerged by way of evolutionary principles of adaptation, both biologically and through cultural transference (which is different from, and not reducible, to biological evolution). "So, when we come to the uniqueness of human knowledge, this process of information processing turns out to be a universal characteristic of all living beings, which again confirms that human rationality . . . can be seen only *as embodied rationality*" (J. Wentzel van Huyssteen, *Are We Alone? Human Uniqueness in Science and Theology* [Grand Rapids, MI: William B. Eerdmans Publishing Company, 2006], 87 [my emphases]; for greater detail, see ibid., 79–93). A different approach is taken by Mark Johnson in his two books: *The Body in the Mind: The Bodily Basis of Meaning, Imagination and Reason* (Chicago and London: University of Chicago Press, 1987) and *The Meaning of the Body: Aesthetics of Human Understanding* (Chicago: University of Chicago Press, 2007). Johnson holds that knowledge and intellectuality are formed through what he calls "image schemata" (Johnson, *The Body in the Mind*, 101), formed in persons from their earliest awareness of themselves in the world; such "image schemata" include, for example, "*in* in contrast to *out*" (sense of containment), or "increase means *up*; decrease means *down*," "balance," and dozens if not hundreds of similar schemata which are then mapped metaphorically onto more abstract life experiences. The point here is that all of these are generated by *bodily* experience—hence the thesis, which forms the subtitle of the earlier of the two books: "the bodily basis of meaning."

45. I have given a slightly more expansive overview of Husserl and his phenomenology in my *Worship as Meaning: A Liturgical Theology for Late Modernity* (Cambridge: Cambridge University Press, 2003), 21–25.

fashion,[46] he sought to locate the one true science in the irrefragable interior of human thought, in the "appearances" (phenomena) grasped by the mind and reflected on by the mind. Standing as he did so emphatically in the Idealist tradition (the true world is the world of ideas), it must or might seem improbable that Husserl's phenomenology would contribute much to overcoming the mind-matter caesura. Two elements of his work have determined otherwise. One of these was his insight and insistence that "consciousness" is always, invariably and inevitably, "consciousness *of* something." He thus distinguished what he called *noesis* (the act of knowing) from its *noema* (that which is known). The active, productive relationship between them he called "intentionality": "From the start Husserl confers on the notion of intentionality its full breadth: every consciousness is a consciousness *of* . . . [thus] signify[ing that] each distinct cogitatio [is] turned toward a distinct cogitatum."[47] Husserl was never able to escape the solipsistic tendencies of his Idealism. His distinction (of *noesis* from *noema*) would nevertheless prove to be of central importance in later, twentieth-century conjoining of consciousness and the external world. So, Ricoeur: "From a strictly descriptive point of view, intentionality avoids the alternatives of realism and idealism."[48] "Intentionality," or "being toward," would be fundamental, for example, in Martin Heidegger's subsequent analysis of *Dasein*:[49]

> Being-in-the-world has always dispersed itself or even split itself up into definite ways of Being-in. The multiplicity of these is indicated in the following examples: having to do with something, producing something, attending to something and looking after it, making use of something, giving something up and letting it go, undertaking, accomplishing, evincing, interrogating, considering, discussing,

---

46. Husserl's more mature thought is to be found in Edmund Husserl, *Cartesian Meditations*, trans. Dorion Cairns (Boston: Kluwer Academic Publishers, 1993).

47. Paul Ricoeur, *Husserl: An Analysis of His Phenomenology*, trans. Edward G. Ballard and Lester E. Embree (Evanston, IL: Northwestern University Press, 1967), 8 (my emphasis).

48. Ibid.

49. *Dasein* literally means "being there."

determining. . . . All these ways of Being-in have *concern* as their kind of Being. . . . [T]he Being of Dasein itself is to be made visible as *care*.[50]

The second striking aspect of Husserl's thought is his recognition that the "phenomena" of consciousness are anchored in, dependent on, human embodiment. This is a sort of logical extension of the *noesis/noema* configuration. It is the recognition, first, that the body is at once both a physical thing and a percipient subject (i.e., the source *and* the vehicle of the phenomena of consciousness); it is thus the recognition that *embodiment* is the *precondition of consciousness*; and it is the recognition that it is the body's mobility that generates the constant variety of perceived phenomena.[51] These insights will lead, again in post-Husserlian phenomenology, to the central place afforded sentient signification in human consciousness *vis-à-vis* the world. As Maurice Merleau-Ponty, the foremost exponent of this form of phenomenology, will have it: "Consciousness is being-toward-the-thing through the intermediary of the body."[52]

My approach to the question will be to trace the path from thought to material representation through the modality of *images* and the human *image-forming* facility. Though seldom citing the established phenomenologists, the theses, first, that thought is "intentional"—i.e., directs itself toward a particular object—and, second, that this intentionality finds its goal in empirical (embodied) forms will be implicit pretty much throughout.

Here at the outset, a fundamental caveat must be entered. I have spoken—and will continue to do so—of the fusion of spirit and physical form. But this—which has been a sort of Holy Grail for the postrationalist philosophies on which we have touched—can, for sacramental thought, only ever be a strictly *qualified* coalescence.

---

50. Martin Heidegger, *Being and Time*, trans. John Macquarrie and Edward Robinson (Oxford: Blackwell, 1962), 83. The translators, Macquarrie and Robinson, suggest that "concern" in Heidegger comes closer to our "be engaged with," "make provision for." Heidegger's definitive treatment of "Dasein as Care" comes at ibid., 235–44.

51. See Ricoeur, *Husserl*, 46–47.

52. Maurice Merleau-Ponty, *Phenomenology of Perception*, trans. Colin Smith (London: Routledge, 1962), 138–39.

Sacramentality can never admit the full identification of the material carrier of sacramental meaning with such meaning or reference. In other words, the physical form only ever *points* to its transcendent reference—which is to say, points away from or points beyond itself.[53] This has nothing to do with the old spirit/body dualism and its hefty disapprobation of the latter element. It derives rather from the one disjunction I have already mentioned, namely, the irresolvable difference between the created order and its Creator. To say this again: it is not its *materiality* which prevents the sacrament from fully representing its own sacramental meaning; it is rather that no *creaturely* thing (physical or otherwise) can encompass the Creator of all things. The desire that it might or could be otherwise is of course endemic. It shows itself in Catholic aspirations for "real presence" and in Protestant suppositions of "immediacy." Both have to be withstood. As the Catholic writer Chauvet says: "The first function of the sacraments is to manifest the vacant place of Christ, his 'absence' as at Emmaus."[54] And the Protestant Tillich says simply: "The unconditional cannot be identified with any given reality whether past or future. . . . A conditional reality set up as something unconditional, a finite reality to which divine predicates are attributed . . . is an 'idol.' "[55] Accepting then that, in speaking of sacramentality, any conception of a "fusion" of spirit energies with a material carrier will necessarily be qualified (in inverted commas, so to speak, whether or not they appear), still, I am urging, the notion is nevertheless not only permissible but proves illuminating and productive.

Reverting, then, to the matter of images—and still with the question of how spirit can merge with physicality—two lines of approach offer themselves. Staying within the broad, anthropo-

53. Another way of saying this, as we shall see, is that the sacramental sign requires *always to be transparent.*

54. Louis-Marie Chauvet, *The Sacraments: The Word of God at the Mercy of the Body* (Collegeville, MN: Liturgical Press, 2001), 85. See also his much more detailed treatment in his *Symbol and Sacrament: A Sacramental Reinterpretation of Christian Existence*, trans. Patrick Madigan and Madeleine E. Beaumont (Collegeville, MN: Liturgical Press, 1995), 161–62, 167–78.

55. Paul Tillich, *The Protestant Era*, trans. and with a concluding essay by James Luther Adams (Chicago: University of Chicago Press, 1948), 37–38.

logical frames so far employed, it transpires that the ability to give *external* form to *mental* pictures is a defining mark of *homo sapiens*. But, second, images and imaging also prove to be highly specific to Christian faith.

In his 2004 Gifford Lectures, Wentzel van Huyssteen undertook an ambitious project in, as he termed it, "interdisciplinary dialogue" between theology and the sciences, taking as his discussion topic "Human Uniqueness," otherwise expressed as the question, "What is it which makes us human?" His objective was to bring together, for their mutual enlargement, key understandings of Christian theology about the human condition and the findings of contemporary anthropologists with respect to human origins. In a detailed review he establishes that professional paleoanthropologists are generally agreed that with the emergence of the so-called Upper Paleolithic hominids, between 80,000 and 40,000 years ago, an exponential leap was gained over their immediate Neanderthaloid predecessors (there is disagreement as to how gradually or "explosively" this happened).[56] This had not so much to do with anatomy or even with brain size, in which the Neanderthals were not so greatly different; it was a vast *cultural* leap. It is with the Upper Paleolithic that the modern human being becomes recognizable: "In a sense we are not simply *more* intelligent than other species, we are *differently* intelligent. . . . *Homo sapiens* is not simply an 'improved version' of its ancestors, but is in fact a new thing altogether."[57] If one asks wherein this dramatically new dimension in human evolution consists, then answers are uniform: in the words of one authority, "attributes like human intelligence, rationality," are unquestionably important, "but [even] more importantly [was] the ability to construct symbolic and ultimately religious meaning."[58] And if one asks *why*—or *what gave rise to*—this exponential gain, attention is drawn to the massive ecological instability of the concluding last Ice Age, which exactly coincides with the emergence of the Upper Paleolithic hominids. It was exactly the new ability to articulate, both in language and in symbolic expression, theorists think, which "greatly

56. Van Huyssteen, *Are We Alone?*, 179 and 196–99.
57. Ibid., 189–90, with reference to Ian Tattersall.
58. Ibid., again drawing on Tattersall.

enhanced the chances of adapting to environmental instability, and this enhancement decoupled the early modern humans from any single ancestral milieu."[59] (The last part of this sentence refers to the survival capacities of the Cro-Magnon peoples [Upper Paleolithic] while other hominid groups [the Neanderthal] succumbed.)

Language was unquestionably crucial. But we should not lose sight in this, as we tend often to do, that language is itself a symbolic system, a way of giving *thought* an *external form*: "Language is not only a highly unusual form of communication, it is also the outward expression of a highly unusual mode of thought, namely *symbolic representation*."[60] Or again, "In this sense, the emergence of language goes hand in hand with the recognition of symbols."[61]

On what evidences are these reconstructions of evolutionary history built? The answer lies in massive proportion in the ancient cave paintings of southeastern France and the Basque country (I wonder that van Huyssteen does not make more of the Australian Aboriginal paintings, many of which date from the same era):

> We seem to grasp that language, self awareness, consciousness and mythology are . . . the defining elements that really make us human. Yet exactly these elements are often the least visible in the prehistoric record. For this reason paleoanthropologists have correctly focussed on . . . the earliest evidences of symbolic behaviour in humans . . . the Paleolithic cave paintings in France and Spain, painted toward the end of the last Ice Age.[62]

But now precisely the point of the paintings is that *they are images*. Their haunting beauty notwithstanding, we are certain that "this prehistoric imagery was never intended to be merely descriptive."[63] It is likely that we shall never know exactly *what* the paintings were meant to represent; what is beyond question is that they were externalizations of some sort of meaning (van Huyssteen, with others, thinks they were *religious* symbols). And if we ask why some motifs

59. Ibid., 225, citing Rick Potts.
60. Ibid., 235 (his emphasis), with reference to Terrence Deacon.
61. Ibid., 229, with reference to Iain Davidson.
62. Ibid., 167.
63. Ibid., 185.

were consistently selected over others, "there must have been some distinct presuppositions in the minds of the people of the Upper Paleolithic. . . . [T]hey were probably 'looking for' certain things and not others. Lewis-Williams takes this to mean that a vocabulary of motifs must have existed in people's minds *before* they were made images."[64] In brief, the markings of these first recognizable humans suggest that *our ability to extrude thought*—to reduce it to, or replicate it in, permanent forms—is a, if not the, fundamental mark of the modern human being.

But now, second (whatever we shall say about humanity generically), images and imaging sit at the heart of the Christian faith. As a religion grounded in its belief in an incarnate God and its hope of bodily resurrection, the interface of spirit and substance is its central confession. Yet—unsurprisingly—the coupling has never been easy. For its first couple of centuries, orthodox faith was forced to contend with versions—deviations, the orthodox claimed—which would have written down or written out the fleshly component of incarnational faith: gnostic schemata and docetic Christologies. Even with the vanquishing of these officially and ostensibly, the uneasy combination of values which is Christian faith has perennially made its presence felt. In the Western church, both elements are found in some degree of compact through the Middle Ages. Nodal points were: Augustine's "doctrine of signs" according to which "things can become signs and these signs can reflect—and even lead us to—the God who is our true home";[65] Pope Gregory's letter to Bishop Serenius (October 600), setting out the idea forever after reiterated by iconophiles (supporters of images) that images are "the books of the illiterate";[66] the so-called Carolingian Books, purportedly sent from the court of Charlemagne in response to the decisions of the Eastern church over images, the authenticity of which however has never been certain;[67] the eucharistic

64. Ibid., 247 (his emphasis).
65. Dyrness, *Visual Culture*, 19.
66. David Freedberg, *The Power of Images: Studies in the History and Theory of Response* (Chicago: University of Chicago Press, 1989), 163.
67. See Margaret Aston, *England's Iconoclasts* (Oxford: Clarendon Press, 1988), 49–50, 52–53, 56–57.

controversies of the ninth and eleventh centuries over the nature of "real presence";[68] and, more generally, the proliferation of images, shrines, and pilgrimages throughout the latter Middle Ages: "The image was not peripheral to medieval Christianity. It was a central means for the individual to establish contact with God."[69] On the other side, simultaneously and with ever new momentum, was what Taylor has called "the work of reform":[70] movements for a "new spirituality," "new forms of inwardness,"[71] wherein the Fourth Lateran Council of 1215 played an important part,[72] in which Cistercians and Carthusians had been influential,[73] as well as Thomas à Kempis and the *devotio moderna*.[74] All this, needless to say, was the setting for the sixteenth-century conflagration over images that we call the Reformation.

The confrontation had come a good deal earlier in the Eastern church. Though "'there is . . . no century between the fourth and the eighth in which there is not some evidence of opposition to images even within Church,' [y]et it was in the eighth and ninth centuries that the doctrinal case against images was articulated more fully than ever before or since."[75] In 753 Emperor Constantine V called the iconoclastic Synod of Hieria where images were deemed to be idols and were ordered to be destroyed. The battle raged for almost a century, until 843, when under the iconophile Empress Theodora images were restored to the church on the first Sunday of Lent,

68. See, notably, Miri Ruben, *Corpus Christi: The Eucharist in Late Medieval Culture* (Cambridge: Cambridge University Press, 1991), 12–35.

69. Aston, *Iconoclasts*, 20.

70. As Taylor calls part 1 of his book: Charles Taylor, *A Secular Age* (Cambridge, MA: Belknap Press of Harvard University Press, 2007), 25–218; but see particularly 63–89.

71. Ibid., 69, 71, etc.

72. Ibid., 243.

73. Dyrness, *Visual Culture*, 31–33.

74. Carlos M. N. Eire, *War Against the Idols: The Reformation of Worship from Erasmus to Calvin* (Cambridge: Cambridge University Press, 1986), 22, 33. See also James F. White, *The Sacraments in Protestant Practice and Faith* (Nashville: Abingdon Press, 1999), 14–17.

75. Jaroslav Pelikan, *The Spirit of Eastern Christendom (600–1700)* (Chicago: University of Chicago Press, 1974), 105, quoting Ernst Kitzinger.

which day has forever subsequently been celebrated as the "Feast of Orthodoxy." The conflict (of iconoclasts and iconophiles) is instructive to our purposes in that the combatants drew diametrically opposite conclusions from pretty well the identical circumstance: namely, the necessary configuration between the image as ectype and its celestial or saintly prototype; in a word, images must *look like* that which they seek to portray. On the one side, iconoclasts claimed that on the basis of its verisimilitude "an image is identical in essence with that which it portrays"[76] and, accordingly, since no material object can represent spiritual verities, every image can only be "false."[77] Oppositely, in his famous first oration to the synod, John of Damascus used the images' likeness to their divine referent precisely as their vindication:

> When we set up an image of Christ in any place, we appeal to the senses. . . . [B]ut it is with the mind that we lay hold of the image. . . . [People are] not worshipping the things in themselves, they [are] being led through them to recall the wonderful works of God, and to adore him whose works they [have] witnessed.[78]

The point which thus emerges for us is that images *occupy an intermediate point* between the spirit realm (whether we are thinking of ideas, of sentiments, or of religious aspiration) and the physical world. This ambivalence or ambiguity will fuel iconoclastic controversies wherever they appear: iconoclasts claiming that an image's material constitution defiles the deity it purports to represent, and iconophiles urging that it is precisely its configuration to its intended referent which enables worshipers to worship through the physical representation. The image, as a figured object, I reiterate, mediates between an idea and raw (unshapen) matter; as I put it earlier, an image is "extruded thought." David Freedberg, then, has it exactly: "Does not the effectiveness of images depend most of all on the possibility of fusion?"[79]

---

76. Constantine V, cited by Pelikan, *The Spirit of Eastern Christendom*, 109.
77. Ibid., 113.
78. John of Damascus, cited by Freedberg, *The Power of Images*, 401.
79. Ibid., 402 (emphases removed).

Coming to the sixteenth century, we know of course that without exception Reformed leaders excoriated every suggestion of faith's material representation. Margaret Aston writes: "In the sixteenth century, idolatry became deeply engraved on the English conscience. The Reformation made it the deadliest of sins and it was one which no believer could be unaware of."[80] We may assume the same to have been true of all the Reformed territories. The startling irony, then, must be that the Reformers themselves spared no effort in giving objective form to their ideas—creating the visible image of their inward vision, we may say. Such is already to be seen in Ulrich Zwingli's joy in "the luminous whiteness of his city churches";[81] in other words, the bare, whitewashed walls set forth exactly the pure, uncluttered faith he so desired in his heart. The tendency is carried forward in Calvin's ambitions for Geneva. His—largely successful—aspiration was to make the entire city "a place of enthusiasm, learning, devotion and determination—truly a godly, reformed city."[82] Churches were thus closed when services were not in progress,[83] since, as William Dyrness says: "[According to Calvin] one does not need special places in which to pray. All of life has become an arena of faith and spirituality."[84] This new Protestant "affirmation of ordinary life"[85] would then soon begin to assume inescapably visual form in social arrangements and built structures. Disorder, irregularity, was said to "stink in God's nostrils."[86] The Reformed

---

80. Aston, *Iconoclasts*, 343.

81. Ibid., 38.

82. William G. Naphy, "Calvin's Geneva," in *The Cambridge Companion to John Calvin*, ed. Donald K. McKim (Cambridge: Cambridge University Press, 2004), 35.

83. See Jean [John] Calvin, "Ordinances for the Supervision of Churches in the Country," in *Calvin: Theological Treatises*, ed. and trans. John Kelman Sutherland Reid, Library of Christian Classics, vol. 22 (Philadelphia: Westminster Press, 1954), 79.

84. Dyrness, *Visual Culture*, 82.

85. See Charles Taylor, *Sources of the Self: The Making of the Modern Identity* (Cambridge: Cambridge University Press, 1989), 211–302, but notably 216–30 on the Reformed impetus to this "sanctification of ordinary life" (221, etc.).

86. Taylor, *Sources*, 228.

Christian's vocation in life was thus to translate the "clarity, harmony and transcendence"[87] that he or she encountered in the new orders of worship into patterns of daily life. Calvinists—particularly those migrating to the new American colonies where they were freer to shape the built environment according to their own vision—thus energetically set themselves to this "remaking of Eden":[88] first, in transforming the wilderness itself into "a new Heaven, and a new Earth";[89] then, in the organization of their towns;[90] and, not least, in the design of their worship spaces.[91] Herein lies the irony: "For the Puritans images were banished from churches, but in place of such sacred imagery, the whole of life, its patterns and structures, took on the character of an icon of God's presence."[92]

Our assignment was to account as well as we could for the fusion of spirit and matter, to say how it is that the ephemeral energies I have subsumed under the description "spirit" (these range considerably; they include ideas, consciousness, or self-awareness, the process of ratiocination, imagination, feelings, memories, religious convictions, etc., to go no further)[93] can combine with external substance, which fusion I have said is what sacramentality is. I do not believe I have *explained* how this happens. What I have undertaken is to show that the need, desire, compulsion even, to give outward form to inward cogitation is endemically human. It shows itself as

87. Ibid., 81.

88. Dyrness, *Visual Culture*, 267.

89. Ibid., 213, citing Edward Johnson, and, in greater detail, ibid., 261–69.

90. Ibid., 115, 214–19, 267.

91. Ibid., 219–21. Also Horton Davies, *The Worship of the American Puritans, 1629–1730* (New York: Peter Lang, 1990), 233–54; and James F. White, "From Protestant to Catholic Plain Style," in *Seeing Beyond the Word: Visual Arts and the Calvinist Tradition*, ed. Paul Corby Finney (Grand Rapids, MI: William B. Eerdmans Publishing Company, 1999), 457–76, but especially 457–66.

92. Dyrness, *Visual Culture*, 238.

93. Murphy, *Bodies and Souls*, 32, speaks of "the very narrow meaning of the word 'spirit' in English" but then goes on to offer, citing Owen Thomas, a range of meanings not dissimilar to mine. Thomas's list includes: "self-awareness, self-transcendence, memory, anticipation, rationality (in its broadest sense), creativity, plus the moral, intellectual, social, political, aesthetic, and religious capacities."

a defining mark of the emergent modern human being (meaning *Homo sapiens*). And it manifests itself as irrepressible even among those who emphatically deny it. As Freedberg puts it: "[Even in non-figurative cultures] the will to image figuratively . . . cannot be suppressed."[94]

My account of the human image-making propensity offered no occasion to refer to Husserlian phenomenology. In fact, it has been Husserl's discernment that there is no act of thought which does not include that which is thought about—no *noesis* apart from its *noema*—which underlies and informs the entire foregoing discussion of images and imaging. Husserl called the dynamic interaction "intentionality"—described by one of his disciples and commentators as "that remarkable property of consciousness to be a consciousness of . . . an intending of transcendence, a bursting out toward the world."[95] It is not too much, then, to see the irresistible impulse to give external form to inner convictions (as exemplified by the opponents of images no less than by their advocates) as precisely this "bursting out toward the world." Intentionality is the compulsion, that is, to fuse thought (or spirit) with expressive form.

Nor have I made much, if any, reference to what I said was Husserl's second groundbreaking insight: that the *noesis-noema* transaction is invariably and necessarily embodied. But again here the question of embodiment has never been absent from the debate over images. Freedberg observes, "[A]ny number of cultures share a belief . . . that the more spiritually developed a religion is, the less need it has for material objects to serve as a channel to the deity."[96] The judgment applies most definitely to the two cases of iconoclasm we have reviewed. Of the eighth-century Greeks, Jaroslav Pelikan writes:

> When they put such an emphasis on the role of the senses in worship, the iconophiles were affirming the role of the body in salvation—of the physical body of Christ as the means of achieving it and the physical body of man as a participant in it together with the soul. The iconoclasts [by contrast] claimed to worship the in-

94. Freedberg, *The Power of Images*, 55 (my emphasis), and see more comprehensively his chapter on "The Myth of Aniconism," ibid., 54–65.

95. Ricoeur, *Husserl*, 16.

96. Freedberg, *The Power of Images*, 65.

visible God in a purely spiritual and mental way, disdaining the use of visual aids such as images.[97]

This, as their opponents saw it, amounted to nothing less than a hatred of God's created order, including human embodiment: "The spiritualism of the iconoclasts seemed to put them into the same class with the ancient Gnostics, who claimed that the body of Christ was not physical but heavenly, and who despised the physically minded believers as less spiritual than they."[98] And the case is hardly different with the sixteenth-century Reformers. Carlos Eire says it simply: "The superiority of the spiritual dimension over the material is at the centre of Calvin's teaching," and quotes the Reformer: "[W]hatever holds down and confines the senses to the earth is contrary to the covenant of God; in which, inviting us unto Himself, He permits us to think of nothing but what is spiritual."[99] It scarcely needs saying that his elevation of spiritual values over materiality is what fires Calvin's lambast against images: "God's majesty is sullied by an unfitting and absurd fiction, when the incorporeal is made to resemble corporeal matter, the invisible a visible likeness, the spirit an inanimate object, the immeasurable a puny bit of wood, stone, or gold." On the contrary, "[T]he best way to contemplate the divine is where *minds* are lifted above themselves with admiration."[100] We shall see that the tendency (described as "sarcophobic" by John Dominic Crossan)[101] has persisted in Reformed Christianity even to our own times.

---

97. Pelikan, *Spirit of Eastern Christendom*, 122.

98. Ibid. See also, ibid., 223, on arguments of iconophiles against the iconoclasts: "The Creator of the world of things and animals was the same as the Redeemer of mankind, and a hatred of the material creation amounted to a contempt for him and for his gifts."

99. Eire, *War Against the Idols*, 201, citing Calvin's *Commentary on the Last Four Books of Moses*.

100. John Calvin, *Institutes of the Christian Religion*, ed. John T. McNeill, trans. Ford Lewis Battles (Philadelphia: Westminster Press, 1960), 1.11.2 (pp. 101–2; my emphasis).

101. See Gordon W. Lathrop, *Holy Ground: A Liturgical Cosmology* (Minneapolis: Augsburg Fortress, 2003), 130, 140–41, citing John Dominic Crossan, *The Birth of Christianity* (San Francisco: HarperCollins, 1998), 36–38.

The Human Image of God

For both the defenders and the opponents of images, the biblical proposition that *persons* constitute the primary image of God, the *imago Dei*, assumed fundamental importance. Opponents insisted that as the singular image of God the human person rendered every other image redundant: "A true living man [is] a closer image of God than a carving of wood or stone, so why should not God and Christ be worshipped in man rather than a dead image."[102] The supporters of images argued on the contrary that God's action in creating a physical image of himself in human persons constituted the vindication of images *per se*.[103]

To move our discussion from iconoclastic disputes to consideration of people as made in God's image is to construct a bridge over which we may pass in either direction between God's extensity in the world and God's intensity. On the one hand, the *imago Dei* directs us back toward the universalist considerations whence we began this discussion: if it says anything, the doctrine of the *imago* declares that every single human being bears the divine image. On the other hand, the belief that humans reflect God's image is unambiguously *biblical* and is thus pointing us in the direction not just of a central conviction of all the Abrahamic faiths[104] but to "one of the most enduring, core traditions of the Christian faith."[105] Moreover, we shall see that a Christian reading of the *imago* does not—cannot—rest before reaching its assertion that only in Jesus Christ is God finally and definitively imaged forth: "He is the image of the invisible God," and "He is . . . the exact imprint of God's very being" (Col 1:15; Heb 1:3; see also 2 Cor 4:4). So that here, finally, the intensity of God's presence in the world achieves its most

102. Aston, *England's Iconoclasts*, 122, with reference to the fifteenth-century Lollard Robert Holcroft.

103. Pelikan, *The Spirit of Eastern Christendom*, 95–96.

104. So, Philip Hefner, "*Imago Dei*: The Possibility and Necessity of the Human Person," in *The Human Person in Science and Theology*, ed. Niels Henrik Gregersen and others (Edinburgh: T&T Clark, 2000), 87–88: "This concept has often been cited as the single most important statement that the Judeo-Christian-Muslim tradition makes concerning human beings."

105. Van Huyssteen, *Are We Alone?*, 117.

resplendent, concentrated form—what Hardy in another place calls "the bright mystery of faith."[106]

"Let us make humankind in our image, according to our likeness"; accordingly, "God created humankind in his image, in the image of God he created them, male and female" (Gen 1:26-27). This pair of sentences, standing virtually at the head of the Jewish and Christian Scriptures, described as "one of the most daring acts of theological imagination within Scripture,"[107] sets before us the startling—and, in the end, profoundly confronting—idea that my neighbor is a sacrament of God (or, since I mean to keep the term "sacrament" for the church's two central symbolic events, I should better say that my neighbor stands before me as God's sacramental presence). Unsurprisingly, the *imago Dei* has, on the one hand, generated an inexhaustible depth of inquiry and reflection[108] and, on the other, yields no final or definitive key as to its meaning. In Philip Hefner's words: "There is no consensus on exactly what it means; there is no single or even standard interpretation of the concept of the image of God."[109] Ricoeur calls it "that indestructible symbol."[110]

We are nevertheless fortunate, from the point of view of reading the *imago* as constituting sacramental presence, that some venerable interpretations have now been eclipsed. One such is certainly the millennia-long assumption that God's image in human

106. Daniel W. Hardy, *God's Ways with the World: Thinking and Practising Christian Faith* (Edinburgh: T&T Clark, 1996), 18–19.

107. J. Richard Middleton, *The Liberating Image: The* Imago Dei *in Genesis 1* (Grand Rapids, MI: Brazos Press, 2005), 231.

108. Ibid., 38–39, notes that "interpretation of the *imago Dei* covers two and a half millennia and crosses the boundaries of two religious traditions"; so that, "to adequately discuss and situate this history of interpretation would require, minimally, expertise in Second Temple, talmudic, and medieval rabbinic Judaism as well as in the history of Christian theology and exegesis from patristic to modern times." As Middleton drily observes, "This expertise is well beyond the capacity of any single scholar."

109. Hefner, "*Imago Dei*: The Possibility and Necessity of the Human Person," 88.

110. Paul Ricoeur, *History and Truth*, trans. and with an introduction by Charles A. Kelbley (Evanston, IL: Northwestern University Press, 1965), 110, as cited by Noreen Herzfeld, *In Our Image: Artificial Intelligence and the Human Spirit* (Minneapolis: Augsburg Fortress, 2002), 32.

beings consisted in our "spiritual" dimension—chiefly meaning human rational powers, self-awareness, and the capacity for self-transcendence.¹¹¹ My thesis is that sacramentality emerges in the fusion of spirit and form. So that as long as the *imago* was conceptualized purely in terms of the human spirit (in whichever of its aspects) sacramentality could hardly apply. As van Huyssteen says of the "substantialist" interpretation, "This image of God is never found in the human body, but only in the rationalist mind."¹¹² We are fortunate, then, that this way of thinking pretty well disappeared from view in the latter half of the twentieth century, largely through the exegetical labor of the Old Testament theologian and exegete, Gerhard von Rad. Whereas earlier attention had concentrated on the question *wherein* does the image consist (and its corollary: wherein is humanity to be distinguished from the animals), von Rad turned the focus to the so-called "mandate of dominion" linked inextricably to the *imago* ("Be fruitful and multiply and fill the earth and subdue it and have dominion over it" [Gen 1:28]) and asked rather, *for what purpose* is the image given to people?¹¹³ The answer: "[The meaning of the image] only becomes clear and explicit when [Genesis] speaks about the purpose of this image in man, that is, *the function committed to man in virtue of it*, namely his status as lord in the world."¹¹⁴ And further, "[M]an is . . . created in the divine image that he may control the whole of creation. . . . [C]reation is referred to man and needs his dominion as an ordering principle."¹¹⁵ The "mandate" presumes a holistic anthropology:

111. Numerous accounts of the so-called substantialist interpretation of the *imago* (the image *consists in* such and such powers) have been compiled; see, for example, Shults, *Reforming Theological Anthropology*, 220–30; Herzfeld, *In Our Image*, 16–20; or van Huyssteen, *Are We Alone?*, 126–34.

112. Van Huyssteen, *Are We Alone?*, 128; van Huyssteen's reference here is to Augustine but the sentence may be extrapolated to the entire "substantialist" tradition.

113. See Gerhard von Rad, *Old Testament Theology*, vol. 1, trans. D. M. G. Stalker (London: SCM Press, 1975), 144–47.

114. Ibid., 146 (my emphases).

115. Von Rad's article on "εἰκών," in *Theological Dictionary of the New Testament*, ed. Gerhard Kittel, vol. 2, trans. and ed. Geoffrey W. Bromiley (Grand Rapids, MI: William B. Eerdmans Publishing Company, 1964), 392.

"The interpretations are . . . to be rejected which . . . one-sidedly limit God's image to man's spiritual nature. . . . [T]he whole man is created in God's image."[116] By way of corroboration, von Rad points to the two succeeding image references in Genesis: Genesis 5:1ff., where Adam's offspring, Seth, is said to continue to bear the divine likeness. According to von Rad, "This statement is most important. . . . [It] tells us that the transmission of the divine likeness is thought of in terms of the physical sequence of generations and therefore obviously in a physical sense."[117] Further, at Genesis 9:6 it is a person's divine image which grounds the prohibition of murder: "Here . . . attack on man's body is [a] violation of God's honour."[118] Since von Rad's time, then, and largely due to him, dualist interpretations of the *imago* have attracted minimal interest. It is the bodied human being who sacramentally stands for God.

A second matter of which we can now thankfully divest ourselves is that of the status of the *imago* subsequent to our original parents' "fall." That the question should have so exercised theological minds from at least patristic times to the Protestant scholastics of the seventeenth century, derived from the conviction or assumption mentioned a moment ago, namely, that the image *consisted in* a certain human quality or attribute, i.e., chiefly in rationality and/or a spiritual aptitude. The question thus became how to continue speaking of the chief distinguishing mark of humanity when precisely this distinguishing quality—our God-likeness, our reason and virtue—has been so seriously disfigured. Various permutations were worked out with variously optimistic and pessimistic readings—the nadir of which was probably the "total depravity" formula of the Reformed Synod of Dort in 1618–1619. With new frames of interpretation, the question has become redundant. To construe the *imago* other than as "substantialist"—for example: as God's commission laid upon humans (von Rad), or as the human

116. Gerhard von Rad, *Genesis: A Commentary*, trans. John H. Marks (London: SCM Press, 1972), 58. And see similarly his article "εἰκών," 391: "If we had to think in terms of . . . an alternative [i.e., between spiritual or physical being] . . . we should have to decide in favour of a predominantly physical likeness."

117. Von Rad, *Genesis*, 58.

118. Ibid.

capacity for relationships (Karl Barth), or as an eschatological goal (Wolfhart Pannenberg)—simply bypasses the question (of the image's postlapsarian status). More pointed, perhaps, the Genesis text itself discounts the question in that it continues to draw on the idea of divine likeness *subsequently* to its account of the fall: namely, in the procreation of Seth (5:3) and the prohibition of murder (9:6). As von Rad says austerely: "The Old Testament says nothing about the divine likeness being lost."[119] Of course it yet remains for us to consider the dreadful depredations suffered by God's image through human willfulness; iconicity is never far removed from its dark side, idolatry. Yet the point here is that it is precisely in, through, and notwithstanding his or her evil intent that a person comes to me as a sacrament of God; it is exactly my *enemy* that I am called to love (Matt 5:44)! The image may be obscured but is never lost; that this contorted creature never ceases to be a manifestation of God to me is the ineluctable mystery.

A third problematic factor which need no longer distract us has been the misunderstanding attaching to the clear link made by Genesis between the divine image and the so-called "mandate of dominion," the charge to "fill the earth and subdue it" (Gen 1:28). The question is asked: "Is the connection between the *imago Dei* and the *dominium terrae* in Genesis 1 about nothing other than the sad and brutal truth of the human species that always powerfully asserts its strength to prevail biologically as well as culturally?"[120] At least one answer must be that historically it has been so: the so-called mandate has consistently been misinterpreted and misappropriated to the lamentable cost of the planet and its other-than-human species. In this case too, however, we are now fortunate to have available to us exegetical findings, particularly and most recently the meticulous work of Richard Middleton, which exegesis answers the question with a resounding No! Middleton shows convincingly, first, that the Genesis story, in strongest—and unquestionably polemical—contrast to the ancient Near Eastern myths which form its background, carries not the faintest suggestion of a contest or conflict between God and alien forces in order to bring the universe

119. Von Rad, "εἰκών," 392.
120. Van Huyssteen, *Are We Alone?*, 155, citing Michael Welker.

into being: "The typical pattern of divine command (for example, 'let there be light') followed by an execution report ('and there was light') pictures God as encountering no resistance in creating the world." "God is pictured here not as warrior, but as a craftsman or artisan."[121] Second, Middleton draws attention to the fact that the so-called "mandate of dominion" is to "fill" the newly formed earth, which action in fact replicates—and continues!—God's own work of creation; this consisted, first, in separating distinctive parts of the cosmos (Gen 1:3-13) and then *filling* these domains with moving and living beings (Gen 1:14-31).[122] Then: God rests from his creative work (Gen 2:1-3)! Middleton draws the conclusion: "God's rest in Genesis 2 represents the delegation to humanity of the royal task of administering the world on his behalf. Humans are entrusted with nothing less than *God's own proper work* as the creator's authorised representatives on earth."[123] Given that the creative work was, in first place, a peaceful and peaceable act—quite oppositely, that is, to the "combat myths" against which Genesis is reacting—and, second, that the "mandate" is to continue this peaceable work in God's name and in the dignity of the image invested in the human race, "[T]his two-pronged ideology critique calls for all humanity . . . to exercise power differently from anything implied by cosmogonic conflict."[124]

We have thus, so far, cleared away some of the distracting elements historically associated with the *imago Dei*. But now we are bound to ask: *How* is this, my neighbor in all her or his ambiguity, a manifestation of God to me? Noreen Herzfeld has observed that the various interpretative frames invoked for the *imago* since about the mid-twentieth century—divine commission, relationality, eschatological goal—are "not necessarily mutually exclusive."[125] I would concur. I would also say, however, that there is a dimension to the divine likeness not caught expressly in any and all of these

---

121. Middleton, *The Liberating Image*, 264 and 266. See more comprehensively, ibid., 263–69.

122. See particularly ibid., 74–77.

123. Ibid., 212 (his emphases).

124. Ibid., 266.

125. Herzfeld, *In Our Image*, 32.

which carries us forward in our question about sacramentality. This finds expression in the writings of the great Jewish philosopher and Talmudist, Emmanuel Levinas: the human person is *endlessly other* to me. It is exactly the *inexhaustible alterity* of my neighbor, which makes her or him a parable—or to recur to our accustomed language here, the sacramental presence—of the Almighty.

Levinas is driven by what he sees as the endemic human preoccupation with the self—as he calls it, "the egoist position,"[126] "the central place the I occupies in the world."[127] This endless turning in upon itself effectively closes the self to an external world, he claims, as though colonizing all exteriority in conformity with its own needs, its own thoughts, its own perceptions: "The subject is 'for itself'—it represents itself and knows itself as long as it is. But in knowing or representing itself it possesses itself, dominates itself, extends its identity to what of itself comes to refute this identity."[128] This is the "totalization" that stands in the title of Levinas's early and seminal work, *Totality and Infinity*. John Wild in his introduction to the book has it this way: "[T]otalizers . . . are satisfied with themselves and with the systems they can organize around themselves as they already are. . . . It is this outwardly directed but self-centred totalistic thinking that organizes men and things into power systems, and gives us control over nature and other people."[129] But this "totalizing" tendency can be broken open, interrupted by an "unquenchable Desire for Infinity."[130] This is the desire truly to encounter an otherness beyond myself. And this opening up of myself, or being accosted by another, exposes me to an incalculable dimension—hence "infinity." The two, totality and infinity, can be distinguished in terms of "need" and "desire." "Need" is the satisfaction of my physical and emotional dependencies; "desire" is the reaching to the other for *its* sake, not my own: "[I]n need I can sink my teeth into the real and satisfy myself in assimilating the

126. Emmanuel Levinas, *Totality and Infinity: An Essay on Exteriority*, trans. Alphonso Lingis (Pittsburgh: Duquesne University Press, 1969), 75.
127. Ibid., 83.
128. Ibid., 87.
129. Ibid.
130. Ibid., 150.

other; in Desire there is no sinking one's teeth into being, no satiety, but an uncharted future before me."[131] As this phrase—"uncharted future"—makes clear, it is the encounter with alterity which exposes me to infinity: "Infinity is characteristic of a transcendent being as transcendent; the infinite is the absolutely other."[132] Levinas can occasionally speak of the "shock" experienced by the self (or "the same" as he regularly calls it) in being accosted by alterity ("the shock of the encounter of the same with the other").[133] But much more characteristically he speaks of the beneficent, almost beatific, effect of such an encounter:

> This extraterritoriality has a positive side. It is produced in the gentleness or the warmth of intimacy. . . . By virtue of its intentional structure gentleness comes to the separated being from the Other. The Other precisely reveals himself in his alterity not in a shock negating the I, but as the primordial phenomenon of gentleness. . . . The welcoming of the face is peaceable from the first, for it answers to the unquenchable Desire for Infinity.[134]

Our interest is in the sacramentality of the person. From this point of view it is striking that Levinas steadily refuses to say *which* or *whose* alterity he has in view: God's or that of persons. He can indeed use such exalted terms to speak of alterity that one might well think that it is not other than God of whom he speaks: "[T]his alterity . . . is understood as the alterity of the Other and of the Most-High."[135] Or: "The dimension of the divine opens forth from the human face."[136] He can describe the encounter with otherness as "religion."[137] On the other hand, neither does Levinas wish to conflate these—as if to apotheosize humanity.[138] It is rather that

131. Ibid., 117.
132. Ibid., 49.
133. Ibid., 42.
134. Ibid., 150.
135. Ibid., 34.
136. Ibid., 78.
137. Ibid., 64.
138. See the dialogue attached to his address "Transcendence and Height," in *Emmanuel Levinas: Basic Philosophical Writings*, ed. Adriaan T. Peperzak,

each, by *reason of their alterity*, opens us to infinity. The very fact that God and the other person, each or both, meet us as infinity—"to receive from the Other . . . means exactly: to have the idea of infinity"[139]—means that there can *be* no clear demarcation between them. It is as if in the infinity of the other person I gain an intuition or apprehension of the infinitude, which is God's. The neighbor, we may say, stands to me as a manifestation of the Most High.

And yet precisely the person, who comes toward me, opens me to the infinitude of otherness, is an embodied human being! Levinas's most famous leitmotif is that it is *the face*, which is the epiphany of alterity: "This new dimension opens in the sensible appearance of the face."[140] In a word, infinity assumes fleshly form, as *in a particular person* it addresses me. It is spirit fused with substance!

Levinas's Jewishness holds him essentially within the prophetic tenets of the Hebrew Scriptures. Accordingly, the quintessential manifestation of the other is for him "the stranger, the widow and the orphan."[141] The Christian gospel, on the other hand, pushes us even further in terms of recognizing the presence of God in other persons. In the first place, of course, is the immediate conjunction of God and one's neighbor in the so-called Great Commandment (Mark 12:29-31; Matt 22:36-40; Luke 10:25-27). Again, this is

---

Simon Critchley, and Robert Bernasconi (Bloomington: Indiana University Press, 1996), 29: "I do not want to define anything through God because it is the human that I know. It is God that I can define through human relations and not the inverse. The notion of God—God knows, I am not opposed to it! But when I have something to say about God, it is always beginning from human relations." And see, from the essay "Meaning and Sense" in the same volume (p. 64): "The God who passed (Exodus 33.18-23) is not the model of which the face would be an image. To be in the image of God does not mean to be an icon of God but to find oneself in his trace. The revealed God of our Judeo-Christian spirituality maintains all the infinity of his absence. . . . He shows himself only by his trace."

139. Levinas, *Totality and Infinity*, 51.

140. Ibid., 198. The face as the site of encounter with otherness occurs not just throughout *Totality and Infinity* but in practically all of Levinas's philosophical writings. See, helpfully, David F. Ford, *Self and Salvation: Being Transformed* (Cambridge: Cambridge University Press, 1999), particularly 37–39, but more generally 19–44.

141. Levinas, *Totality and Infinity*, 215.

not to conflate or merge the two: love of God is one thing, and has priority, and neighborly love another. But neither is it possible or permissible to separate them. As the First Letter of John would catch it exactly: "Those who say, 'I love God' and hate their brothers and sisters are liars" (1 John 4:20). This finds yet more concrete expression in the so-called "parable of sheep and goats" where the nations of the world are assembled for judgment and where "the Son of Man seated on the throne of his glory" draws an exact identification between himself and "the least of these, the members of my family," namely, the hungry and thirsty, the sick, strangers, the naked and imprisoned (Matt 25:31-46).[142] And the gospel has not finished with me yet! It is not only in the outcasts of society that I am to see God's or Christ's image reflected. Ultimately it is *my enemy* who approaches me in God's stead: "I say to you, love your enemies and pray for those who persecute you" (Matt 5:44). Here at last and at any rate is the shock of alterity! The coda, "those who persecute you," makes clear that this person, in all his or her otherness, comes toward me with the intention of damaging if not destroying me. And yet I am required to *love* her or him. To ask how this can possibly make sense is to be returned to the *imago Dei* inherent, we saw, in every human being. The commentator Douglas Hare thus writes (of the injunction to pray for those who persecute us): "Praying for enemies involves a serious attempt to see them from God's point of view. We cannot earnestly pray for our enemies without acknowledging our common humanity; they too have been created in the image of God, and no behavior, no matter how nefarious, can erase that image."[143] This is why Gerrit C. Berkouwer can conclude that the meaning of the *imago Dei* is finally "the harmony of the new commandment, the commandment of love, the fulfilling

142. Levinas had no good reason to be especially enamored of Christianity. He did however find this parable impressive where, as he says, "people are quite astonished to learn . . . that when they turned away the poor who knocked on their doors, it was really God in person they were shutting out" (Emmanuel Levinas, *In the Time of the Nations*, trans. Michael B. Smith [Bloomington: Indiana University Press, 1994], 162).

143. Douglas R. A. Hare, *Matthew: Interpretation Bible Commentary for Teaching and Preaching* (Louisville, KY: John Knox Press, 1993), 59.

of the law,"[144] or Robert Jenson can say, "[T]he final specification of 'the image of God' is *love*."[145]

We have yet to consider the dreadful deformation of the image in human history. That the human person is—for all his or her ambiguity—nevertheless a sacramental manifestation of God is secured by the conviction, shared by every sacramental theologian, that Jesus Christ was and is *the* primordial sacrament. For Christ was a human being.

The "Other Likeness"

In an essay on "the self" in the Hebrew Scriptures, James Mays has drawn attention to "the other likeness" mentioned in the Genesis creation stories.[146] The "other" likeness comes initially in the tempter's words, "You will be like God," then in God's subsequent recognition that the human creatures indeed "have become like one of us, knowing good and evil" (Gen 3:5 and 22). Mays sets this account of "the other likeness" in a larger canonical context, chiefly consisting in the prayers of invocation of the psalter. He distills from such prayers a "self" of the following lineaments: it is a self able to translate consciousness into communication; it is a relational being, conscious of "I," "you," and "them"; it exists in three spheres, physical, social, and theological; it is a dependent self, urgently conscious of its needs; and it is "inextricably religious," addressing

144. Gerrit Cornelis Berkouwer, *Man: The Image of God* (Grand Rapids, MI: William B. Eerdmans Publishing Company, 1962), 116. By all means, Berkouwer is writing here not so much of the *imago* as originally given but as reconstituted "in Christ." On the other hand, he has argued at length, in some dependence on Barth and beyond Barth on Calvin, that the image is most properly to be understood in terms of "man in his new *conformitas*," in other words, "in the renewal of the image of the Creator" (ibid., 100; see in detail, ibid., 87–100).

145. Robert W. Jenson, *Systematic Theology*, vol. 2 (New York: Oxford University Press, 1999), 72 (his emphasis).

146. James L. Mays, "The Self in the Psalms and the Image of God," in *Preaching and Teaching the Psalms*, ed. Patrick D. Miller and Gene M. Tucker (Louisville, KY: Westminster John Knox Press, 2006), 51–67. The reference to "the other likeness" is found on pp. 61–62 of the essay.

itself to God as the source of its succor and as its ultimate point of reference.[147] Its chief characteristic, however, is that it is a deeply conflicted self—conscious of an inherent self-worth which has been damaged or lost, sometimes through sickness or misadventure but much more regularly through the nefarious actions of "them," its attackers and defrauders. Mays draws a line, via the "image" allusion of Psalm 8, from this portrait of a fractured self to the Genesis account of God's image in humans, which has been so traduced by the same humans' will to independence, their aspiration to a "likeness" other than that of the original gift:

> This likeness is not a representing and resembling God . . . but rather the opposite. . . . It is the autonomous prerogative to decide what is nourishing and beautiful and best for living. . . . "Like Elohim, knowing good and evil," means assuming divine autonomy. . . . [I]t is a misuse of reason that is centered radically in the self.[148]

The stories that follow (in Genesis) thus depict "a corporate and individual self that has become its own center and reference in the matter of life and death." "[N]othing . . . reconciles the contradiction between the two likenesses. . . . The self-centered enterprise to take possession of life is a radical disconnection with the original likeness. The two identify the human creature in their contradiction."[149] It is just this contradiction, thinks Mays, which then displays itself in the invocatory psalms: "The prayers are a litany of a longing to be what the psalmists are: creatures created in the image of God."[150]

The deep complicity, entanglement we may say, between iconicity and idolatry has often been noticed.[151] Everything turns around the

147. Mays, "The Self in the Psalms," 55–56.
148. Ibid., 61–62.
149. Ibid., 62.
150. Ibid., 64.
151. Jean-Luc Marion, for instance, begins his well-known essay on idols and icons as follows: "That the idol can be approached only in the antagonism that infallibly unites it with the icon is certainly unnecessary to argue" (Jean-Luc Marion, "The Idol and the Icon," in *God without Being*, trans. Thomas A.

central matter of this essay: the physicality, or visibility, of spiritual verities. Freedberg says, for instance, "In order to grasp the divinity, man must figure it,"[152] and then he can equally say, "Through sight we fall into idolatry."[153] In a word, to give physicality, visibility, to spiritual values both gains sentient access to them and risks idolatry.

Jean-Luc Marion, in his analysis of "the two phenomenologies"[154]— namely, idolatry and iconicity—insists that materiality is not, as so regularly supposed, the issue: "The decisive moment in the erection of an idol stems not from its fabrication, but from its investment as gazeable, as that which will fill a gaze."[155] The decisive point about an idol, he is saying, is that it is an artifact—and not necessarily just a material object; later we will learn that concepts can be just as idolatrous—which has the power "to stop the gaze" of its viewer:[156] "The idol fascinates and captivates the gaze precisely because everything in it must expose itself to the gaze, attract, fill and hold it."[157] It becomes an object for itself, an end in its own right. Its power as idol is that it allows no further reference: "[T]he gaze no longer pierces things, no longer sees them in transparency . . .; a last one finally presents itself as visible, splendid, and luminous enough to be the first to attract, capture and fill [the gaze]."[158] But more: not only does it enthrall its beholder; the idol then reflects to him or her the power of this fascination. Something like a radar signal

---

Carlson, with a foreword by David Tracy [Chicago: University of Chicago Press, 1991], 7). Pelikan, in his account of images in the Eastern church of the eighth and ninth centuries, observes: "[T]here is a consensus among modern historians that 'at the root of image worship lay the concept that material objects can be the seat of divine power . . .' [it] was in fact a concept held in common by the opponents and the supporters of images" (Pelikan, *Spirit of Eastern Christendom*, 93). And Freedberg makes the same point: "[The issue is] the inseparability of the iconoclast and the iconodule positions. Both are predicated on the possibility of reconstitution and fusion. Both are based on the cherishing that turns to fear" (Freedberg, *The Power of Images*, 427).

152. Freedberg, *The Power of Images*, 60.
153. Ibid., 384.
154. Marion, "The Idol and the Icon," 7.
155. Ibid., 10.
156. Ibid., 11.
157. Ibid., 10.
158. Ibid., 11.

bounced back to its source, or, in more homely metaphor, "the idol thus acts as a mirror . . .; a mirror that reflects the gaze's image, or more exactly, the image of its aim and of the scope of that aim."[159] Yet such is the bedazzlement of this transaction that it is wholly unbeknown to the enraptured viewer; the idol is, as it were, "an *invisible* mirror."[160] She or he, the idolater, is *ravished*![161] The icon, by contrast, "attempts to render visible the invisible as such, hence to allow that the visible [i.e., the icon's material composition] not cease to refer to an other than itself. . . . The icon summons the gaze to surpass itself by never freezing on a visible. . . . [T]he icon makes visible only by giving rise to an infinite gaze."[162] The distinguishing mark of an icon, in other words, is its transparency, its referentiality.

It remains implicit in Marion's text, though by no means obscurely, that the differences between iconicity and idolatry derive both from the *nature of the gaze* directed toward each and also from the *physical configuration* of the objects themselves. He can say, on the one hand, for instance, "[T]he manner of seeing decides what can be seen."[163] But then he can equally say of the idol's fabricator, "[T]his is what the artist tries to bring out in his material: he wants to fix in stone, strictly to solidify, an ultimate visible, worthy of the point where his gaze froze,"[164] or oppositely, "[T]he icon allows itself to be traversed by an infinite depth."[165] What this comes to is that both a spiritual and a material dimension inhere in both iconicity and idolatry.

I want to direct all this back to the creature, which is at one and the same time God's icon ("icon" is the Greek word for "image" in Gen 1:26, etc.) and yet has also determined on its own "likeness" to God. It is impossible to overlook the congruences between the self-referentiality of the idol according to Marion's review and the "autonomous prerogative to decide what is nourishing . . . and best" on the part of the creature electing for "the other likeness" of

159. Ibid., 12.
160. Ibid., 11–12.
161. Ibid.
162. Ibid., 18.
163. Ibid., 9.
164. Ibid., 14.
165. Ibid., 20.

Genesis 3. Mays finds such terms as *"assuming divine autonomy* in discerning and deciding what is beneficial to life and what is detrimental,"* or, "a corporate and individual self that *has become its own center* and reference in the matter of life and death," or again, "the self-centered enterprise to take possession of life."[166] All these are just the hallmarks of the idol and idolatry. It is as if the creature has idolized itself.

Jesus Christ as the Image of God

A human being is thus both icon and idol, inextricably mixed or confused. Which is why, already from New Testament times, Christian writers have consistently pointed to Jesus Christ as *the* singular image of God—the one human icon, that is, not compounded with or compromised by idolatry. As one New Testament writer has it, "He became like his brothers and sisters in every respect . . . yet without sin" (Heb 2:17 and 4:15). Here—and only here—do we see the *imago Dei* as it was, and is, supposed to be: "He is the image [*eikon*] of the invisible God" (Col 1:15), or again, "the glory of Christ, who is the image [*eikon*] of God" (2 Cor 4:4). And the writer to the Hebrews calls him "the reflection [*apaugasma*] of God's glory, the exact imprint [*charakter*] of God's very being" (Heb 1:3). In the person of Jesus Christ we thus reach the culmination of our movement from generalization to particularity, from God's extensity in the world to the "bright mystery" of God's most intense presence. As sacramental theologians are wont to say, Jesus Christ is the primordial sacrament.[167]

166. All these references are on p. 62 of Mays, "The Self in the Psalms."

167. Osborne, *Christian Sacramentality in a Postmodern World*, 84–111 (and see also 64, 138, 146), makes extensive objection to the naming of Jesus as "primordial sacrament." His argument turns around the claim that "primordial" could only mean that Jesus was *different* from all other humans, whereas the creeds insist that Jesus was "of one nature with us," "truly human," and so on. The upshot: "Jesus, in his humanness, must be presented constitutively in the same kind of humanness all other men and women share. To do anything else would render his humanness different from ours and would make the

Christ images God for us. The thing is, "God"—whether we mean by that the reality we are trying to express or simply the term by which we usually name the reality—is impossibly *big*. As the catechism itself says: "God is a Spirit, infinite, eternal and unchangeable in his being, wisdom, power, holiness, justice, goodness and truth."[168] That means that "God" remains beyond definition (other than by the series of negations), finally impossible to conceptualize or imagine. And as the cosmos in which we find ourselves grows ever, and exponentially, larger, by the same token, even with the best will in the world, or for the most devout among us, a Creator and Sustainer of that universe is ever more difficult to grasp.[169] But Jesus Christ was a human being—as we read earlier, "like his brothers and sisters in every respect." It is Jesus, as the image of God, who

---

Christian doctrine of Incarnation a meaningless statement and a meaningless reality" (103). Jesus cannot therefore be seen as somehow "primordial."

Osborne's view appears to me quite to overlook the insistence of the New Testament and subsequent Christian conviction that, unlike all other human beings, Jesus was not susceptible to what I have called "the idolatrous tendency" (i.e., sin). It seems to me one has to say, either that sin is not embedded in all human behavior (disputed by the New Testament), or that Jesus partook of sin (also disputed), or that, in this respect, Jesus *was* different from all other human beings.

168. Westminster Shorter Catechism, question 4; in *Confession of Faith: The Larger Catechism, The Shorter Catechism, The Directory for Public Worship, and the Form of Presbyteral Church Government* (Edinburgh and London: William Blackwood and Sons, 1955), 115.

169. In earlier generations, God's "unreachableness" was conceived in terms of human culpability (sin, guilt, eternal death, wrath, etc.). See, for example, Randall C. Zachman, "Jesus Christ as the Image of God in Calvin's Theology," in *Calvin Theological Journal* 25, no. 1 (April 1990): 45–62, on "the wonderful exchange" in Calvin's theology. In the present age, on the contrary, one senses that the difficulty people have is much more nearly a conceptual one, or, better, a difficulty in *imagining* God. See Taylor, *A Secular Age*, 159ff., on "the social imaginary"; specifically, p. 192: "The . . . newness of the [contemporary] public sphere has to be defined by its radical secularity. . . . [This is] a notion of secularity [which] is radical, because it stands not only in contrast with a divine foundation for society, but with any idea of society as constituted in something which transcends contemporary common action." I will come back to the idea of "salvation" as the finding of meaning in an otherwise meaningless universe.

gives definition, focus, concreteness, and visibility to the otherwise indefinite, diffused, generalized sense of transcendence, which is our best apprehension of God.

The hymnic Colossians reference (Col 1:15) offers only a personal pronoun, "who" (*hos*), but the subject is not in doubt. The writer has just spoken of "the kingdom of [God's] beloved Son" (1:13) and earlier references have been to "our Lord Jesus Christ" and "Christ Jesus" (1:3, 4). Both names are important in determining his status as "image" of God: "Jesus" anchors the person so named in recognizable human history and "Christ" (the Greek version of "Messiah") represents the several honorific titles ("Son of Man," "Son of God," "Lord," etc.) which the followers of Jesus subsequently found to express their belief in the transcendent eminence and power of the Nazarene prophet.

"Jesus" is his proper name. This is the name that locates him in time and place, in a human family, that makes him identifiable (Mark 3:32; cf. Luke 4:22). It is, however, not just the *fact* that "he became flesh and lived among us" (John 1:14); Jesus, prophet of Nazareth, created both by his manner of life and his teachings an indelible impression of what "God's Rule" is like when it is allowed to affect human lives.[170] It is of course unquestionably true that the drawing of exact distinctions between the things said and done by Jesus and those attributed to him by the later, believing community is probably finally impossible. The circumstance may, however, by no means lead to a skepticism or despair about our knowledge of Jesus. As Edward Schillebeeckx affirms in his magisterial study:

> It is not denied that the four gospels are extensively conditioned by the confessional affirmation, proclamation, catechesis, paraenesis and liturgy of the first Christian congregations, and so are overlaid with the evangelists' own theology; but they are thought nonetheless to contain *sufficient basic information about Jesus* and

---

170. This in contrast to "the mere that" (*das bloße Dass*) of Rudolf Bultmann: "The message of Jesus is a presupposition for the theology of the New Testament rather than part of that theology itself," and "for the Church, as for Jesus himself, the content of his message was not the decisive thing" (Rudolf Bultmann, *Theology of the New Testament*, vol. 1, trans. Kendrick Grobel [London: SCM Press, 1965], 3, 43).

recollections of him, in respect of his message, his attitude to life and his conduct as a whole.[171]

Jesus apparently saw himself as standing in the line of Israel's prophets, calling people to a renewal of faith and the observance of God's law ("turning" or "returning," *metanoia*; Mark 1:15). Several characteristics distinguish him and his message, however.[172] In the first place, in sharp contradistinction to his immediate predecessor in this tradition, John the Baptizer (whose preaching Jesus did nevertheless take entirely seriously), for Jesus the imminent "Rule of God" (*basileia tou Theou*) was not, as for John, a matter of wrath and judgment but meant rather "the proximity of God's unconditional will to salvation, of reconciling clemency and sufficing graciousness, and along with them opposition to all forms of evil: suffering and sin."[173] "The one thing that Jesus is getting at is that this God [the God of the *basileia*] is a 'God of human kind.' "[174] The in-breaking "Rule" is thus a matter of joy and festivity for all who will receive it. A second distinctive mark as expressed in his preaching and actions was Jesus' certainty about the inclusiveness, the humanizing intention, of God's law as this was to be found within the in-breaking "Rule": "Jesus was not against the law; he radicalized it by bringing into the open its deepest purposes of salvation: a freedom 'to do good.' "[175] And yet a third feature of his ministry was his conviction that this whole-making, division-destroying "Rule of God" was immediately at hand, perhaps already breaking in in his own words and actions: "It is plain from the life of Jesus that 'present' and 'future,' although distinguished, are essentially bound up together; Jesus proclaims the salvation to come, and at the same time by his conduct makes it present."[176] It is this

171. Edward Schillebeeckx, *Jesus: An Experiment in Christology*, trans. Hubert Hoskins (New York: Crossroad Publishing Company, 1981), 72 (my emphases).

172. As the references will show, I am significantly dependent in what follows on Schillebeeckx's *Jesus*.

173. Ibid., 140.

174. Ibid., 142.

175. Ibid., 242.

176. Ibid., 152.

embodiment of the in-breaking "Rule"—his "breaking" of Sabbath rules in the interests of the person, for example (Mark 3:1-6), or his insistence on God's favor even for those scarcely deserving of it (Matt 20:1-15) and, perhaps most infuriatingly, his blatant disregard for table-fellowship protocols (Matt 9:10-13, etc.)—which attracted the bitter opposition of the religious leaders of the time, for whom such ritual distinctions were of utmost importance.

None of this is to say that the call to repentance was without its cost. The receiving of "God's Rule" entailed an abandonment of all the normal human dependencies: family (Matt 8:21-22), finances (Mark 10:17-22), and, most particularly, the prestige of religious, ethnic, and ritual purity (Luke 18:9-14). The Jesus of the gospel tradition could call this unqualified trust in God "dying to self" and "taking up one's cross" (Mark 8:34-38); and even if the actual formulation of such expressions is colored by the communities' later experience, there can scarcely be doubt that at some point in his ministry Jesus recognized that his mission must end in his own demise. The question then arises, doubtless for Jesus himself, and most assuredly for his followers, about the contradiction between his, Jesus', total confidence in God's providential care and the fate that clearly confronted and eventually overtook him. The tradition remembers sayings such as "the Son of Man came . . . to give his life as a ransom for many" (Mark 10:45) and "I am among you as one who serves" (Luke 22:27; cf. John 13:3-5). Again in this case, even if the sayings are refracted through later community experience, "this one thing is certain: Jesus [stood] open to God's future for man and, on the other hand, his whole life [was] a service to people, a service of love."[177]

Our interest here is in the way Jesus images God for us. One dimension of this is, then, the showing forth in his life and teaching of "a God of human kind," a God impatient with religious scruples and generous "to a fault" (so to speak) with those normally reckoned to be unworthy. But we have also to recall that the "image of God" originally invested in every human being has been disastrously compromised by "the idolatrous tendency," the "autonomous prerogative to decide what is nourishing and best" for oneself. So that it is in this respect too that we see in the actions and resolve of the

---

177. Ibid., 309.

prophet of Nazareth a true reflection of the *imago Dei.* For here was one who lived and died, expressly *not* for himself, but "open to God's future . . . [and as] a service to people, a service of love." In both his embodiment of God's generosity and his repudiation of self, so the later community came to believe, "Whoever has seen [Jesus] has seen the Father" (John 14:9).

But was a selfless life enough? Enough, that is, to validate Jesus as the sacrament of *God*? For he is not the only person to have lived and died a courageous and selfless life. As Schillebeeckx says, all that we have so far said attests "the fact that Jesus put into words and practised profoundly . . . human and yet simple 'things of life' . . . accepted even by non-Christians."[178] And then of course there is no avoiding the fact that like so many outstandingly good people before and since, Jesus' mission crashed on the reefs of human obduracy and intolerance. He was put to death.

The claim that Jesus is the sacrament of God, then, cannot side-step the event which Christians celebrate as Jesus' resurrection from death, the sign that his, Jesus', implacable trust in God was *not* misplaced and that there is a force in the universe greater than human machinations and the power of death. As Schillebeeckx goes on from the passage just now cited: "Jesus' message . . . and . . . conduct was certainly the cause of man—but . . . *what was truly distinctive* about Jesus . . . what was closest to his heart [was] *the God* mindful of humanity."[179] In short, to speak of Jesus as the sacrament of God, there is no avoiding the question of a divine presence and involvement.

And that in turn means there is no avoiding the teasing questions attending the historicity of the event we call the resurrection. In some degree, the issue seems to me (the protagonists hotly dispute this!) to be a semantic one: what sort of happening can be brought under the description "historical"? Pannenberg is one who reso-lutely claims the term for the resurrection:

> [T]hese events [the resurrection appearances] are to be affirmed also as historical events, as occurrences that actually happened at

178. Ibid., 607.
179. Ibid. (my emphases).

a definite time in the past. If we would forgo the concept of a historical event here, then it is no longer possible at all to affirm that the resurrection of Jesus or that the appearances of the resurrected Jesus really happened at a definite time in our world.[180]

Pannenberg may well be justified in his claim that the uniqueness of an event does not, in itself, put it beyond the range of historical inquiry.[181] The "resurrection" is not simply unique among other mundane events, however. From the earliest times, the followers of Jesus were clear that whatever it was that had happened was an *extra*ordinary event, one not able to be accounted for (even as something astonishing) within the normal categories of human reckoning, a divine action in fact. The point about the applicability or otherwise of the term "historical" has to do with whether "an action of God" can be read off the surface of terrestrial events, in short, whether the "resurrection" can, so to speak, be claimed as a "proof" for the existence and intervention of God in human affairs. And here, theologians are as one: God cannot finally be a matter of demonstration but of belief.

This is by no means to gainsay that *something happened*—only that the word "historical" is not the most appropriate description—and that this something was of epochal significance. Schillebeeckx is one who, for the reasons given, eschews the term "historical" but asks:

> *What was it then* that after a time gave these same disciples [who had fled in dismay] reason to assert that they were once more drawn into a living and present relationship with Jesus, whom they now proclaimed to be the living one, risen from the dead . . . ? *What took place* between Jesus' death and the proclamation of the church?[182]

He answers his own question thus: "[E]ven the historian must face the problem here; something must surely have happened to make

180. Wolfhart Pannenberg, *Jesus—God and Man*, trans. Lewis L. Wilkins and Duane A. Priebe (London: SCM Press, 1969), 99.

181. Ibid., 98.

182. Schillebeeckx, *Jesus*, 331 (my emphases).

this transformation at any rate psychologically intelligible."[183] Charles F. D. Moule, who entertains no hesitation about the facticity of the resurrection, posits much the same question:

> All I am trying to do is to present certain undoubted phenomena of the New Testament writings and to ask how the reader proposes to account for them. If the coming into existence of the Nazarenes, a phenomenon undeniably attested by the New Testament, *rips a great hole in history*, a hole the size and shape of Resurrection, what does the secular historian propose to stop it up with?[184]

Schillebeeckx thinks that "resurrection," as an explanatory category, may not have been equally available to all the earliest Christian groups.[185] What is factually undeniable is that *something clearly happened* to change the despair of the disciples into a vibrant assurance that the Jesus whom they had known so intimately had assumed a new form of life which made it possible to resume their earlier sense of fellowship with him—which experience they came to call, eventually and perhaps quite rapidly, "resurrection from death to life." Such an event, they believed, could only be the action of the same God whom Jesus had so confidently proclaimed and manifested; his faith had not, after all, been misplaced. So it was that their earlier decision to "follow" Jesus—to leave everything, that is, and to believe his message about God's in-breaking "Rule"—though temporarily badly shaken by events became their faith in Jesus Christ, Jesus Messiah, Jesus the Lord.

I began these reflections by noting the elusiveness of God, God's absence of definition, inscrutability—which is presumably why there are nearly as many representations of God as there are human beings who contemplate the divine.[186] But I said that for Christians, it is Jesus Christ, the "image of the invisible God," who does furnish

183. Ibid., 381.

184. Charles Francis Digby Moule, *The Phenomenon of the New Testament: An Inquiry into the Implications of Certain Features of the New Testament* (London: SCM Press, 1967), 3 (my emphases).

185. Schillebeeckx, *Jesus*, 396.

186. See Robert Banks, *And Man Created God: Is God a Human Invention?* (Oxford: Lion Hudson, 2011), 138–42.

this definition, visibility, distinctiveness; it is in, or through, Christ, Christians say, that we are able to say with some confidence and clarity who God is, and the nature of God's relationship to us as his creatures.[187] I said that as the image of God, both names of Jesus are important predicates: "Jesus" locates the person so named in visible history—this man left an indelible mark on those who knew him and then transmitted these impressions to those who came after them; and "Christ" or "Lord" stands for the several honorific titles by which they sought to express their encounter with the same person, now transformed, they could only believe, by God's power and vindication. So is concreteness, visibility afforded of what would otherwise remain to us, admittedly real, but intangible, vague, diffused. Schillebeeckx writes accordingly:

> The question of God only has meaning for us human beings in so far as, being a human question, it speaks to our humanity; that is, if we come to realize that the whole issue of man is in the end the issue of God himself. . . . The historically accessible human being, Jesus, becomes a new and more profound question for us as soon as, and because, he is the one with something crucial and definite to say about God.[188]

And: "His pro-existence as man is the sacrament among us of the pro-existence or self-giving of God's own being. In Jesus God has willed, in his Son, and 'in fashion as a man,' to be God for us."[189]

There remains the question *of what* Jesus Christ is the disclosure? Otherwise expressed: wherein does "salvation" consist for a now deeply secularized people? Some dimensions of Jesus' earthly life and teaching clearly transcend cultural barriers: for example, his selflessness and his resolute inclusion of "outsiders," or the precepts of the Sermon on the Mount. Other aspects of "the gospel" appear to have gained or lost ground according to cultural climates. I referred earlier to Calvin's enthusiasm for "the wonderful exchange"

187. In so putting it, I am not intending to discount the millennia-long experiences of the Hebrew people; Jesus was a Jew and his faith in God was the faith of Israel.
188. Schillebeeckx, *Jesus*, 404.
189. Ibid., 670.

in which Christ's "work" was couched in terms of human sinful-
ness, God's wrath, and eternal life or death (note 169 above). And
Schillebeeckx has compiled an extensive list of the ways in which
"Christ" has "made sense" across successive generations:

> [E]very period has its own way of representing Jesus. . . . Just
> as in the Letter to the Hebrews Jesus was already the heavenly
> high priest, for the early Fathers God "who became man in order
> to make man divine" and give him everlasting life, in Byzantium
> the "Christus Victor," Pantocrator and Sun-god, "Light of Light";
> so in in the early and high Middle Ages he became the one who
> makes satisfaction, who has ransomed us, and at the same time
> the "Jesus of the *via crucis*" and the Christmas manger. Later on,
> for Luther, he was one who achieved reconciliation with God in
> a free and sovereign act that covers our guilt and invites us to
> rely unconditionally on God's favourable verdict; then came the
> Christ-mystique of the incarnate Word in French spirituality of the
> seventeenth century, the veneration of the "childhood of Jesus" and
> of "Christ, the Sacred Heart"; the Enlightenment saw in him the
> prototype of human morality, the basis of true camaraderie. The
> Romantics felt Jesus to be the model of genuine human personality;
> and our [sic] twentieth century amid its now fully-fledged *raison
> d'état*, proceeded to extol him as Christ the King. Then after this
> triumphalism and the experience of two world wars came Jesus
> "our brother," our fellow-man, whose example anticipates what
> we have to do, the "man for others" and the contemporary "Jesus
> of human liberation" (in some quarters even Jesus the combatant
> and revolutionary), and so forth.[190]

Precarious as it doubtless is to generalize for an entire populace,
it is nevertheless difficult to suppose that many of the above-listed
representations of Jesus—some of the later "humanistic" ones possibly—carry much appeal for late-modern people. Otherwise than
in earlier centuries, there seems little anxiety about life after death,
or at any rate any great perturbation about eternal punishment.
On the other hand, this essay set out from the presupposition that
there is a residual sacramentality in our deepest humanity, and

190. Ibid., 64.

perhaps John Calvin's *divinitatus sensum* should not be too quickly dismissed even in a secular age.[191]

For millions in our time, "salvation" surely means an adequate supply of food and water; it means shelter and security; it means freedom from war and oppression. But for millions of others who are able to take these things for granted, there is a strong case for coupling "salvation" with "meaning." Ours is an age that has heard (relentlessly I am inclined to say) for over a century that we are here, we exist, simply as products of an unimaginably unlikely chemical combination about three and a half billion years ago, whence human life has emerged by random selection, and that the planet we are accustomed to call "home" is in fact a speck of cosmic dust in a galaxy consisting in one hundred thousand million stars similar to our own sun, and that beyond our galaxy there are at least a hundred thousand million more. Ours is a generation that has lived through the age of permissiveness in which one of the most successful advertising slogans has been "just do it." Though most "people in the street" are unacquainted with the arcane divagations of postmodernist theorists, there can be little doubt that "the breaking up the grand Narratives," which once legitimized society—one of the chief distinguishing marks of postmodernity[192]—makes its

191. For *divinitatus sensum*, see Calvin, *Institutes*, 1.3.1. One cannot but be struck that a similar sentiment should appear in the late-modern, thoroughly secularized philosopher, Jürgen Habermas: "In the wake of metaphysics, philosophy surrenders its extraordinary status. Explosive experiences of the extraordinary [*das Außeralltägliche*] have migrated into an art that has become autonomous. . . . Viewed from without, religion, which has largely been deprived of its worldview functions, is still indispensable in ordinary life for normalizing intercourse with the extraordinary" (Jürgen Habermas, "Themes in Postmetaphysical Thinking," in *Postmetaphysical Thinking*, trans. William Mark Hohengarten [Cambridge, MA: MIT Press, 1992], 51, cited by Peter Dews, *The Limits of Disenchantment: Essays in Contemporary European Philosophy* [London and New York: Verso, 1995], 10). See p. 210 of this volume for a similar statement.

192. Jean-François Lyotard, *The Postmodern Condition: A Report on Knowledge*, trans. Geoff Bennington and Brian Massumi, foreword by Frederic Jameson (Minneapolis: University of Minnesota Press, 1984), 15, 37, 51, 60, etc.

impact on such people, if not directly then certainly indirectly.[193] Finally, this is a generation that has confronted the fact that there is not ever going to be "the war to end war," and that the terrorist can be waiting in any city café. The judgment: "Never in any previous civilization have the great metaphysical questions of being and of the meaning of life, seemed so utterly remote and pointless."[194]

In a noteworthy sermon, Stanley Hauerwas addresses just this circumstance.[195] He cites at some length William James's conclusion to *The Varieties of Religious Experience*, where James traverses pretty much the territory I have touched on; Hauerwas calls the passage "this eloquent hymn to our nothingness." But of course Hauerwas will not allow that this dismal view of our human condition is the only possible, let alone an inevitable, one: "To have seen the face of God in Jesus Christ," he claims, "gives us confidence that time is not a tale told by an idiot. . . . We are not abandoned. The heavens do declare the glory of God."[196] Jesus Christ, I said, is God's visibility—or in the biblical phrase, "the image of the invisible God." To claim that the life, the death, and the resurrection of this man has been a manifestation of God among us is not to lapse into some kind of "proof" of God; it is to say that belief that the universe amounts to much more than "bubbles on the foam [of] a stormy sea" (so, James), belief that at its heart are principles of justice and truth, belief that it is devised and upheld by an infinitely loving Creator, such belief is *by no means unreasonable*. As the scientist-theologian John Polkinghorne says in a different context: "It [is] not claimed that theistic answers [are] logically inevitable, but that they [are]

---

193. See Osborne, *Christian Sacraments in a Postmodern World*, and Nathan D. Mitchell, *Meeting Mystery: Liturgy, Worship, Sacraments* (Maryknoll, NY: Orbis Books, 2006), 6–46, for a discussion of the significance of postmodernity for sacramental theology.

194. Frederic Jameson, "The Silence of the Real: Theology at the End of the Century," in *Theology at the End of the Century: A Dialogue on the Postmodern*, ed. Robert P. Scharlemann (Charlottesville, VA, and London: University of Virginia Press, 1990), 14 (cited without reference by Charles E. Winquist).

195. Stanley Hauerwas, "Facing Nothingness—Facing God," in *Without Apology: Sermons for Christ's Church* (New York: Seabury Books, 2013), 48–55. I owe this reference to Grahame Ellis.

196. Ibid., 54.

insightful and intellectually satisfying."[197] To claim Christ as the sacrament of God is to claim that this man's advent in human history offers *permission* to believe, indeed it is the *encouragement* so to believe in a personal universe. For a great many doubtful souls in our time, I am saying, to be persuaded of this would be none other than a form of "salvation." We have yet to see how it is that the sacraments of baptism and the Lord's Supper can or might affect this assurance. For it is these, Christian faith asserts, which join us to, and sustain us in, Christ the primordial sacrament.

The Sacraments of Baptism and the Lord's Supper

The question is: how is this "salvation" *made effective* for women and men? Schillebeeckx writes:

> [W]e, earthly men, cannot encounter [Christ] in the living body because his glorification has made him invisible to us. From this it follows that if Christ did not make his heavenly bodiliness visible in some way in our earthly sphere, his redemption would after all no longer be for us; redemption would no longer turn its face toward us. . . . [But] this is precisely what the sacraments are: the face of redemption turned visibly toward us, so that in them we are truly to encounter the living Christ.[198]

197. John Polkinghorne, *Science and Theology: An Introduction* (London and Minneapolis: SPCK and Fortress Press, 1998), 77.

198. Edward Schillebeeckx, *Christ the Sacrament of the Encounter with God*, trans. Paul Barrett and N. D. Smith, English text revised by Mark Schoof and Laurence Bright (Kansas City, MO: Sheed and Ward, 1963), 43–44. My borrowing of these sentences should in no wise be taken as implying that I subscribe to Schillebeeckx's further thesis that the church (meaning exclusively the Roman Catholic Church) is the extension in history of the incarnation: "In its entirety . . . the Church is the sacramental or mystical Christ" (ibid., 49). This view has never been acceptable to Reformed theology. See, for example, Donald Macpherson Baillie, *The Theology of the Sacraments and Other Papers* (London: Faber and Faber, 1957), 61–67. This view now encounters criticism from within Catholicism itself. See Osborne, *Christian Sacraments in a Postmodern World*, 112–36.

Of utmost importance in this respect must be the recognition that both the sacrament of Christian baptism and the sacrament of Holy Communion are themselves *images*; that is, through material forms they give concreteness, visibility, access to matters which would otherwise remain conceptual, rather abstract ideas, matters of spirit. Both sacraments are multivalent in their imagery: beginning probably with John's baptismal ministry in the wilderness (Mark 1:5 and parallels) but carried over into Christian symbolism (Acts 22:16; 1 Cor 6:11; Titus 3:5; and Heb 10:22) baptism was a form of *washing*; but, in all likelihood through the creative genius of Paul, the image was taken to entirely new depths, to become the enactment of *death* (burial in the baptismal waters) and *emergence* (rising) into the new life Christ offers (Rom 6:4-8; Col 2:12). Of the former passage, Vorgrimler writes: "Paul describes an event in which 'we' are quite concretely united with the crucifixion, burial, and raising up of Jesus . . . a real being-buried-with Jesus."[199] The Eucharist, at least as obviously, is *meal* imagery: that is, standing for the satisfaction of hunger and thirst. Baptism is the visible sign of being incorporated into the new dimension of human existence, which Christ in his death and resurrection has initiated, which really means the death of the baptismal candidate to the self-directed life; and the Lord's Supper of Holy Communion is the receiving of sustenance and communion with Jesus for the maintenance of this new life. I will come back to the fact that both sacraments are images.

---

199. Herbert Vorgrimler, *Sacramental Theology*, trans. Linda M. Maloney (Collegeville, MN: Liturgical Press, 1992), 104.

Chapter Three

The Uncertain Place of Materiality in the Reformed Tradition

To celebrate the five-hundredth anniversary of someone's birth is in fact to celebrate the enduring legacy of that person's life and work. And in this case the legacy is momentous. Whereas the Lutheran reform never really struck root in other than Germanic or Nordic populations, within a few decades Calvin's style of Reformation had crossed most northern European frontiers and had become *the* face of Reformation.[1] Five centuries later it is arguably still the dominant form of Protestantism on all five continents, though of course in recent decades Pentecostalism has seriously challenged this hegemony.

Historical explanations are invariably precarious. But some strong element of Reformed Christianity's phenomenal success must lie in the close conjunction it was able to achieve from its beginnings between itself and the emerging temper of the age, namely, what we would come to call modernity.

---

1. So, David E. Wright, "Calvin's Role in Church History," in *The Cambridge Companion to John Calvin*, ed. Donald K. McKim (Cambridge: Cambridge University Press, 2004), 287: "Calvinism proved itself eminently more exportable than Lutheranism."

And yet, precisely to couch Reformed Christianity in these terms may be to lay one's finger on its present predicament. For, equally arguably, it has been churches of this persuasion that have proven most susceptible to the ravages of secularization. (This might seem to be contradicted by the prosperity of the so-called evangelical churches, most of which would see themselves in one way or another as "Calvinist" but which are grounded more nearly in precritical precepts than the humanism of Reformed Christianity.)

Somewhat encouraged by the conference title and agenda, it is from this contemporary vantage point that I wish to approach Calvin and his legacy. A persistent characteristic of this tradition, I shall argue, has been the doubtful place it has accorded embodiment, physicality, or materiality (all used here more or less synonymously), and, I shall further want to say, this now shows itself as a considerable liability. Calvin and the style of Christianity he forged do have a place for physicality—chiefly in terms of the created order and the dignity of the human person—as manifestations of God's creative goodness and grace. What seems to be a persistent strain, however, is that this material revelation is regarded generically, universally, assuming a form I shall describe as "disseminated sacrality." Otherwise expressed, what Reformed styles of faith have never been comfortable with is a *particular* representation of God's presence, whether in terms of designated spaces, of physical depictions of the sacred (images), or of human representatives of God (priestly persons). Even the canonical sacraments, we shall see, have been hedged about as carriers of God's or Christ's presence.

This rejection of particular sacramentality in favor of an "affirmation of ordinary life" unquestionably dovetailed with the already emerging culture[2] and ensured Reformed Christianity's mainline place in Western societies for the bulk of the ensuing five centuries. In today's climate, I shall want to say, where such a disseminated sa-

---

2. Charles Taylor, in his *Sources of the Self: The Making of the Modern Identity* (Cambridge: Cambridge University Press, 1989), devotes a long section of his account of modern self-understanding to the emergence, in the sixteenth and seventeenth centuries, of "ordinary life" as the basic cultural frame of reference; see ibid., esp. 211–47.

crality must find its way in post-Christian and post-secular societies,[3] a clearer perception of wherein Christian sacramentality consists has become necessary. As Calvin's legatees, we need to revisit his abhorrence of particular physicality as a vehicle of God's presence.

I

Western intellection has long distrusted materiality. From the time of Plato until only very recently it has depended on a dualist split between form and matter, between the noetic and the ontic, between an idea and its utterance, between theory and practice, and so on (the permutations must be almost endless), and the valorization of the former: "Platonism distrusts and condemns the senses. The eyes and ears are not, for the Platonist, windows of the soul, opening upon reality. The soul sees best when these windows are closed and she holds silent converse with herself in the citadel of thought."[4] In our own time postmodernism or post-structuralism has sought to collapse such dichotomies. In the sixteenth century, however, the tendency was still ascending to its apogee in the Cartesian separation of reality between *res cogitans* and *res extensa*—named by one prominent observer as "the chief girder in [the] framework of modernity."[5] That the Reformers and their successors should draw heavily on this cultural and intellectual assumption, then, was virtually inevitable.

Though the Catholic Church against which they ranged themselves had also long been susceptible to these influences,[6] it was still

3. The book *Sacred Australia: Post-Secular Considerations*, ed. Makarand Paranjape (Melbourne: Clouds of Magellan, 2009), on which I will draw later in this essay, makes a good deal of the point of view that much of Australian society has moved on beyond its atheistic modernity to a new resacralizing of reality.

4. Francis M. Cornford, *Before and After Socrates* (Cambridge: Cambridge University Press, 1960 [1st ed., 1932]), 86.

5. Stephen Toulmin, *Cosmopolis: The Hidden Agenda of Modernity* (Chicago: University of Chicago Press, 1990), 108.

6. Taylor, in his recent narrative of Western secularization, devotes his first two hundred pages to what he calls "the work of reform" within medieval Catholicism, by which he means a centuries-long effort to encourage a more contemplative, spiritualistic faith in preference to a dependence on physical

essentially a materialistic church. For these believers, faith consisted in doing things: "[F]asting and abstaining from work at the appropriate times . . . attendance at Mass on Sunday, Penance and Communion at least once a year . . . as well as a rich gamut of devotional acts . . . like 'creeping to the Cross' on Good Friday, blessing candles on Candlemas, [or] taking part in Corpus Christi parades."[7] And this "doing of things" depended on particular locations and artifacts: sacred things, places, and times. At the heart of it all, the Real Presence of Christ was to be discerned in the consecrated wafer and cup. In the church's institution, and through its consecrated priesthood, the medieval believer—so it was held—had access to God's presence on earth.[8]

From the Reformers' point of view it was exactly this dependence on outward forms that most attracted their ire. For them, faith was—by definition, we may say—an inward, personal volition of spirit. It consisted not in ritual actions, in seeing and doing certain things, but in hearing and responding to God's Word. The church was not, essentially, an institution but the invisible communion of those who truly believe. And the person of faith needs no human intermediary, since his or her faith is directly in Christ as the only necessary intermediary between people and God.

The degree to which the Reformers' attack on Catholicism depended on the old spirit/matter dichotomy varied. At one end of a spectrum, humanists like Erasmus and Jacques Lefèvre d'Etaples (usually known as Faber Stapulensis) could certainly, on occasions, appeal to a recognizably Neoplatonic dualism.[9] At this end

---

artifacts and actions; Charles Taylor, *A Secular Age* (Cambridge, MA: Belknap Press of Harvard University Press, 2007), particularly 61–75.

7. Ibid., 63.

8. "The medieval believer before 1500 took it for granted that the human relationship to God and the supernatural world was visually reflected and was mediated through this visible order of things" (William A. Dyrness, *Reformed Theology and Visual Culture: The Protestant Imagination from Calvin to Edwards* [New York: Cambridge University Press, 2004], 26).

9. Carlos M. N. Eire, *War Against the Idols: The Reformation of Worship from Erasmus to Calvin* (Cambridge: Cambridge University Press, 1986), 28–52. Professor Bruce Mansfield, in personal correspondence, advises me that one has to add to Erasmus's dualism ("which is certainly there, especially

of the spectrum one must also place Zwingli, Reformer of Zürich, whose antimaterialism would subsequently influence some parts of Reformed Christianity more deeply even than Calvin's mediating stance. Thus Zwingli draws an absolute line between spirit and matter or between the invisible and visible worlds.[10] For Zwingli, unbelief *is* unbelief *because* it looks to the sentient world while faith is faith insofar as, or because, it believes in God as pure Spirit, is only ever brought into being by God, and thereafter entrusts itself to God's Word alone: "If your faith is not so perfect as to need a ceremonial sign to confirm it, *it is not faith*," he could say; or, "A substance that is incorporeal [i.e., the inner person] cannot be purified by a corporeal element."[11] Luther, on the other hand, is well known to have stood at the opposite end of such a spectrum. For him, the dichotomy at the heart of the Reformation was decidedly *not* the ancient one of spirit/matter but that of faith *versus* works (or, we can equally say, of gospel *versus* law). That is why he could regard the religious images not as idols crying out for destruction but as a matter of indifference—iconoclasm, in fact, he saw as dangerously like a "work." And, of course, of absolute importance for Luther was to be able to speak of Christ's bodily presence in the sacramental elements.

For his part, Calvin cannot be called a dualist.[12] For him, it is not some lower corporeality that constitutes the human predicament;

---

in the earlier works") a practical ethic: it is better to stay at home and attend to one's responsibilities than to go on a pilgrimage looking at relics or sacred sites. "Here," writes Mansfield, "Erasmus links up to Reformation thinking about vocation and family."

10. W. Peter Stephens (*The Theology of Huldrych Zwingli* [Oxford: Clarendon, 1986], 139) speaks of the "profound ambiguity" in Zwingli's anthropology—that it is "both biblical and Neoplatonist"; on p. 153 he describes Zwingli's theology as "both Paulinist and Greek dualist"; and on p. 187 he says: "Zwingli's profound suspicion of outward things in religion is derived in part from Augustine's Neoplatonism with its stress on the inward over against the outward."

11. Ibid., 162 (emphasis added) and 182.

12. So he distances himself from the traditional scheme: "The philosophers . . . imagine that the reason is located in the mind, which like a lamp illuminates all counsels, and like a queen governs the will. . . . On the other hand,

rather, it is the *entire person*—mind, heart, and body—that is consumed in darkness: "Not only did a lower appetite seduce [Adam],
but unspeakable impiety occupied the very citadel of his mind,
and pride penetrated to the depths of his heart."[13] One observer
writes: "Calvin makes it clear that the root of idolatry lies not in the
material world *per se*, but in man himself."[14] And we have already
indicated—to which aspect of Calvin's thought we will return in
greater detail—that the created order is for him "the theatre of God's
glory" and "the mirror of divinity."[15]

And yet, neither is it possible to think that Calvin escaped the
lure of the spirit/matter bifurcation.[16] He may see the whole person
as ensnared in sin. This by no means leads him to suppose that body
and soul are of equal dignity; he thus cites Plato approvingly in this
respect;[17] the body, he says repeatedly, is our "prison house";[18]
our body is "this unstable, defective, corruptible, fleeting, wasting,
rotting tabernacle";[19] it "fetters" us.[20] And it is the soul alone that
bears God's image, definitely *not* the whole person, body and soul.[21]

For Calvin, the key seems to lie in his absolute conviction that
there can be *no admixture of the created order and its Creator*. And

---

they imagine that sense perception is gripped by torpor and dimness of sight;
so that it always creeps along the ground, is entangled in lesser things and
never rises up to true discernment" (John Calvin, *Institutes of the Christian
Religion*, ed. John T. McNeil, trans. Ford Lewis Battles [Philadelphia: Westminster Press, 1960], II.2.2).

13. Ibid., II.1.9.
14. Eire, *War Against the Idols*, 206.
15. See Dennis E. Tamburello, "Calvin and Sacramentality: A Catholic
Perspective," in *John Calvin and Roman Catholicism: Critique and Engagement, Then and Now*, ed. Randall C. Zachman (Grand Rapids, MI: Baker
Academic, 2008), esp. 202–8.
16. Alasdair Heron thus speaks of "a certain lingering dualism which even
Calvin did not entirely overcome"; see his *Table and Tradition: Towards
an Ecumenical Understanding of the Eucharist* (Edinburgh: Handsel Press,
1983), 132.
17. Calvin, *Institutes*, I.15.6.
18. Ibid., II.7.13; III.3.20; III.9.4.
19. Ibid., III.9.5.
20. Ibid., III.2.19.
21. Ibid., I.15.3.

since God is pure Spirit, everything, which pertains to him, must similarly be spiritual in nature: "God's nature is immeasurable and spiritual. . . . Surely, his infinity ought to make us afraid to try to measure him by our own senses [and] his spiritual nature forbids our imagining anything earthly or carnal of him";[22] "nothing belonging to his divinity is to be transferred to another."[23]

From this radical separation flows a series of consequences. For a start, worship must be preserved from any and all material impurity. Calvin thus regularly issues the call for "spiritual worship."[24] He accordingly takes the Second Commandment[25] as the directive for the "spiritual worship of the Invisible God"; God is said here to make clear "with what kind of worship he should be honoured, lest we dare attribute anything carnal to him." The commandment is given to "restrain our licence from daring to subject God, who is incomprehensible, to our sense perceptions, or to try to represent him by any form."[26] Of course this is the premise for Calvin's unrelenting attack on images in Catholic practice. It is sometimes said that Calvin disapproved iconoclasm, holding the destruction of images to be the responsibility of elected councils rather than popular uprisings. His chapter on "Images in Worship" (*Institutes* I.12), however, leaves no doubt that any such restraint had more to do with his sense of civic order than any tolerance of images in worship.

His distrust of materiality, we may also say, determines his fixation on the Word as God's singular medium of self-communication; for language must seem to be the most ephemeral, instantaneous, and transparent form of utterance known to us.[27] Hardy thus speaks

22. Ibid., I.13.1.
23. Ibid., I.12.1.
24. See, notably, Eire, *War Against the Idols*, 200–202.
25. It is perhaps important to note that the separation of the prohibition of images in the Decalogue as a separate, self-contained commandment (the "Second Commandment") was a Reformed innovation; Catholic and Lutheran Bibles included this within the First Commandment (and then reached a total of ten by dividing the tenth commandment).
26. Calvin, *Institutes*, II.8.17.
27. An oversight on the part of the Reformers, both interesting and hugely significant for subsequent Reformed Christianity, was the assumption that language has no material content. The deconstructionist analyses of Derrida particularly

of a "double invisibility of the Word" in Reformed theology: "Language . . . has the advantage of allowing the invisibility of that to which it refers. . . . And its reception is also invisible, the quality being dependent on the power of its referent—in the reading or hearing—to convince the recipient."[28] Calvin is rightly famous for his wonderful theory of "accommodation";[29] that God might thus "accommodate" himself to human language is for Calvin more than thinkable. But that God might—wholly analogously—accommodate himself within a visible image is not simply inconceivable to him; it is an idea utterly blasphemous.

Finally, in this all-too-brief survey, we should make reference to Calvin's elusive eucharistic theology. Nowhere in Reformation studies, one may say, is the spirit/matter interface drawn more sharply than with respect to the Lord's Supper. Though coming to the discussion after its initial lines had been laid down, Calvin sought, as is well known, to strike a mediating line between the Lutheran and Zwinglian factions. The perduring outcome has mostly been dissension from both sides![30] I think one is bound to say that Calvin does achieve some genuinely reassuring sentences with respect to the apprehension of

---

have in recent times disclosed the fallacy: "Now a word is already a unity of sense and sound, of concept and voice, or . . . of the signified and the signifier" (Jacques Derrida, *Of Grammatology*, trans. Gayatri Chakravorty Spivak [Baltimore: Johns Hopkins University Press, 1974], 31). See, even more explicitly, Terry Eagleton, *Criticism and Ideology: A Study in Marxist Literary Theory* (London: NLB, 1976), 54–55: "Language, that most innocent and spontaneous of common currencies, is in reality a terrain scarred, fissured and divided by the cataclysms of political history. . . . Language is first of all a physical, material reality, and as such is part of the forces of material production."

28. Daniel W. Hardy, "Calvin and the Visual Arts: A Theological Introduction," in *Seeing Beyond the Word: Visual Arts and the Calvinist Tradition*, ed. Paul Corby Finney (Grand Rapids, MI: William B. Eerdmans Publishing Company, 1999), 5.

29. "[A]s nurses commonly do with infants, God is wont in a measure to 'lisp' in speaking to us. Thus forms of speaking do not so much express clearly what God is like as accommodate the knowledge of him to our slight capacity. To do this he must descend far beneath his loftiness" (Calvin, *Institutes*, I.13.1, and often).

30. See especially Brian A. Gerrish, *Grace and Gratitude: The Eucharistic Theology of John Calvin* (Eugene, OR: Wipf and Stock Publishers, 2002), 2–14.

Christ in the Eucharist: "We must then really receive in the Supper the body and blood of Jesus Christ, since the Lord there represents to us the communion of both." Or, "[W]e have good reason to be satisfied when we realize that Jesus Christ gives us in the Supper the real substance of his body and blood, so that we may possess him fully."[31] Or yet again: "We all confess, then, with the mouth that, in receiving the sacrament in faith, according to the ordinance of the Lord, we are truly made partakers of the real substance of the body and blood of Jesus Christ."[32] The problem, to the consternation of Lutherans ever since, is that this *eating and drinking* is actually a *spiritual* business, and the "substance" turns out to be—Calvin seems to resort to an oxymoron—"the *substance* of our *spiritual* life."[33] As opposed to Zwingli, he does insist that "the sacraments of the Lord ought not and cannot at all be separated from their ['the visible signs'] reality and substance."[34] But these, the sacramental elements, can never be more than instruments. There can be no question of Christ being present in the bread and wine: "That the body of Christ is enclosed within the sign, or is joined locally to it, is not only a dream but a damnable error."[35] The reason is that, since his ascension, Christ is not at all to be found in bodily form upon the earth; he is at the right hand of his Father. So, Calvin says time without number, "We have always to raise our thoughts on high" so as not to "abase him under the corruptible elements of this world."[36] It is pretty well impossible to escape the idea that what is directing Calvin in this is his unbending refusal to allow an admixture, contamination he might say, between God and matter or, here, between the ascended Christ and any suggestion of "earthly and corruptible elements."[37]

31. Jean [John] Calvin, "Short Treatise on the Holy Supper of our Lord and only Saviour Jesus Christ," in *Calvin: Theological Treatises*, ed. and trans. John Kelman Sutherland Reid, Library of Christian Classics, vol. 22 (Philadelphia: Westminster Press, 1954), 148.
32. Ibid., 166.
33. Ibid., 147.
34. Ibid.
35. Ibid., 158–59.
36. Ibid., 159.
37. So, Calvin's eucharistic Order of Service, "The Form of Church Prayers," in *Prayers of the Eucharist: Early and Reformed*, ed. Ronald Claud Dudley

II

I have remarked in passing now a couple of times that Calvin, and subsequent Reformed theology, does have a place for materiality. Perhaps this is nowhere seen more clearly than in his ambitions for Geneva. His—largely successful—aspiration was to make the *entire city* "a place of enthusiasm, learning, devotion and determination—truly a godly, reformed city."[38] That is, it was not to be a city with *some* holy places—the churches were deliberately closed when services were not in progress "in order that no one outside the hours may enter for superstitious reasons"[39]—but a city in which "*all of life* [would be] an arena of faith and spirituality."[40]

This demonstrates rather well what I earlier called Calvin's "disseminated sacrality": sacredness or holiness that is not identified with *particular* places, things, actions, or persons (an idea repulsive to Calvin, we have seen) but is distributed through the whole of one's life as this is undertaken before God and is then found in the community at large.

Two forms of material existence appeal to Calvin especially as "sacramental" manifestations of God:[41] the order of the natural world and the dignity of the human person. The tortuous debate

Jasper and Geoffrey J. Cuming (New York: Pueblo, 1987), 218: "With this in mind, let us raise our hearts and minds on high, where Jesus Christ is, in the glory of his Father, and from whence we look for him at our redemption. Let us not be bemused by these earthly and corruptible elements which we see with the eye, and touch with the hand, in order to seek him there, as if he were enclosed in the bread or wine. . . . Let us therefore be content to have the bread and wine as signs and evidences, spiritually seeking the reality where the word of God promises that we shall find it."

38. William G. Naphy, "Calvin's Geneva," in *The Cambridge Companion to John Calvin*, ed. Donald K. McKim (Cambridge: Cambridge University Press, 2004), 35.

39. Jean [John] Calvin, "Ordinances for the Supervision of Churches in the Country," in *Calvin: Theological Treatises*, ed. John Kelman Sutherland Reid (Philadelphia: Westminster Press, 1954), 79.

40. Dyrness, *Visual Culture*, 82 (emphasis added).

41. Tamburello, "Calvin and Sacramentality," 201, draws attention to the fact that Calvin can name certain material things in the Bible (notably the Tree of Life and Noah's rainbow) as "sacraments."

as to whether Calvin espoused a natural theology need no longer delay us; there is general agreement that "[in Calvin] there *is* a revelation in creation, even if it is, to use Edward Dowey's famous phrase, a 'sin-negated natural theology' "[42]—that is, a clear revelation of God in creation, albeit one not apprehended by a fallen human race apart from, or prior to, God's gracious regeneration in the gift of faith. Calvin can write, "[God] revealed himself and daily discloses himself in the whole workmanship of the universe. . . . Upon his individual works he has engraved unmistakable marks of his glory."[43] He speaks frequently of creation as "the mirror of revelation" and as "the theatre of God's glory."[44]

But, second, surprising perhaps in view of Calvin's dismal view of unredeemed humanity, the created dignity of human beings is also revelatory. As with the natural order, Calvin is clear that this, its own worth and stature, is wholly obscured from humankind in its fallen state. That in no way diminishes, however, the nobility which is God's image in a person and which is, and always was, there, though becoming apparent only to the eyes of faith. We have already seen that for Calvin this dignity resides preeminently in the soul, and yet he can bring himself even to allow the body some share in this: "[A]lthough the primary seat of the divine image was in the mind and heart, or in the soul and its powers, yet there was no part of man, not even the body itself, in which some sparks did not glow."[45]

It is the affirmation of divine disclosure in nature and in human existence that led me earlier to speak of the close congruity between Reformed theology and the emerging temper of the age. It is unquestionably anachronistic so to describe it, yet, retrospectively, we can see at least an implicit secularization—a secularizing tendency, perhaps—in the new theology. The demolition (I use the word advisedly) of particular or "condensed" holiness in things, times, places, and people, and its consequent distribution in human existence and

42. Ibid., 203, citing Edward A. Dowey, *The Knowledge of God in Calvin's Theology* (New York: Columbia University Press, 1965), 72–73.

43. Calvin, *Institutes*, I.5.1.

44. Copious references are given in Tamburello, "Calvin and Sacramentality," 202–8.

45. Calvin, *Institutes*, I.15.3; again, Tamburello has assembled multiple references in his "Calvin and Sacramentality," 208–13.

the natural order, entailed a leveling of hierarchies which would continue to be the hallmark not just of Protestant sensibilities but of the modern spirit *in toto*.

This flattening of distinctions is seen, not least, in spatial configuration. We have noted this already in relationship to the churches in Geneva—it is the entire habitat which is to be "a godly, reformed city."[46] And this beginning would be replicated in Reformed spatial perception generally. In place of the extended nave of the medieval church or cathedral, thus distinguishing priests and people and greatly distancing the latter from the former, the Huguenots and Puritans built round or rectangular worship edifices, enabling direct sight of other worshipers and audition of a preacher. Spatial significance was thus distributed within the building, and the building itself was not sacramentally distinguished from other space. The French temples and Puritan meetinghouses were available for any sort of communal or civic business.[47]

But time, too, is rendered uniform: the Catholic calendar of saints' days and festivals was abandoned and the distinctively Reformed style of *lectio continua* was introduced—a method of preaching through entire books of the Bible from one end to the other, which of course afforded us, among other things, Calvin's vast series of commentaries.[48]

46. See, further, Andrew Pettegree, "The Spread of Calvin's Thought," in *The Cambridge Companion to John Calvin*, ed. Donald K. McKim (Cambridge: Cambridge University Press, 2004), 217: "No aspect of Calvin's achievement was so influential in sixteenth-century society as this perception of the perfectibility of the Christian commonwealth."

47. See notably Raymond A. Mentzer Jr., "The Reformed Churches of France and the Visual Arts," in *Seeing Beyond the Word: Visual Arts and the Calvinist Tradition*, ed. Paul Corby Finney (Grand Rapids, MI: William B. Eerdmans Publishing Company, 1999), 200–210; in the same volume, George Starr, "Art and Architecture in the Hungarian Reformed Church," esp. 304, 321–27, and James F. White, "From Protestant to Catholic Plain Style," notably 458–59. On Puritan meetinghouses, see also Horton Davies, *The Worship of American Puritans, 1629–1730* (New York: Peter Lang, 1990), 233–54.

48. Dawn DeVries, "Calvin's Preaching," in *The Cambridge Companion to John Calvin*, ed. Donald K. McKim (Cambridge: Cambridge University Press, 2004), 111–12.

Possibly even more significant than the flattening of space and time was the equality between Christian people that Reformed theology stood for and worked for. There is a nice moment in the *Institutes* where Calvin is discussing auricular confession. He notes that St. James had urged his readers to confess their sins "to one another" and to pray "for each other." He accordingly mocks the church's penitential rite: James nowhere speaks of making confession to "a priestling(!)." And then, "Away with trifles of this sort! Let us take the apostle's view which is simple and open: namely that we should lay our infirmities on one another's breasts, to receive among ourselves mutual counsel, mutual compassion and mutual consolation. Then, as we are aware of [each other's] infirmities, let us pray to God for these."[49] Again, this presages things to come culturally. Perhaps it was fortunate that religious reform coincided with civic reform in the Swiss republics; things were not so simple in royalist lands (not that Calvin always had his way with the Genevan councilors!). Over the long term, however, we can see how the kind of Christianity Calvin shaped would eventuate in the kind of conciliar governance we now take for granted. And still in this area, we may not lose sight of the social reforms Calvin put in place in Geneva, in striking contrast to the profligacy of so much of the Catholic hierarchy.

Third, but in the same general direction, we can perhaps point to the dignity of the individual in his or her daily work which became such a distinguishing mark of Reformed Christianity. Of central importance here is the reworking of the notion of "vocation": for example, "God prefers [to monastic renunciation] devoted care in ruling a household, where the devout householder, clear and free of all greed, ambition and other lusts of the flesh, keeps before him the purpose of serving God in a definite calling,"[50] or "[The gospel] must enter our heart and pass into our daily living."[51] Weber would make much of this in his controversial (but I think not at all inaccurate) account of Calvinism and capitalism.[52]

49. Calvin, *Institutes*, III.4.6.
50. Ibid., IV.13.16.
51. Ibid., III.7.4.
52. Max Weber, *The Protestant Ethic and the Spirit of Capitalism*, trans. Talcott Parsons, with an introduction by Anthony Giddens (London and

In such points of reference as these, materiality is unquestionably in view: in terms both of the *world* as "the mirror of God's immense riches" or as "the theatre of God's action," and of one's *neighbor* as "the most excellent example of God's works." This view of materiality will empower Reformed Christianity through vast social and political experiments for centuries to come. But, as I have now said several times, it is also a distinctively modern view of materiality. Taylor opines: "[T]he entire modern development of the affirmation of ordinary life was . . . foreshadowed and initiated, in all its facets, in the spirituality of the Reformers."[53] More recently, he names Calvinism particularly in this regard.[54]

III

The question, it seems to me, is whether the affinities between a disseminated sacrality—emblematic, I have argued, of Reformed Christianity—and the modern or postmodern, and therefore unreservedly secular, spirit of our times have reached a point at which it is no longer easy to say what is distinctively *Christian* about the Reformed style. And because—as must now be apparent—I do think something like this obtains, I shall further argue that it has become urgently necessary to revisit the sixteenth-century "war against the idols"[55] with a view toward reappropriating at least to some degree the "compressed" sacramentality which our forebears viewed with such abhorrence.

There is a minority opinion in this country, and very possibly in other so-called developed nations, that we are now entering a cultural moment that may be described as "post-secular." It is acknowledged that the dominant master-narrative is still the secularist,

---

New York: Routledge, 1992), 79–92. That Weber titles his chapter "Luther's Conception of the Calling" is quite misleading; the chapter is as much about Calvinism and Puritanism as it is about Lutheranism.

53. Taylor, *Sources of the Self*, 218.

54. Taylor, *A Secular Age*, 77–79, 83–84, 105, 230, etc.

55. This is the title Eire gave his book on sixteenth-century iconoclasm; see above, note 9.

modernist one; but several of the contributors to a recent collection of essays subtitled *Post-Secular Considerations*[56] advance the view that in the vacuum created by the collapse of conventional religious observance, "a [new] sacred dimension [has] asserted itself."[57] The writers are emphatic that this repristination of sacrality has no relationship to the structures which preceded it: "My faith has nothing to do with the churches," the novelist Patrick White is quoted as saying.[58] (White, together with several other prominent Australian literary figures, is regarded here as both harbinger and agent of the revolution.)

If the sacred is not to be identified with traditional religion, then wherein does it consist? Several contributors address themselves to this. The editor in his preface speaks of "that which is worthy of worship" (a definition also held traditionally) and of "something secured against violation or interference . . . off-limits or exclusive."[59] Peter Murphy, whom I have just now cited, expands on this: "[T]he sacred is distinct from ordinary or profane life. It is what elevates, expands, and edifies."[60] Geoff Cheong says it comprises "things of ultimate meaning and value."[61] It is of course clear that "God," around which the conventional descriptions were built, nowhere features in these post-secular definitions.

Two characteristics—additionally, that is, to their renunciation of conventional religious categories—consistently appear in these accounts of the rediscovery of the sacred in Australian consciousness: first, the sacred discloses itself in what may be called epiphanic moments (though this term is not much used by the

56. *Sacred Australia: Post-Secular Considerations.* See n. 3 above.

57. Peter Murphy, "Sacred Icon: Jørn Utzon's Sydney Opera House," in Paranjape, *Sacred Australia*, 287, 289.

58. David Tacey, "Spirituality in Australia Today," in Paranjape, *Sacred Australia*, 50.

59. Makarand Paranjape, "Preface," in Paranjape, *Sacred Australia*, x, xi.

60. Murphy, "Sacred Icon," 287.

61. Geoff Cheong, "Sports Loving Australians: A Sacred Obsession," in Paranjape, *Sacred Australia*, 238.

writers in question)—glimpses of the uncanny,[62] the wonderful,[63] the mysterious,[64] or the transcendent[65] in or through incidents, circumstances, or persons where the recipient of the epiphany had least expected such disclosure—and, second and consequently, both the vehicles and the recipients of such insights are thoroughly "ordinary" people or events. The development is described as "the sacralisation of the everyday, the enchantment of the ordinary"[66] and as "the sacred imagined as earthed, embodied, humbled, local, demotic, ordinary and proximate."[67]

One can be genuinely thankful for these stirrings in Australian consciousness, given the spiritual bleakness of mid-twentieth-century positivism. Even so, from a Christian point of view they leave a great deal still to be desired. Particularly, one cannot but be struck by the essential passivity of the experiences here recorded. That is, any sense of "claim" upon the receivers of such insights, such that they are impelled or called to make an answering response—as is always and necessarily the case with a theistic revelation—is practically absent. This is not to say that many of the poets and writers here named are not active protagonists of the point of view they enunciate; some indeed are politically engaged. That said, anything like a "vocative dimension," an answering *response* to the epiphany, as this is understood in Christian worship and/or discipleship is hard to detect.[68] Given the elusive and imprecise nature of the sacrality so cognized, it is difficult to see how it could be otherwise.

---

62. Bill Ashcroft on the *Unheimlichkeit* of the continent itself in his "The Sacred in Australian Culture," in Paranjape, *Sacred Australia*, 23.

63. Paranjape on a rainbow over Uluru. See his "A Passage to Uluru: Rethinking Sacred Australia," in Paranjape, *Sacred Australia*, 11.

64. Dennis Haskell, "The Sardonic and the Sacred: Australian Identity and Australian Poetic Language," in Paranjape, *Sacred Australia*, 126.

65. Ibid., 129.

66. Tacey, "Spirituality in Australia Today," 59.

67. Ashcroft, "The Sacred in Australian Culture," 22.

68. The "vocative dimension" of Christian worship is an idea I appropriated from Ninian Smart and used extensively in my book on meaning in worship: see Graham Hughes, *Worship as Meaning: A Liturgical Theology for Late Modernity* (Cambridge: Cambridge University Press, 2003), 280–85. Smart had written: "[T]he language of worship begins with the vocative. In worship

Perhaps even more disconcerting from a theistic point of view is that not only are the participants of the new sacrality left unconstrained in terms of any reciprocating response to their epiphany, but at least some forms of it espouse a search for "God within": "The new man and woman are looking for God within. . . . They find it impossible to concentrate on the old external God in heaven, but the new interest is in locating a sense of the divine in the interior life."[69] This *need* not end up in an apotheosis of oneself, perhaps; on the other hand, and *at very least*, a clearly defined Other, one who graciously makes himself apparent to me and then solicits my joyful allegiance in response, is scarcely to be seen.

IV

One will not generally draw a comparison between the religious intuitions just now canvassed and a congregation of Reformed worshipers. The connections between this style of Christianity and the tenets of modernity, to which conjunction I have now sometimes drawn attention, suggests nevertheless that there may be some deeply implicit "family resemblances." That presentiment appears borne out in sentences such as these: "The discussions followed on from [Dutch Reformed theologian] Abraham Kuyper, that all of our life is religion, all is worship, whether I'm washing the dishes or writing a poem or cleaning out the rubbish bin or feeding the dog, it's all done in the service of God."[70] Assuredly, God is clearly in view here, unlike the asseverations of the new sacralists. And yet, as with them, sacrality is "distributed"; *everything* is, if not actually epiphanic, potentially so: "cleaning out the rubbish bin" sits on the same level as "worship."

The problem can be stated remarkably simply: when everything is sacred, nothing is any longer sacred.[71] Some essential part of

---

one *addresses* the focus of worship" (Ninian Smart, *The Concept of Worship* [London: Macmillan Press, 1972], 10 [emphasis added]).

69. Tacey, "Spirituality in Australia Today," 57.

70. *Sydney Morning Herald*, "Good Weekend" (December 18–20, 2009), 12.

71. Kevin Hart is cited in *Sacred Australia* as saying: "[Y]ou can claim . . . that . . . all poetry is at heart sacred. This certainly expands the category of

sacrality, as the contributors to *Sacred Australia* themselves make clear, is that it must be "something secured against violation or interference . . . off limits or exclusive," that it be experienced as "distinct from ordinary or profane life. It is what elevates, expands, and edifies."[72] It is this perception that Protestants in the Reformed tradition, schooled as they are over now five centuries, seem to me to be in serious danger of missing. And the clue to this seems to me to lie in the uncertain place, which has been accorded materiality over this long stretch of time. Physicality has had a place, but, generally, as I have said, it has served as the vehicle of a "disseminated" or "distributed" sacrality. Physicality *in its particularity*, on the other hand—as special or particular sacred space, in terms of sacramental objects, as sacrally infused time, as designated persons—has not usually been given high importance. So it is in our own time (the examples are anecdotal but can be multiplied at random) that worshipers generally detect no especial significance in passing from the church foyer to the worship space itself. Churches are even deliberately designed to serve multiple functions, having a concert platform at one end and liturgical furnishings at the other. The table is the communion table on the Sundays it is so needed, but it may serve any convenient function at other times. Anyone in the congregation may declare God's absolution and now, increasingly, preside over Holy Communion. And so on.

In proposing some sort of recuperation of material sacramentality, it is paramount that we do so fully conscious of what it was the Reformers were doing and why. The danger from which they sheered away so violently was the ever-present one of reification: the temptation to exchange the signifying thing for that which it seeks to signify—of worshiping the image rather than the One of whom it is the image (the icon, we may say). Any return to objective sacramentality may therefore not be *at the expense* of Calvin's centrifugal emphases but as their corrective complement. It was not, and is not, *wrong* to see God as active in all of life. It is rather

---

religious poetry, so much so, though, that in effect it abolishes it" (Haskell, "The Sardonic and the Sacred," 127).

72. Above, notes 59 and 60.

that for this to be possible, we need among us *particular* bearers of holiness.[73]

I need here to introduce a distinction which I have mostly observed through the essay but which now needs to be made explicit (I am bound to say it is not a distinction which writers on the subject observe with any consistency). I want clearly to distinguish between "sacrality" and "sacramentality." The former, I want to say, denotes what I have called through the paper "disseminated" holiness; the sacramental, on the other hand, appertains to *particular things, places, times, and persons* who or which are *in some way so designated* (they have some manner of public recognition or "canonicity," I shall want to say), and they are purposely designed or designated *in order to elicit an active response* to the holiness they thus manifest.

I discern three necessary qualities in such sacramentality.

First, and perhaps easiest to grasp: the things we deem to be sacred must be semiotically capable of such signification. That is, their physicality *must be able to bear* the significance we want to attribute to them. In some cases this will occur naturally or spontaneously as with some of the epiphanic moments or places attested by the writers I called above "the new sacralists." In other cases, this physical propensity must be fashioned. I have in mind the way in which churches, galleries, or memorials are able to be designed in such ways so as *in themselves* to evoke the sense of otherness which is a mark of the sacred. This all sounds obvious perhaps, excepting that Reformed Christians have generally been inept, or unaccustomed, to such semiotic investment in the physical apparatus of their worship. A preponderant reason *why* these Christians feel no change as they cross the threshold from foyer to worship space is that the building *elicits* no such awareness. Or the reason that anyone at all can preside over Holy Communion is that those persons who have been authorized to do so appear for all the world just like everyone else. And so on. An enabling of sacramental rehabilitation will require a

---

73. Tamburello, "Calvin and Sacramentality," 198, cites the evangelical theologian Brian McLaren: "[T]hrough learning that a few things can carry the sacred, we become open to the fact that all things . . . can ultimately carry the sacred."

profound revision in Protestant understanding of the ways in which sentient signification can be, or is, a carrier of holiness.

But second, we must understand that sacramental meaning also requires *to be invested* in the designated event, object, or person. That is, I said just now that the event or object must be able actually to bear the significance accorded it, but now we must also say that this significance is, to some strong degree, *given* or *ascribed* to it—i.e., by some act of ritual consecration. Such investment may be compared to human rites of passage: it formalizes in a public way the status of the thing or event or person. But it does more: it *changes* the status and so in some important degree it *brings into being* the sacramental person or object; it makes it or her or him *what* it or she or he *is*. This perhaps is what the endless disputation over the nature of consecrated communion elements was about. Zwinglians wanted to say that bread is bread, consecrated or not; Catholics, on the other hand, knew that something indeed happens in the sacramental action, that it cannot be *just* bread anymore— whether they found the most expeditious way of saying that, of course, remains open to debate. "Trans-signification" is the term now most often drawn upon and speaks to the nature of the change I am reaching for.[74]

Third, I believe there is required for sacramentality some order of canonicity. This specification is directed chiefly toward the largely private epiphanic experiences hailed by the writers on Australian spirituality. I am here not much concerned that we should be able to say whether there are two, or five, or seven sacraments. I am concerned to say that sacramentality consists not simply in the apotheosis of each individual's experience. The requirement is to be able to determine how closely or otherwise such experiences cohere with the received view of God *Christianly*. Possibly paradoxically, it is Calvin who here comes to our assistance. Calvin (following Augustine, in fact) held that it is the fusion of the Word of God with a material object which creates a sacrament: "[I]ndeed, the tree

---

74. So, Edward Schillebeeckx (*The Eucharist*, trans. N. D. Smith [London: Sheed and Ward, 1968], 113) speaks of the way cloth can be fashioned into a flag: "Physically, nothing has changed, but its *being* is essentially changed" (emphasis added).

was previously a tree, the rainbow a rainbow. [But] when they were inscribed by God's Word a new form was put upon them, so that they began to be what previously they were not."[75] If we assume the freedom to interpret "Word" more broadly, as the biblical or *Judeo-Christian understanding of God*, then the formula suggests that it is inasmuch as we can re-cognize (cognize anew) in this or that disclosive event, place, or person the presence of the God who is confessed in the Christian church, that we may speak with some degree of confidence of a sacramental presence.

Robert Gribben, a foremost spokesperson on liturgy in the Uniting Church of Australia, once cited C. S. Lewis as saying that Christianity is "the most materialistic of all religions."[76] The purpose of my essay has been to bring that fact, assuming it is true, into a slightly sharper realization in the awareness of John Calvin's latter-day successors.

75. Calvin, *Institutes*, IV.14.18.
76. *Living Stones—Theological Guidelines for Uniting Church Worship Buildings* (Melbourne: The UCA Synod of Victoria Office of the General Secretary, Property, Insurance Services, 1997), 1.

Chapter Four

The Embodied Word: In Search of a Reformed Sacramentality

I

The cliché runs: "Protestants read the Bible and Catholics do sacraments."[1] Clichés seldom catch the entire truth. So, in this case Catholics will quickly point to the reforms of the Second Vatican Council, including the now celebrated three-year Lectionary once described as "Catholicism's greatest gift to Protestant preaching,"[2] while Protestant protesters might point to the thousands of worshipers, admittedly in centuries past, gathered for an annual communion service in the Scottish Highlands[3] or the great nineteenth-century Methodist camp meetings and Presbyterian "sacramental occasions"

1. Ray R. Noll, *Sacraments: A New Understanding for a New Generation* (Mystic, CT: Twenty-Third Publications, 2003), 1; similarly, F. J. Leenhardt, "This Is My Body," in Oscar Cullmann and F. J. Leenhardt, *Essays on the Lord's Supper* (London: Lutterworth Press, 1958), 32.

2. James White, as cited by William Skudlarek, *The Word in Worship: Preaching in Liturgical Context* (Nashville: Abingdon Press, 1981), 31.

3. George B. Burnet, *The Holy Communion in the Reformed Church of Scotland 1560–1960* (Edinburgh and London: Oliver and Boyd, 1960), 244, 274.

in the United States.[4] Still, the cliché does carry some sort of intuitive conviction. The sacraments as such, and sacramentality as a more general principle, have hardly been accorded the weight of importance given to the Bible and preaching in Protestant churches, particularly those stemming from the Swiss Reformation. Don Wardlaw observes: "The language for worship the Reformers trusted least was the visual/tactile."[5]

It may be assumed that anything said on church and theology in the present straightened circumstances of the churches in the West is impelled by the wish or intention to rectify the situation. And since it is the so-called mainline churches, including the Reformed confession from within which the following remarks arise and to which confession they are addressed, that find themselves in the direst of these straits, I need not disguise my conviction that the attenuated sacramental life characteristic of this confession is a major contributor to its present plight.[6] And neither am I in illusion as to how improbable the proposal will sound to many readers, not least those of Reformed conviction.[7] Notwithstanding, my thesis is that a reevaluation of the sacraments and of sacramentality more gener-

4. Lester Ruth, "Reconsidering the Emergence of the Second Great Awakening and Camp Meetings Among Early Methodists," *Worship* 75, no. 4 (July 2001): 341, 350.

5. Don M. Wardlaw, "Realigning the Three Languages in Worship," *Reformed Liturgy and Music* 21, no. 1 (Winter 1987): 21.

6. "[T]he four movements which are most likely to dictate the shape of a future Christianity [are]: Roman Catholicism, Pentecostalism, evangelicalism and Eastern Orthodoxy. . . . Mainline Protestantism seems very unlikely to survive the next century in the west, at least in its present form" (Alister E. McGrath, *The Future of Christianity* [Oxford: Blackwell Manifestos, 2002], 99, as cited by Robert Gribben, "The Future of Christianity?," *Uniting Church Studies* 18, no. 1 [June 2012]: 3).

7. The essay did not in the first instance envisage a Uniting Church readership. That it now appears in *Uniting Church Studies* perhaps raises the question of Methodist ethos in the UCA. My impression on arriving in Australia in the 1970s—which impression was and is doubtless open to correction—was that in comparison with other Methodist communions, Methodism in this country had imbibed some elements of a Reformed style. However that may or may not have been, much of what follows in the essay does seem to me to appertain to current Uniting Church habits and presuppositions.

ally is a key to the future well-being, survival even, of the churches naming themselves Calvinist or Reformed.[8]

The heart of the matter is whether, where, and how people encounter some sense of a divine dimension in ordinary lives. Sacraments are "signs of the way the divine is manifested in the human, of the sacred in our secular world."[9] Since without such a dimension Christianity becomes either a society of like-minded people with a more-or-less religious bent or an agency directed (admittedly, with religious motivation) to social improvement, sacramentality is actually the *sine qua non* of authentic Christian life.

As crucial as it may be, sacramentality is both elusive and contested. Christians of practically every persuasion—Orthodox,[10] Catholic,[11] or Reformed[12]—share the conviction that there is no

8. On the terms "Calvinism" and "Reformed," and the preferability of the latter, see Philip Benedict, "Calvinism as a Culture: Preliminary Remarks on Calvinism and the Visual Arts," in *Seeing Beyond the Word: Visual Arts and the Calvinist Tradition*, ed. Paul Corby Finney (Grand Rapids, MI: William B. Eerdmans Publishing Company, 1999), 20.

9. Kevin W. Irwin, "A Sacramental World—Sacramentality as the Primary Language for Sacraments," *Worship* 76, no. 3 (May 2002): 198.

10. "The Christian *leitourgia* [liturgy] is not a 'cult' if by this term we mean a sacred action, or rite, performed in order to establish 'contact' between the community and God. . . . A cult by its very essence presupposes a radical distinction between the 'sacred' and 'profane,' and, being a means of reaching or expressing the 'sacred,' it posits all the non-sacred as 'profane' "; so, Alexander Schmemann, "Theology and Liturgical Tradition," in *Worship in Scripture and Tradition*, ed. Massey H. Shepherd (New York: Oxford University Press, 1963) (reprinted in *Liturgy and Tradition: Theological Reflections of Alexander Schmemann*, ed. Thomas Fisch [Crestwood, NY: St Vladimir's Seminary Press, 1990], 16). See similarly, perhaps, Schmemann's *The Eucharist* (Crestwood, NY: St Vladimir's Seminary Press, 1988), 33: "[I]n the Orthodox experience a sacrament is primarily a revelation of the sacramentality of creation itself, for the world was created and given to man for conversion of creaturely life into participation in divine life."

11. "We do not live in 'two different worlds,' the sacred and secular, with liturgy and sacraments offering an escape from the mundane to the eternal. Rather we live in one world, called 'good' in Genesis 1:3" (Irwin, "A Sacramental World," 198).

12. The Reformed sociologist Roger Mehl writes, "The polarity between sacred and profane is [in Christian theology] constantly placed in question.

sharp cutoff point between a sacred and a secular realm. On the other hand, neither will any Christian theology, not even so-called natural theologies, allow that the divine can be deduced directly from the created order or from human experience. No substantial form can contain, or adequately represent, divinity; the Creator remains forever beyond the signifying power of the created order. This ancient conviction has found recent sacramental application through postmodern criticisms of so-called ontotheology or theories of "presence."[13] Sacraments thus occupy this indeterminate space between world affirmation and world supersession, between physicality and spirituality; they consist in material signs claiming a transcendent reference; they point to what cannot finally be comprehended.

Hence is generated in the churches not just sharply divergent estimations of the place and the value of the sacraments *per se*; the notion of sacramentality itself varies widely. At one end of a spectrum, so to speak ("aniconic," more conventionally called "low" church), the world of ordinary sense experience is reckoned to be the locus of divine disclosure—admittedly ambiguously but, for all that, in ways that are immediate, democratic, accessible. Here—in one way confusing, given its valorization of everyday experience, but in another way quite consistent—sacramentality consists essentially in spiritual or noetic values, i.e., in personal apprehensions, insights, intuitions. The logic runs: *because* the sentient signifiers here in question remain within everyday experience, the sacramental encounter *must* be of an inward, personal, subjective kind. At an opposite extreme ("iconic," or so-called high church), sacramentality is held to depend on or derive from "saturated" or "dense" sentient signification—elaborate ritual actions, for example, or enriched aesthetic experiences. In this case too, sacramentality is governed by

_____

Although Christianity has replaced other religions in large parts of the world . . . and has taken over the functions which these religions assumed in society, the sociologist must never neglect the fact that this situation is a sort of permanent temptation for Christianity (to which it often succumbs)" (*The Sociology of Protestantism* [London: SCM Press, 1970], 3).

13. See, for example, Nathan Mitchell's discussion of Jean-Luc Marion in Nathan D. Mitchell, *Meeting Mystery: Liturgy, Worship, Sacraments* (Maryknoll, NY: Orbis Books, 2006), 269–76.

material signification pointing beyond itself. But here the materiality in question is deliberate, explicit, select, and augmented. The transcendental reference is assumed to be gained *through* materiality rather than being found (inferentially, so to speak) *within* it. Tillich rather famously dubbed the alternative approaches "Protestant Principle" and "Catholic Substance," respectively.[14] One way of describing the task before us might then be an attempt to evaluate the two options or, perhaps better, to search for the optimal point on the spectrum for a sacramental life and theology in the church(es).

It is common knowledge that from its earliest moments Reformed Christianity has opted strongly for the spiritualizing, noetic end of this spectrum. It is not entirely easy to account for this marked antimaterialist stance. Of course, there had been a millennium-long preferment of spirit over substance in the West, which tendency had been in ascendency in the centuries immediately preceding the Reformation; Swiss Reformers seem to have been rather more inclined in this direction than their German counterparts; and, as is everywhere acknowledged, Calvin himself was inexorably opposed to every material embodiment of human belief in God and/or of God's self-disclosure to us. Yet Calvin's actual sacramental theology was very much more substantialist and realist than has often been supposed. In what follows we shall attend in detail to Calvin's writings; though it is at least conceivable that subsequent Reformed tendencies owe at least as much to Zwinglian influences as those of this confession's

14. The pair is often attributed to Tillich as though he had been accustomed regularly to set the two terms in juxtaposition (see, for example, Gabriel Daly, "Protestant Principle and Catholic Substance," *Uniting Church Studies* 3, no. 2 [August 1997]: 3–4). Actually, Tillich seldom used the pair in explicit antithesis; to my knowledge, there are just two such occurrences, both in the third volume of his *Systematic Theology* (Paul Tillich, *Systematic Theology*, vol. 3 [London: James Nisbet and Co., 1964], 7, 130). Tillich in fact had a great deal more to say about "Protestant Principle" than about "Catholic Substance," though it is most certainly true that he did see the two confessions as each in need of, and as complementary to, the other (see particularly, "The Permanent Significance of the Catholic Church for Protestantism," in *Paul Tillich: Main Works*, ed. Carl Heinz Ratschow, vol. 6, *Theological Writings*, ed. Gert Hummel [Berlin and New York: Walter de Gruyter, 1992], 235–45—where Tillich's pairing is in fact "prophetic" and "priestly" rather than "principle" and "substance").

most renowned theologian. Whence ever, the genetic strain is unmistakable. It quickly emerged in iconoclastic outbursts. It is seen in the consistent preference in this tradition for oral/aural modes of communication over visual and tactile forms. It remains to this day in the diminished signifying power of the sacraments themselves in churches of this lineage, in a disdain for liturgical forms in favor of colloquial immediacy, in a predilection for "secular" or "multipurpose" worship places, in far-reaching uncertainties about anything inherently "special" in ordained ministries, and in convictions about "ordinariness" as the normal condition of divine disclosure.[15]

II

Tillich may well have been justified in thinking: "No theologian has broader and profounder discussions of the meaning of idolatry than Calvin."[16] And he was no less right, perhaps, in his judgment that "the Reformation starts . . . [in] . . . the divinity of the Divine, the ultimacy of the Ultimate, the unconditional character of the Unconditioned."[17] Thus: "This God is transcendent in such a radical way, for Calvin, that every visible incorporation must be denied; Calvin says that we may not dare to form any carnal conceptions of God."[18]

15. In his magisterial study of the evolution of modern identity, Charles Taylor named "the affirmation of ordinary life" as a distinguishing mark of emergent modern consciousness (Charles Taylor, *Sources of the Self: The Making of the Modern Identity* [Cambridge: Cambridge University Press, 1989], 211–302). Taylor attributed an especial importance to the Protestant Reformers in the promotion of ordinariness as the theater of God's action (ibid., 215–18; and see, similarly, his more recent *A Secular Age* [Cambridge, MA: Belknap Press of Harvard University Press, 2007], 79–84).

16. Paul Tillich, "The Recovery of the Prophetic Tradition in the Reformation," in *Paul Tillich: Main Works*, ed. Carl Heinz Ratschow, vol. 6, *Theological Writings*, ed. Gert Hummel (Berlin and New York: Walter de Gruyter, 1992), 323.

17. Ibid., 326.

18. Ibid., 322.

Though he does not pursue the subject in these terms, Tillich in these sentences touches on a fusion or conflation of notions which I suspect has haunted Reformed Christianity since its origin and which I also suspect has governed the question of sacramentality of the churches in this tradition. I do not doubt that the linkage is thoroughly instinctive—to those who assume it, practically self-evident. Yet it is a linkage, a conjoining of separable ideas, which, for the sake of clarity, do need to be distinguished. For *physicality* is not necessarily the same thing as *idolatry*. Calvin, I am suggesting, has immense difficulty—perhaps understandably—in seeing the difference.

Hence one is struck by how he moves, seemingly instinctively, from the matter of *images* (a question of material forms) to *idolatry* (which is a tendency of the human heart, a matter of human aggrandizement, of self-satisfaction, self-justification):

> But . . . Scripture . . . where it would distinguish the true God from the false it particularly contrasts him with idols. . . . [S]ince this brute stupidity gripped the whole world—to pant after visible figures of God and thus form gods of wood, stone, gold, silver, or other dead and corruptible matter—we must cling to this principle: God's glory is corrupted by an impious falsehood whenever any form is attached to him.[19]

> [Isaiah] teaches that God's majesty is sullied by an unfitting and absurd fiction, when the incorporeal is made to resemble corporeal matter, the invisible a visible likeness, the spirit an inanimate object, the immeasurable a puny bit of wood, stone, or gold.[20]

Or, again:

> The purpose of this [second] commandment . . . is that he does not will that his lawful worship be profaned by superstitious rites. . . . He wholly calls us back and withdraws us from petty

19. Both sentences from John Calvin, *Institutes of the Christian Religion*, ed. John T. McNeill, trans. Ford Lewis Battles (Philadelphia: Westminster Press, 1960), 1.11.1.
    20. Ibid. 1.11.2.

carnal observances, which our stupid minds, crassly conceiving God, are wont to devise. And . . . he makes us conform to his lawful worship, that is, a spiritual worship established by himself. . . . He marks the grossest fault in this transgression, outward idolatry.[21]

Our analysis must move with subtlety and sophistication: we have at the same time to recognize that physicality is not the same thing as idolatry, yet neither are they unrelated. Calvin is of course right: our idolatrous disposition does manifest itself, assume visibility, in physicality. To vest our highest hopes, our most ardent aspirations, our deepest trust in some*thing* is to suppose that the thing is somehow at our disposal, that it reflects our glory, that we can shape it according to our will or dispose of it as we please: in a word, that it reflects to us our self-sufficiency. This is the concupiscence of the human heart and it finds its opportunity in material objects. It is the source of all human misery; it issues in greed, envy, jealousy; it pits the strong against the weak, those who have against those who do not; it tears at the fabric of society whether we speak of petty resentments, of murder, or of international warfare. Materiality provides the stage on which idolatry plays its deadly game. But now we must equally deny that idolatry is *simply* to be equated with materiality. People can be consumed with things other than physical realities: with health, with their career,

21. Ibid., 2.8.17. We speak today, influenced not a little by Calvin, easily of "the second commandment" as prohibiting images. In fact, major exegetical and interpretative questions are thereby glossed (a) as to whether the prohibition of images is indeed a self-standing commandment or is not simply the extension of the first commandment about having no gods other than Yahweh (as Augustine and the medieval church supposed). In this case it refers not to images *per se* but to images of *other gods* (i.e., idols). (b) What precisely is to be understood by the Hebrew words *pesel*, Greek *eikon* or *eidolon*, or Latin *imago*? See the extensive discussion in Margaret Aston, *England's Iconoclasts* (Oxford: Clarendon, 1988), 371–92 and 392–400. Aston points out that Protestant reformers were operating as much out of ideological conviction as exegetical insight in arguing so strenuously for "the second commandment." She also notes that at the heart of the matter was the question of physicality: "A prohibition that had its origin in the threat that images presented to the deity . . . became part of a code secluding Creator from created. God was pure spirit: all images were alien to his being" (ibid., 391–92).

or with a relationship. People become obsessed with their ideas or political opinions. A sense of racial or of gendered superiority is no less territorial than any struggle over possessions. For Calvin's "idolatry" we might better speak of "reification" or "apotheosis": whenever some *human energy assumes preeminent importance* for people, there we have *the malevolent energy* about which Calvin was so sensitive.

Interestingly, Calvin did know that "idolatry" was not just a question of (external) images. Perhaps uniquely, he could see that it arises in human hearts, in human imaginations: idolatry is "each [person] cling[ing] to his own speculations," "the divinity that men fashion for themselves out of their own opinion."[22] "[M]an tries to express in his work the sort of God he has inwardly conceived . . . the mind begets an idol; the hand gives it birth."[23] And, most famous, "Man's nature . . . is a perpetual factory of idols."[24]

One is then prompted to wonder what was happening for Calvin that this link or equation between spiritual debility and corporeal constitution should have seemed so self-evident. On one hand, Calvin was unquestionably a person possessed—not just by his vision of God's absolute supremacy as Tillich has reminded us, but by his certainty that religion is above all a matter of the heart, of inward fidelity, and has little if anything to do with what he calls "this outward mask," "the outward pomp," of formal church life.[25] On the other hand, we know too that these intimations did not come from nowhere: they had been building over centuries, even if now in the early and middle sixteenth century they exploded in unprecedented force. It is impossible, for example, to overlook the millennia-long suspicion in the West of physicality generally (and of images particularly!)—at least as old as Plato and not reaching its apogee until Descartes's bifurcation of reality into *res cogitans* and *res extensa* roughly a century after Calvin. And, though by the late medieval

22. Calvin, *Institutes.*, 1.11.1.
23. Ibid., 1.11.8.
24. Ibid.
25. In the "Prefatory Letter to King Francis I of France" of the *Institutes*, section 6. Terms like these are found throughout the *Institutes*; for example, the "ceremonial pomp . . . the tricks . . . the trifling follies" of Roman Catholic worship (ibid., 4.10.12).

period, the Western church had evolved an all-embracing system in which "God's power [was] somehow concentrated in certain people, times, places or actions,"[26] yet, as Taylor and others have made clear, there had been a consistent spiritualizing tendency, a "work of reform"[27] in which the Fourth Lateran Council of 1215 had played a part,[28] in which Cistercians and Carthusians had been influential,[29] as well as Thomas à Kempis and the *devotio moderna*,[30] to say nothing of the groundbreaking work of Calvin's predecessors in Switzerland: Zwingli, Bucer, and Bullinger.[31]

Precedent, then, there had been. But Calvin's towering zeal for God's unalloyed majesty, and for what he called "the altar of the heart"[32] (and not least, perhaps, his rhetorical skills in bringing these to expression[33]) effected a hitherto unexampled mistrust of physicality as a vehicle of faith.

It is important to notice that Calvin cannot be called a dualist in any classical sense, i.e., dividing reality into opposing material and spiritual spheres.[34] The human predicament, for instance, lies not

26. Taylor, *A Secular Age*, 76.

27. As Taylor calls part 1 of his book (ibid., 25–218); but see particularly 63–89.

28. Ibid., 243.

29. William A. Dyrness, *Reformed Theology and Visual Culture: The Protestant Imagination from Calvin to Edwards* (New York: Cambridge University Press, 2004), 31–33.

30. Carlos M. N. Eire, *War Against the Idols: The Reformation of Worship from Erasmus to Calvin* (Cambridge: Cambridge University Press, 1986), 22, 33. See also James F. White, *The Sacraments in Protestant Practice and Faith* (Nashville: Abingdon Press, 1999), 14–17.

31. See notably Eire, *War Against the Idols*, 74–104.

32. Calvin, *Institutes*, 3.3.16.

33. See Dyrness's reference to John Bossy: "John Calvin did more than anyone to explore the use of printed word as 'art': [He] wrote more eloquently than was decent for a theologian" (Dyrness, *Visual Culture*, 67n48, citing John Bossy, *Christianity in the West 1400–1700* [Oxford: Oxford University Press, 1988], 102).

34. Here a sharp contrast must be drawn with Calvin's predecessor, Zwingli, for whom spirit and matter were irreconcilable opposites and for whom faith thus *is* faith insofar as it looks away from the physical world, while unbelief is what it is because and insofar as it entangles itself in corporeality. See

in the entrapment of a benevolent spirit within a pernicious body; it is the *entire person*—mind, will, body—that is consumed in perfidy and is restored to perfection in Christ.[35] Nor, again in distinction from classical dualism, does the physical universe constitute for Calvin some evil circumstance from which the soul must find release; quite contrarily, it is "the theatre of God's glory" and "the mirror of divinity,"[36] the world of God's good making, which Christians are commissioned to restore to its original design.

Yet neither is it possible to suppose that Calvin was able to extricate himself from the Western prejudice against materiality (nor to imagine how he could have done so).

Though human beings do "have within themselves a workshop graced with God's unnumbered works,"[37] "very remarkable gifts that attest the divine nature within us,"[38] yet Calvin has not the slightest doubt that it is the *soul* which bears the divine image.[39] The *body*, quite contrariwise, is called over and over again "our prison house";[40] it is "this unstable, defective, corruptible, fleeting, wasting, rotting tabernacle."[41] Nor can there be doubt that

---

W. Peter Stephens, *The Theology of Huldrych Zwingli* (Oxford: Clarendon, 1986), 139, 187.

35. On the one side: "Paul . . . teaches that corruption subsists not in one part only, but that none of the soul remains pure or untouched by that mortal disease. . . . Not only [are] the inordinate impulses of the appetites [condemned] . . . but especially . . . the mind is given over to blindness and the heart to depravity" (Calvin, *Institutes*, 2.1.9 or similarly 2.3.2). And on the other: "[W]e see how Christ is the most perfect image of God; if we are conformed to it, we are so restored that with true piety, righteousness, purity and intelligence we bear God's image" (ibid., 1.15.4).

36. Ibid., 1.14.20, 21. See esp. Dennis E. Tamburello, "Calvin and Sacramentality: A Catholic Perspective," in *John Calvin and Roman Catholicism*, ed. Randall C. Zachman (Grand Rapids, MI: Baker Academic, 2008), 202–5.

37. Calvin, *Institutes*, 1.5.4.

38. Ibid., 1.5.6.

39. Ibid., 1.15.3.

40. Ibid., 1.15.2; 2.7.13; 3.2.19; 3.3.20; 3.9.4, to name just some such references.

41. Ibid., 3.9.5. A fundamental qualification to this disparagement of human bodiliness is Calvin's esteem of *Christ's* human body. As numerous commentators point out, it was precisely the seriousness with which he took Christ's

it is this disdain of corporeality that fuels Calvin's fury against any and every visible, tactile vehicle of religious devotion. "God's nature [as] immeasurable and spiritual . . . forbids our imagining anything earthly or carnal of him."[42] Any admission of materiality into worship is thus branded as "superstition"[43]—whether this be the use of candles,[44] representations of the cross,[45] set hours for prayer,[46] pilgrimage to sacred sites,[47] or ritual actions in general.[48] Of course, one understands that we are never done (as Calvin tirelessly reminds us) with what I earlier called "reification"—that is, the *substitution* of the artifact for God. That said, his hostility to all physicality seems to make it inconceivable to Calvin that one might actually pray to God *through* material forms; such worship for him will only, can only, ever be offered *to* the image.

Hardy observes: "[There is] a longstanding Western conviction . . . that there is such an unbridgeable gulf between the spiritual and the material that the material is incapable of representing the

---

physical body which moved him to question the so-called *communicatio idiomatum* (the "communication of properties"—the interchangeability of Christ's human and divine natures). See, e.g., Brian A. Gerrish, *Grace and Gratitude: The Eucharistic Theology of John Calvin*, 2nd ed. (Eugene, OR: Wipf and Stock Publishers, 2002 [1st ed., 1993]), 54; Alasdair Heron, *Table and Tradition: Toward an Ecumenical Understanding of the Eucharist* (Edinburgh: The Handsel Press, 1983), 118, 126–27; and, most recently, Nathan R. Kerr, "*Corpus Verum*: On the Ecclesial Recovery of Real Presence in John Calvin's Doctrine of the Eucharist," in *Radical Orthodoxy and the Reformed Tradition: Creation, Covenant and Participation*, ed. James K. A. Smith and James H. Olthuis (Grand Rapids, MI: Baker Academic, 2005), 229–42, but particularly p. 233. As these commentators make clear, Calvin insisted that a *body* must exist some*where*—it cannot be in two places at once, let alone everywhere as Lutherans and Catholics claimed—and in Christ's case his glorified and ascended body *is in heaven* (whither believers are lifted up in their eucharistic celebration).

42. Calvin, *Institutes*, 1.13.1.
43. Ibid., 1.11.9; 2.8.17; 4.10.24; 4.10.28, 29; etc.
44. Ibid., 4.15.19.
45. Ibid., 1.11.7.
46. Ibid., 3.20.50.
47. Ibid., 1.11.10.
48. Ibid., 4.18.20; 4.19.18; etc.

spiritual—*finitum non capax infiniti*—except where this is made possible by God." "In the Western view [then], the question is *how* the material may represent the spiritual."[49] We have seen that given Calvin's convictions about God's absolute transcendence, and the correlative poverty of material representation, this becomes exactly the question for him: *how* is communication between divine and human existence effected? Calvin's solution takes two forms. The first is rightly hailed as among his most creative insights: God *accommodates himself*—for the sake of self-disclosure—to human frames of reference: "[A]s nurses commonly do with infants, God is wont in a measure to 'lisp' in speaking to us. Thus such forms of speaking do not so much express clearly what God is like as accommodate the knowledge of him to our slight capacity. To do this he must descend far below his loftiness."[50] His second response, however, remains within the antimaterialist trajectory we have already traced: of the five senses, *audition* is singled out as the divinely chosen medium of communication; visibility and tactility, we have seen, are deemed to be the outward and inevitable forms of idolatry; and the olfactory and gustatory senses scarcely offer themselves for consideration. It is as though, contrarily, language is absented of any trace of physicality.[51] It is difficult to overstate

49. Daniel W. Hardy, "Calvinism and the Visual Arts: A Theological Introduction," in *Seeing Beyond the Word: Visual Arts and the Calvinist Tradition*, ed. Paul Corby Finney (Grand Rapids, MI: William B. Eerdmans Publishing Company, 1999), 4 (his emphasis).

50. Calvin, *Institutes*, 1.13.1; see also ibid., 1.8.1; 1.17.13; and 2.16.2.

51. It is, of course, a fallacy that language has no material content (a fallacy to which Reformed theologians have long seemed susceptible). The first person known to me to draw attention to linguistic materiality was the neo-Kantian philosopher Ernst Cassirer: "[T]he sensuous character of expression and the logical factor of signification cannot be separated in the actual reality of language" (*The Philosophy of Symbolic Forms*, vol. 3, *The Phenomenology of Knowledge*, trans. Ralph Manheim [New Haven, CT: Yale University Press, 1957; but published in German in 1929], 111). Since then, of course, the so-called deconstructionists have made much of the fact that "a word is already a unity of sense and sound, of concept and voice, or . . . of the signified and the signifier" (Jacques Derrida, *Of Grammatology*, trans. Gayatri Chakravorty Spivak [Baltimore: Johns Hopkins University Press, 1974], 31; and see Roland Barthes, "The Grain of the Voice," in *Image Music Text*, essays selected and

Calvin's recourse (in company with the other Swiss Reformers) to this assumption.

One must by all means be clear that Calvin's eucharistic theology is very much more realist, substantialist, than is often allowed (we shall elaborate on this later in the essay).[52] Further, Calvin applies his "accommodation" theory to the sacraments (just as he had to God's Word) by way of explaining God's "condescension" in using earthly elements for his purposes.[53] When all this has been duly acknowledged, one is yet bound to recognize that the sacraments, for Calvin, are extensions or predications of God's Word. Their entire point is to function as the bearers of God's Promise: so, "a sacrament is never without a preceding promise but is joined to it as a sort of appendix";[54] it is "an outward sign by which the Lord seals on our consciences the promises of his goodwill toward us in order to sustain the weakness of our faith."[55] Strictly, sacraments should not be necessary. Were we better attuned to God's Word in the first place they would be redundant: "[P]roperly speaking, [a sacrament] is not so much needed to confirm his Sacred Word as to establish us in faith. For God's truth is of itself firm and sure enough, and it cannot receive better confirmation from any other source than from itself. But our faith is slight and feeble unless it

---

trans. by Stephen Heath [London: Fontana Press, 1977], 179–89). But perhaps the most trenchant statement of the case is by the British literary critic, Terry Eagleton: "Language, that most innocent and spontaneous of common currencies, is in reality a terrain scarred, fissured and divided by the cataclysms of political history. . . . Language is first of all a physical, material reality, and as such is part of the forces of material production" (*Criticism and Ideology: A Study in Marxist Literary Theory* [London: NLB, 1976], 54–55). Finally, see the Reformed sacramental theologian, Leenhardt, "This Is My Body," 35.

52. See, notably, the essay by Kerr already referenced, "*Corpus Verum*: On the Ecclesial Recovery of Real Presence in John Calvin's Doctrine of the Eucharist"; and the essay by Laura Smit, "'The Depth Behind Things': Toward a Calvinist Sacramental Theology," in *Radical Orthodoxy and the Reformed Tradition: Creation, Covenant and Participation*, ed. James K. A. Smith and James H. Olthuis (Grand Rapids, MI: Baker Academic, 2005), 205–27.

53. Calvin, *Institutes*, 4.14.3, 4.17.1.

54. Ibid., 4.14.3.

55. Ibid., 4.14.1.

is propped on all sides and sustained by every means, it trembles, wavers, totters, and at last gives way."[56]

Since the operative power of sacraments is the promise they contain, it follows that the signs themselves (their semiosis, we might say) is more or less incidental: sprinkling, pouring, immersion in baptism for instance? Such details "are of no importance."[57] Any additional ceremony is dismissed as "alien hodgepodge."[58] What does remain indispensable for the celebration of a sacrament is preaching![59]

The dominance of language over every other human communicative or sentient faculty is thus prominent in Calvin's sacramental theology but is by no means so confined. In fact, the trend is virtually ubiquitous. Other examples, almost at random, might include: his complaint that decent *doctrine* would have circumvented images in the church;[60] the "power of the keys" should more properly be considered in terms of "the *preaching of the gospel*";[61] of central importance for Calvin's theology/anthropology is his conviction that the *Scriptures* provide "the spectacles" apart from which we

---

56. Ibid., 4.14.3.

57. Ibid., 4.15.19. In other places Calvin does accord more importance to the elements' semiosis. Of baptism, for example, it is said: "These things . . . he performs for our soul within as truly and surely as we see our body outwardly cleansed, submerged, and surrounded with water. For this analogy or similitude is the surest rule of the sacraments: that we should see spiritual things in physical, as if set before our very eyes" (ibid., 4.15.14); and, of the Supper: "[T]he signification would have no fitness if the truth there represented had no living image in the outward sign" (4.17.4). Yet the impression is consistent that the concrete physicality of "these earthly and corruptible elements which we see with the eye and touch with the hand" (from "The Form of Church Prayers 1542," in *Prayers of the Eucharist: Early and Reformed*, ed. Ronald Claud Dudley Jasper and Geoffrey J. Cuming [Collegeville, MN: Liturgical Press, 1992], 218; but see also Calvin, *Institutes*, 4.17.19) is invariably depreciated before their spiritual signification: "[God] condescends to lead us to himself *even by these earthly elements*, and to set before us in the flesh a mirror of spiritual blessings" (Calvin, *Institutes*, 4.14.3; my emphases).

58. Calvin, *Institutes*, 4.15.19.

59. Ibid., 4.14.4.

60. Ibid., 1.11.7 and 13.

61. Ibid., 3.4.14 and 4.6.4.

can never read the world aright;[62] and, "consequently, those for whom prophetic doctrine is tasteless ought to be thought of as lacking tastebuds"![63]

Calvin's theory of accommodation is rightly hailed as among his strokes of genius. But now one of the most urgent questions of this essay presents itself: if God is able, and glad, to accommodate himself to human linguistic forms, is it not reasonable to ask whether he cannot similarly be found, approached through, or comprehended in other sentient forms? On balance, there seems no clear reason why this could, or might, not be so. But for Calvin, and for his Reformed successors, we have seen, their absolute mistrust of materiality as a sign of divine disclosure, and then the instinctive identification of physical representation with idolatry, meant that this path was closed forever. And this circumstance, it seems to me, has governed the notion of sacramentality in churches of this provenance through the five centuries of their existence and is with us to the present day.

III

We have learned in the past several decades that all thought, all comprehension, perception even, is contextually conditioned. What has seemed irrefragable to one generation has become open to query, at least, in another. To inquire whether John Calvin's theological convictions and insights in the mid-sixteenth century entail certain asymmetries or lacunae is not to *criticize* his prodigious achievement. I have said in another place that to celebrate a person's quincentenary is to celebrate the perduring value of that person's life and work. To locate, in the twenty-first century, certain aspects of his work which now appear to us to be imbalanced, in need of augmentation, or perhaps even hazardous is simply to *observe*: to note how things seemed to a great theologian in the sixteenth century and how the same things now seem to us. I have drawn attention to Calvin's preoccupation with audition as seemingly offering the most

---

62. Ibid., 1.6.1.
63. Ibid., 1.8.2.

transparent, immaterial means of meaning-exchange and his correlative disparagement of the human body, of physicality generally,
and of sentient signification other than language. In this section of
the essay I hope to draw out some implications of this perspective
as these appear to us roughly four and a half centuries later. I will
address three issues: Reformed theology's curtailment of bodily
sensation; the problems this raises for God's Otherness (alterity);
and the proximities of a desacralized (disembodied) religion and
secular modernity.

1. The Attenuation of Sentient Signification

"Among the paradigm shifts associated with 'postmodernity,' none
is more basic and pervasive than the changed attitude to human
bodiliness."[64] This "changed attitude" manifests itself not just in
all levels and forms of critical and cultural studies but has become
embedded in everyday assumptions of what it is to be human—
questions of body image and of sensual gratification being among
the more prominent of these.[65] My purpose in the following brief
remarks is contrastingly limited: I wish simply to note the severe
curtailment (as it now seems to us from within the new cultural
paradigm) of human sensibility—both in apprehension and expres-
siveness—imposed by Reformed theology's restriction of the senses
to audition. Another way of describing this is in terms of this tradition's virtual elimination of the body and of bodily sensation from
theological and liturgical consideration. The irony in this, incalculable irony, is that of course the body is never absent: "Bodiliness is

64. Bernard J. Cooke, "Body and Mystical Body: The Church as *Communio*," in *Bodies of Worship: Explorations in Theory and Practice*, ed. Bruce T.
Morrill (Collegeville, MN: Liturgical Press, 1999), 43.

65. For a convenient overview of modern and late-modern attitudes to the
body, see Bryan S. Turner, "The Body in Western Society: Social Theory and
Its Perspectives," in *Religion and the Body*, ed. Sarah Coakley (Cambridge:
Cambridge University Press, 1997), 15–41. See also James F. Keenan, "Current Theology Note: Christian Perspectives on the Human Body," *Theological
Studies* 55, no. 2 (June 1994): 330–31, on the plethora of new ethical questions
surrounding the body.

an inescapable fact of human existence. One can attempt to ignore this multivalent space or consider it."[66]

Over the Christian church's two millennia, estimations of the place and importance of the body have (predictably) varied greatly. Anchored as it was in its conviction of a Word become flesh (John 1:14; 1 John 1:1) and empowered in its expectation of bodily resurrection, Christianity began as a religion committed unambiguously to human physicality. By the twelfth century, however, the Western church had largely replaced this with a spirituality of "heart speaking to heart" (Bernard of Clairvaux).[67] This, we saw earlier, was the world inherited by Calvin and which he, in turn, bequeathed to subsequent Reformed Christianity.[68]

It is, however, no longer our world. In certain respects (not in others!) we are closer again to a biblical worldview than in intervening centuries—the body is once more a unifying ground of personal identity. Our interest here is confined to the body as receptor, interpreter, and expressive modality—all this in terms of what Michael Polanyi dubbed "personal knowledge." In the latter decades of the twentieth century any number of theorists worked to secure this new vantage point: Polanyi whom we have just mentioned, but preeminently Merleau-Ponty in his studies of perception, Gabriel Marcel

---

66. Colleen M. Griffith, "Spirituality and the Body," in *Bodies of Worship: Explorations in Theory and Practice*, ed. Bruce T. Morrill (Collegeville, MN: Liturgical Press, 1999), 79.

67. For the evolution of ideas on the body in the Western church, see especially Andrew Louth, "The Body in Western Catholic Christianity," in *Religion and the Body*, ed. Sarah Coakley (Cambridge: Cambridge University Press, 1997), 116–22; and for the Eastern church, Kallistos Ware, "'My Helper and my Enemy': The Body in Greek Christianity," also in Coakley, *Religion and the Body*, 90–110.

68. It is to be noted that the Reformers were by no means uniform in their antipathy to the body, the generally prevailing attitudes notwithstanding. David Tripp has compared the attitudes of Luther, Zwingli, and Calvin to corporeality, and has found that Calvin's disfavor—with effects running on into seventeenth- and eighteenth-century Reformed and Puritan theology—was markedly more hostile than that of either his fellow reformers. See David Tripp, "The Image of the Body in the Formative Phases of the Protestant Reformation," in Coakley, *Religion and the Body*, 138–47.

and Ricoeur on personal identity, and Michel Foucault particularly on sexuality as a cultural construct.

The unique quality of a human body, according to Merleau-Ponty, is that at one and the same time it both perceives and is perceptible; it is an object in the world but one that is capable of engaging with other physicality around it:

> Visible and mobile, my body is a thing among things; it is caught in the fabric of the world, and its cohesion is that of a thing. But because it moves itself and sees, it holds things in a circle around itself. . . . There is a human body when, between seeing and the seen, between touching and the touched, between one eye and the other, between hand and hand, a blending of some sort takes place.[69]

It is this "reversible" identity-with-and-difference-from the world within which it finds itself that permits what Merleau-Ponty remarkably calls the body's "communication or communion" with the world:

> We are now in a position to approach the analysis of the thing as an *inter-sensory entity*. . . . [I]nsofar as my hand knows hardness and softness, and my gaze knows the moon's light, it is *a certain way of linking up* with the phenomenon and *communicating with it*.
>
> The passing of sensory givens before our eyes or under our hands is, as it were, a language which teaches itself, and in which meaning is secreted by the very structure of the signs, and this is why it can literally be said that *our senses question things* and that *things reply to them*.
>
> The relations between things or aspects of things having always our body as their vehicle, the whole of nature is . . . our interlocutor in a sort of dialogue. . . . To this extent, *every perception* is a *communication or communion*.[70]

---

69. Maurice Merleau-Ponty, *The Primacy of Perception: And Other Essays on Phenomenological Psychology, the Philosophy of Arts, History, and Politics*, ed. with an intro. by James M. Edie (Evanston, IL: Northwestern University Press, 1964), 163.

70. Maurice Merleau-Ponty, *Phenomenology of Perception*, trans. Colin Smith (London: Routledge, 1962), 317, 319, and 320 (my emphases).

"The sensory . . . is, as it were, a language which teaches itself, and in which meaning is secreted by the very structure of the signs." Though coming from the world of exact sciences rather than phenomenology, Polanyi nevertheless reached similar conclusions.[71] Or perhaps we could cite Ricoeur's reflections on the body as constituting our "twofold identification as an objective person and as a reflecting subject."[72] In a word, what all these late-modern theorists are saying is that *our bodies are our interface with the world*; everything we know either about ourselves or about the world beyond us comes to us through sentient signification.

Merleau-Ponty was not (intentionally, anyway) writing sacramental theology. But if "communication and communion" struck him as the most apt way to describe the normal processes of human perception, we can scarcely not hear in such description either the account of (or an impulsion to!) the engagement by worshiping Christians with the particular signs which are set before them in a worship service—the space, the arrangement of objects within the space, the sounds, the light, other worshipers and official ministers, to mention just some of the sensations that offer themselves for "communication and communion." But, to insist once more, *all* these are transmitted through sensory media. Xavier John Seubert thus writes: "Sacramentality is the orchestration of the diverse elements of a time-space embodied world for manifestation. . . . This

71. "[T]here is one single thing in the world we normally know only by relying on our awareness of it for attending to other things. Our own body is this unique thing. . . . The localisation of an object in space [for example] is based on a slight difference between the two images thrown on our retinas, the accommodation of our eyes, and on our control of our eye motion, supplemented by impulses received from the inner ear, which vary according to the head in space. . . . You dwell in [this knowledge] as you dwell in your own body. . . . *All* knowing is personal knowing—participation through indwelling" (Michael Polanyi and Harry Prosch, *Meaning* [Chicago: University of Chicago Press, 1975], 36–37, 44 [his emphasis]).

72. "[T]he body is at once a fact belonging to the world [people identify me as so-and-so] *and* the organ of a subject that does not belong to the objects of which it speaks [I sense my own identity as not being just another object in the world]" (Paul Ricoeur, *Oneself as Another*, trans. Kathleen Blamey [Chicago: University of Chicago Press, 1992], 54 [my emphasis and inclusions]).

is a very basic sacramental principle . . . : without the body, the actual presence of the spiritual and deeply emotional cannot function among us."[73]

The present professor of liturgy and music at Yale Divinity School (the J. Edgar and Ruth Cox Lantz Professor of Christian Communication, to give him his full title), Thomas Troeger, offers this childhood recollection: "I remember as a boy, sitting in my mother's lap during long Presbyterian sermons. I had not one idea of what was said. But I was ever impressed with how seriously my mother listened. I was in fact getting something out of the sermon: I was learning the importance of understanding the Bible."[74] Perhaps the anecdote should be allowed, in its simplicity, to speak for itself. Yet one cannot help noticing that here audition, conscious appropriation of a spoken utterance, plays virtually no part of the signification; *everything* is transmitted through *the tactile proximity of the two bodies*, the mother's and the child's, and the sensations that are thus conveyed. The story encapsulates Chauvet's dictum: "To be initiated is not to have learned 'truths to believe' but to have received a tradition, in a way *through the pores of one's skin*."[75] Today, anyway, the child so formed is a Yale professor of divinity.

Yet we heard earlier that "one can attempt [either] to ignore this multivalent space [the body] or [to] consider it."[76] An "inescapable fact of human existence" though it may be, much Reformed worship tends still, under the perduring influence of its founding fathers we may surmise, to ignore our bodily constitution. In the next two sections I want to highlight what seem to me two deleterious effects of this oversight in this tradition.

---

73. Xavier John Seubert, "The Trivialization of Matter: Development of Ritual Incapacity," *Worship* 67, no. 1 (January 1993): 41.

74. Thomas H. Troeger, unpublished lecture, "The Landscape of the Heart: The Function of the Conventional Imagination in Worship," given at United Theological College, North Parramatta, Sydney, 15 August 1995.

75. Louis-Marie Chauvet, "The Liturgy in Its Symbolic Space," in *Concilium*, vol. 3: *Liturgy and the Body*, ed. Louis-Marie Chauvet and François Kabasele Lumbala (London: SCM Press, 1995), 31 (my emphases).

76. Griffith, "Spirituality and the Body," 79.

2. The Question of Alterity

Bodiliness enables "communication and communion." Bodies also, however, are substantial. They stand over against us; at certain points and in certain ways they *resist* us; we encounter them or they encounter us. In a word, they stand for, stand before, us as *otherness*, alterity.

Noesis, when not grounded in externality, is unfettered. It is free to imagine, contemplate what it may—and regularly does so: sometimes envisaging the worst conceivable scenario but, also equally, sometimes impossibly optimistic ones. It is physicality, which anchors us, binds us to reality.

Noesis, when not tethered to the external world is also, or at least tends toward being, solipsistic; it is other people's bodiliness that perpetually notifies me that I am not alone. That is to say, it is my neighbor's physicality that demands my accountability, responsibility. No one has probed this in greater depth than the twentieth-century Talmudic scholar and philosopher Levinas in his meditations on the human face: "The presence of a face thus signifies an irrecusable order, a command, which calls a halt to the availability of consciousness. Consciousness is put into question by a face. . . . The I loses its sovereign coincidence with itself, its identification, in which consciousness returned triumphantly to itself and rested on itself."[77]

Not only does the other person—in bodied presence!—deliver me from my perennial preoccupation with myself; he or she symbolizes, in some sense represents, the fact that *God* is other than myself. This was Bonhoeffer's lastingly important insight in his reflections on confession:

> Why is it that it is often easier for us to confess our sins to God than to a brother? God is holy and sinless, he is a just judge of evil and the enemy of all disobedience. But a brother is as sinful as we are. He knows from his own experience the dark night of secret sin. Why should we not find it easier to go to a brother than to the

77. Emmanuel Levinas, "Meaning and Sense," now in *Emmanuel Levinas: Basic Philosophical Writings*, ed. Adriaan T. Peperzak, Simon Critchley, and Robert Bernasconi (Bloomington: Indiana University Press, 1996), 54.

holy God? But if we do, we must ask ourselves whether we have not often been deceiving ourselves with our confession of sin to God, whether we have not rather been confessing our sins to ourselves and also granting ourselves absolution. . . .

Who can give us the certainty that, in the confession and the forgiveness of sins, we are not dealing with ourselves but with the living God? God gives us this certainty through the brother. *Our brother breaks the circle of self-deception.* A man who confesses his sins in the presence of a brother knows that he is no longer alone with himself, he experiences the presence of God in the reality of the other person.[78]

In a similar vein, the contemporary liturgical theologian Nathan D. Mitchell asks "whether [in a postmodern age] we can 'name' God at all—and whether, if we do, we have really encountered *God* or merely heard ourselves talking."[79] In looking to answer this question, another present-day liturgical theologian, Lathrop, turns to what must be nearly the oldest extant text on Christian worship, the First Apology of Justin (middle-second century), where Justin is giving an account of Christian baptism and where he notes in passing, "For no one has a name for the unspeakable God. . . . [A]nyone who dares to say there is such a name raves in incurable madness."[80] Lathrop then goes on to show that it is in the *things* of worship that the unnamable God may be approximated:

Christians learn that there is no name for God. . . . Nonetheless, at the bath [Justin had been discussing baptism, we recall] . . . in a striking, tension-laden paradox, they call upon the God with names. . . . The teaching of the community will be continually exploring this name, the combination of no name with the name of Jesus Christ, and leading to the pairing of this name with the bath.[81]

---

78. Dietrich Bonhoeffer, *Life Together*, trans. and with an intro. by John W. Doberstein (London: SCM Press, 1954), 90–91 (my emphasis).

79. Mitchell, *Meeting Mystery*, 137 (his emphasis).

80. Justin, *I Apology*, 62, cited by Gordon W. Lathrop, *Holy Things: A Liturgical Theology* (Minneapolis: Augsburg Fortress, 1993), 62.

81. Lathrop, *Holy Things*, 68.

And

> The primary theology of the liturgy, the liturgy itself searching "for words appropriate to the nature of God" *begins with things*, with *people* gathered around certain central things, and these things, by their juxtapositions, speaking truly of God and suggesting a meaning for all things. . . . These central things [Lathrop has chiefly in mind what he calls "book, bath and table"] provide the "words" that the assembly uses to speak of God.[82]

Calvin was himself deeply sensitive to the dangers of an unfettered "spiritism."[83] The necessary corrective seemed to him to lie in the "judgment" of Spirit impulses before the testing of Scripture: "Word and Spirit belong inseparably together."[84] It is of course the case that textuality carries an important degree of critical control over subjectivity, over arbitrariness. Our problem is that we have learned to be rather less sanguine than Calvin appears to have been about the clarity, objectivity, certainty of the scriptural texts. Interpretations abound! And these are often scarcely less malleable than are uncluttered appeals to the Spirit's inspiration.

I noticed much earlier that "aniconic" religious traditions (styles of belief with low estimations of "special" or "intensified" places, times, objects, or persons) necessarily depend exactly to that extent on personal intuitions—subjective apprehensions—of sacral presence. Reformed worship, in its disapprobation of Christianity's symbolic representations (Lathrop's "central things") is particularly vulnerable in this respect. The instinct is for "ordinariness," "familiarity." But it is the *objective* world, the world beyond our own cogitations, we said, which confronts us with alterity, an alternative view. The "central things," when allowed their appropriate status and significance, may not be direct manifestations of the divine; they do, however, most assuredly point us in this direction; they allow us, in all our provisionality, to "speak of God," indeed, to speak *to* God, rather than "merely hearing ourselves talking."

---

82. Ibid., 90 (my emphases).
83. Calvin, *Institutes*, 1.9.1.
84. Ibid., 1.9.2,3.

3. Secular Colonization?

The interface between Christian worship and its enveloping culture is a matter for perennial reflection. On the one hand, Christians know that they belong to a tradition that distinguishes itself from the cultural goals and values by which they are surrounded: "in the world but not of the world," "having here no continuing city" are classic expressions of this. And, on the other hand, they are always and inevitably immersed in a particular culture; only in the language into which they have been born, only in the ways in which the world is construed, only in the fundamental structures of thought they receive from the culture of which they are part, can they make any sense of themselves, of God, and indeed of the believing tradition within which they stand.[85] That means there is always a dialectic which must be held up to, or for, conscious reflection; to fail so to do is to collapse into one or the other of the two dialectical elements—i.e., into a ghetto-like traditional*ism* or, more usually, into an unwitting identification with the prevalent culture at the expense of fidelity to the tradition.

This "enculturation of the tradition" certainly comes to expression in intellectual convictions—the *theology*, we may say, of any particular believing community. It is then also manifested in their *values*: their estimation of others, whether of similar or different outlook, and thus in attitudes and behavior. But, by no means least, the fusion of tradition and culture makes itself apparent in the physical artifacts, which Christians construct as expressive of what they believe—in a word, their *symbols*—and in the *rituals* they enact with and around such material objects/structures.[86] These substantial expressive forms do certainly declare the faith or tradition as it has come to be understood by those whose expressive forms they

---

85. Of any number of possible references, see, most recently, Mitchell, *Meeting Mystery*, chap. 1; e.g., p. 3: "Culture is thus not merely the inevitable context within which Christians celebrate the liturgy; it is the indispensable means by which they recognize and respond to God's action among them."

86. Edward Schillebeeckx, *Christ the Sacrament of the Encounter with God*, trans. Paul Barrett and N. D. Smith, English text revised by Mark Schoof and Laurence Bright (Kansas City, MO: Sheed and Ward, 1963), 64.

are; but, by the sheer fact that they are substantial forms, they also perpetuate such understandings of the tradition.

The places of worship—their construction, furnishings, and deployment—offer one instance of such objectification. Chauvet thus writes of liturgical spaces:

> Space is something other than simple extent. It is a place which has been constructed culturally and has psychological connotations. As liturgical space, it is a place which is "informed" . . . by the tradition and collective memory of Christians.
>
> Thus liturgical space constitutes as it were a quasi-sacramental crystallization of the whole of the value system specific to Christianity. The whole ecclesial tradition is presented here.[87]

The liturgical space is "informed by the tradition and collective memory of Christians." If this judgment holds, far-reaching questions are raised for present-day Christians of Reformed persuasion in terms of the dialectic between tradition-fidelity and cultural colonization.[88] For space, in these Christians' estimation, hardly counts: all space is continuous, particular spaces are indistinguishable. In Chauvet's terms, no spaces can be recognized as "quasi-sacramental."

In some instances, this homogeneity of space seems almost deliberate: so-called "worship spaces" (churches) are designed and constructed as "multipurpose" buildings. Arguments are given: it is hopelessly uneconomic to put so much expense and effort into a space used for not more than an hour or so each week; or, if the area is "multifunctional," it can serve groups other than the worshiping congregation. Similar "practical" considerations are advanced, all plausible and difficult to withstand.

Other examples of "flattened" space are not as deliberate as this: they are more nearly the unconscious demeanor of those entering and occupying older, more intentionally constructed worship spaces.

---

87. Chauvet, "The Liturgy in its Symbolic Space," 29, 30.

88. I borrow this term from an important essay by Gary J. Deverell, "Uniting in Worship? Proposals towards a Liturgical Ecumenics," *Uniting Church Studies* 11, no. 1 (March 2005): 21–36; see p. 35 where Deverell suggests that "the colonisation of Christianity by secular modernity is . . . already complete."

But the same values show themselves: sanctuary areas (supposedly so) are convenient "stages" for the drums and other equipment of the song leaders; communion tables are useful for displaying various objects; no incongruity is sensed in using the space as a whole for various nonliturgical purposes—"arts and crafts" presentations, for instance.

But in this case too arguments similar to those offered for the multipurpose buildings will be forthcoming: "practicality," "sensibleness," "economy." But the arguments are themselves revealing: they are arguments drawn not from the worshiping tradition but directly from the prevalent culture. It is difficult to resist the conviction that the requisite dialectic between culture and tradition has here collapsed, extensively anyway, in favor of the values of secular modernity. At the very least, any sense of the spaces used for worship as "quasisacramental" seems largely to have evaporated.

One must admittedly beware the temptation of prescribing a particular style for worship. James White, in an essay titled "How Do We Know It Is Us?,"[89] noted that attempting to evaluate whether people gather in "expectation of encounter[ing] the divine" is "indeed a risky business."[90] Gary Deverell compiles a taxonomy of six "worship-based theologies," ranging from "traditional sacramental churches" through "praise and worship" and "seeker churches," to what he calls "ancient-future" churches.[91] With reference to the utilization of space, it is noteworthy that some at least of these groups are "very accepting of contemporary suburban culture" and/ or "the building [in which they meet] resembles an auditorium."[92] Recalling White, the question must indeed be allowed as to whether

89. James F. White, "How Do We Know It Is Us?," in *Liturgy and the Moral Self: Humanity at Full Stretch before God; Essays in Honor of Don E. Saliers*, ed. E. Byron Anderson and Bruce T. Morrill (Collegeville, MN: Liturgical Press, 1998), 55–65.

90. See Maxwell E. Johnson, "Can We Avoid Relativism in Worship? Liturgical Norms in the Light of Contemporary Liturgical Scholarship," *Worship* 74, no. 2 (March 2000): 135–55, whence I have taken these references to White; see esp. ibid., 140–41.

91. Deverell, "Uniting in Worship?," 31–35.

92. Ibid., 33.

such Christians are "coming together in Christ's name" and in an "expectation of encounter[ing] the divine." Maxwell Johnson, in his considerations on "relativism in worship," does take the questions seriously. But he also concludes that "descriptive analyses of any phenomenon are not necessarily the *primary* task of the *theologian*, who may well be required to make *prescriptive* statements as well for the life of the church here and now as it seeks to appropriate, even selectively, various elements from that tradition in its own practice and interpretation today."[93]

One can hardly not notice White's interrogative title: "How do we know it is us?" The question might better run: "How do we know who we are?" with a decided emphasis on the "how." At the imprecise interface between contemporary culture and received tradition, which is where Christian faith, witness, and worship are forged, the first of the two elements is ever-present and unmistakable. It is in allowing the *symbols* of faith (its "central things") to have their power (while not overlooking the importance of the received body of knowledge), which can secure a place for this—the traditional or "traditioning" dimension of the dialogical assignment. In its extensive devaluation of physicality—as, I have argued, exemplified in its nonchalance about spatiality and objective relationships—Reformed Christianity seems to be peculiarly vulnerable to a colonization by modernity.

IV

We are now perhaps in a position to formulate a Reformed understanding of sacramentality. I need to revert to two observations made earlier: first, that sacraments and sacramentality occupy an indeterminate place between physical and transcendent worlds; and, second, Calvin's apparently instinctive conflation of physicality and idolatry. It is the second of these two earlier points to which we must first attend.

Calvin, I wanted to say, sees the physical representation of holy things—images of God and of Christ, naturally, but including every-

---

93. Johnson, "Can We Avoid Relativism?," 147 (his emphases).

thing else which he brands as "superstitious": the sign of the cross, other ritual gestures, sacred times and places of pilgrimage—as idolatry. And I further wanted to say that while Calvin and his immediate successors doubtless had good reason at the time for the assumption,[94] we are now bound to distinguish idolatry and physicality. Both, we may say, are irreducibly aspects of our human condition; the one, though, is to our ruination, and the other, the very possibility of life. The one is our predilection for the "worship of the gifts in place of the Giver himself";[95] the other is precisely the Giver's gift to us. And yet, we also said, that while being different things, not to be confused, they are also (almost) inextricably entwined. For it is the projection of the love, loyalty, dependence, and devotion that, as creatures, is due only to our Creator into some *thing* (or person, or ambition), which is what idolatry is. As Calvin saw more clearly than almost anyone else (we recall the judgment of Tillich, above), it is the ensconcement of our hearts' desires in such artifacts of our own making which seduces us into the belief that—as their artificers—we can manipulate, adore, and also serve these representations of ourselves. The descriptions, which came to mind earlier in our discussion were "reification" and/or "apotheosis." It is therefore an inviolate principle of Reformed theology that, as Calvin has it, "nothing belonging to [God's] divinity is to be transferred to another."[96] In other words, an absolute distinction between the created order and its Creator is not negotiable.

94. Any number of instances of trickery and exploitation for pecuniary gain by way of relics and images can be documented in the late Middle Ages. See, for example, the chapter on "Selling the Sacred: Reformation and Dissolution at the Abbey of Hailes," in Ethan H. Shagan, *Popular Politics and the English Reformation* (Cambridge: Cambridge University Press, 2003), 162–96, but esp. pp. 165–66; or Margaret Aston, "Iconoclasm in England: Official and Clandestine," in *The Impact of the English Reformation 1500–1640*, ed. Peter Marshall (London: Arnold, 1997), 167–92, but most notably p. 172 (on an image so constructed as to be able to move its eyes and lips—subsequently exposed by the reformist bishop, Bishop Hilsey of Rochester, as a mechanical puppet).

95. Calvin, *Institutes*, 4.17.36.

96. Ibid., 1.12.1.

These twinned considerations—that physicality is not just necessary but is our glorious opportunity and that physicality is nevertheless and at the same time the invitation to idolatry—is the nexus within which a Reformed sacramentality is to be formed. On the one hand, the stricture against the least identification of creatureliness and the Creator means that sacraments must always point beyond themselves; they can never "contain" or "embody" the divine presence; this means that, from a Reformed perspective, all notions of "presence" must be strictly qualified, written in inverted commas so to speak. Over against this, however, our extended reflections on embodied meaning sound an urgent warning to churches of this style: without the objectivity brought by externality, Reformed Christianity is exposed (dangerously, I thought) to interior speculation, an absence of alterity and to cultural assimilation. Sacraments and sacramental *loci* (such as symbolic space or ritual actions) do indeed signify; they do refer us to an Other whom we name, Christianly, as Almighty God (or Christ the Lord). From this point of view, "presence" will not be strictly ruled out—providing, of course, it is always understood in the above-mentioned qualified sense.

The first of these considerations (sacraments can never subsume divine presence) defines a Reformed sacramentality over against some versions at least, or aspects, of its Roman Catholic counterpart. A fairly standard view of the church in contemporary Catholicism, for example, is as "the fundamental sacrament."[97] Of course, everything depends on what is meant by the description. Schillebeeckx is widely acclaimed as a theologian whose reconceptualization of the sacraments as "encounter with God" importantly laid part of the groundwork for the Second Vatican Council, and, later in this essay, we shall ourselves thankfully draw on this fertile idea. Yet Reformed sensibilities do become more than uneasy when Schillebeeckx can apparently describe the church as

97. See, e.g., Karl Rahner, *The Church and the Sacraments*, trans. W. J. O'Hara (New York: Herder and Herder, 1964), 11–19; or Herbert Vorgrimler, *Sacramental Theology*, trans. Linda M. Maloney (Collegeville, MN: Liturgical Press, 1992), 32–40.

"the earthly prolongation of Christ's visible humanity"[98] or can say of the sacraments: "What was visible in Christ has now passed over into the sacraments of the Church."[99] (Is it accidental that the term "primordial sacrament," used of *Christ* in Schillebeeckx's first chapter,[100] subsequently turns out to apply to the *church*?[101]) Though the council's Dogmatic Constitution on the Church also draws on the notion of "the church as sacrament,"[102] it does avoid speaking of this as "the prolongation of the incarnation." Even so, Reformed (or Protestant) readers will know the same disquiet about its confidence in an infallible church: "Although individual bishops do not enjoy the prerogative of infallibility, they do, however, proclaim infallibly the doctrine of Christ . . . [especially when] . . . assembled in an ecumenical council they are, for the universal church, teachers of and judges in matters of faith and morals, whose definitions must be adhered to with the obedience of faith."[103] A Reformed misgiving—actually, critical rejection—of what seems to them the conflation of the church and Christ is what Tillich meant by the "Protestant Principle": "Protestantism [cannot] accept the Roman Catholic . . . sacramental idea of the Church: The identification of an organized Church with the presence of the Divine in history and the consequent claim for absoluteness by this Church."[104] And:

98. Schillebeeckx, *Christ the Sacrament of the Encounter with God*, 41; or, again, p. 59: "[T]he plan of the incarnation requires a prolongation of [Christ's] bodily mediation in time. . . . [T]his sacramental body of the Lord is the Church."

99. Ibid., 41.

100. Ibid., 13–39.

101. Ibid., 52, 54.

102. The Dogmatic Constitution on the Church, paragraphs 1 and 9, in *The Basic Sixteen Documents of Vatican Council II: Constitutions and Declarations*, ed. Austin Flannery (Northport, NY: Costello Publishing Company, 1996), 1, 14.

103. Ibid., par. 25 (p. 35).

104. Tillich, "The Permanent Significance of the Catholic Church for Protestantism," 239. It is doubtless important to note that Tillich goes on immediately to say: "But Protestantism must admit the necessity of a new understanding of the sacramental foundation of the Church as it has been maintained in all Catholic traditions and never was entirely lost in the majority of the Protestant churches, especially those of Lutheran type."

The concept of "infallibility" of a decision by a council or bishop or a book excludes doubt as an element of faith in those who subject themselves to these authorities. . . . [C]reedal expressions of the ultimate concern of the community must include their own criticism. . . . [T]hey are not ultimate. Rather, their function is to point to the ultimate which is beyond all of them. This is what I call "the Protestant Principle", the critical element in the expression of the community of faith and consequently the element of doubt in the act of faith.[105]

Should we briefly touch on perhaps the most tortured point of disputation between Reformed Christianity and Roman Catholicism: the issue of Christ's "presence" in the eucharistic elements? Notwithstanding the considerable convergences achieved, Catholics (and, for that matter, Lutherans too) will still be dismayed at the Reformed insistence that "presence" here must be inscribed within inverted commas. For Catholics, there is, can be, no ambiguity: the consecrated elements *are* the body and blood of Christ. To the best of my knowledge, principally among the functions of the ordained priest remains the power to confect the elements: "The ministerial priest, by the sacred power that he has . . . in the Person of Christ . . . brings about the Eucharistic sacrifice and offers it to God in the name of all the people."[106] To return to Schillebeeckx, in his treatment of the Eucharist, undertaken as he says "to make [the dogma of transubstantiation] capable of being freshly experienced by modern man,"[107] Schillebeeckx presents numerous studies, essentially phenomenological, showing that what something *is* derives very much from how it is apprehended: "A Greek temple is something different for its builders, for those who worship in it, and for modern tourists. . . . The *being* itself of things changes when the relationship is altered"; and, "A coloured cloth is purely

105. Paul Tillich, "Dynamics of Faith," in *Paul Tillich: Main Works*, ed. Carl Heinz Ratschow, vol. 5, *Writings on Religion*, ed. Robert P. Scharlemann (Berlin and New York: Walter de Gruyter, 1988), 244–45.

106. The Dogmatic Constitution on the Church, par. 10 (Flannery, *Basic Documents*, 14).

107. Edward Schillebeeckx, *The Eucharist*, trans. N. D. Smith (London: Sheed and Ward, 1977), 90.

decorative, but if a government decides to raise it to the level of a national flag, then the same cloth is really and objectively no longer the same. Physically, nothing has been changed but its being is essentially changed. Indeed, a new meaning of this kind is more real and more profound than a physical or chemical change."[108] And yet, after nearly fifty pages of similar examples, Schillebeeckx cannot allow that "transsignification," as he calls it, is the same thing as "transubstantiation": "I cannot personally be satisfied with a purely phenomenological interpretation without metaphysical density."[109]

Calvin, we heard earlier, held a view of the Eucharist considerably more realistic than is often supposed: "I say, therefore, that in the mystery of the Supper, Christ is truly shown to us through the symbols of bread and wine, his very body and blood."[110] Or, "We all confess . . . that in receiving the sacrament in faith, according to the ordinance of the Lord, we are truly made partakers of the real substance of his body and blood, so that we may possess him fully."[111] His disavowal of a divine/creaturely admixture meant, however, these high and positive evaluations of the sacramental significance of the elements notwithstanding, there can be no question here of a change of substance. His "metonymy" language—"because [the symbol] *not only* symbolizes the thing it has been consecrated to represent . . . but also *truly exhibits it*"[112]—draws him as close as he could have come, we might risk saying, had the language been available to him, to "transsignification"; or, more simply perhaps, to "metaphor": the eucharistic elements both *are* and *are not* what they say they are. *Both* copulative verbs have to be taken with equal seriousness.[113]

All this has been by way of distinguishing a putative Reformed sacramentality over against more recognizably "catholic" tendencies

---

108. Ibid., 113 (his emphasis).

109. Ibid., 150 (emphasis removed).

110. Calvin, *Institutes*, 4.17.11.

111. Jean [John] Calvin, "Short Treatise on the Holy Supper of our Lord and Saviour Jesus Christ," in *Calvin's Theological Treatises*, ed. John Kelman Sutherland Reid (Philadelphia: Westminster Press, 1954), 166.

112. Calvin, *Institutes*, 4.17.21 (emphases added).

113. Nathan Mitchell, writing from an essentially Catholic point of view, devotes an entire chapter to the metaphoric quality of liturgical language. See Mitchell, *Meeting Mystery*, 189–227.

(by which I mean not just Roman Catholicism but aspects of Lutheranism and some branches of Anglicanism). This has been the outworking of the fundamental mistrust in this confession of what I earlier called "reification" or "apotheosis": the substitution of the sign itself for that which is signified. As such, the tendency represents the faithful maintenance of one of Calvin's most passionate convictions.

But now we must turn in another—opposite in fact—direction: namely, in attending to all that we heard above about the indispensable place of the body in our knowledge of ourselves, of others, and of the world around us. We observed, also earlier, the instinctive recoil from physicality in Reformed theology, showing itself, I suggested, in Calvin's direct identification of materiality with idolatry. And I said that this conflation seems to me to have had permanent and deleterious consequences over the now several centuries of Reformed Christianity, arguably even more damagingly in the face of modern, postmodern, secularism. A Reformed sacramentality will then wish to correct that trajectory.

We might begin this assay where we had just left off: in the celebration of the Holy Supper. I was at pains to underline Calvin's high estimation of the eucharistic elements as signifying Christ's body and blood though being unable to allow their substantial change. Now, however, one must seriously lament the fact that—doubtless driven by the exigencies of disputation—he could speak as disparagingly as he sometimes did of the elements' physicality: "the corruptible elements of this world," he could call them, or "an ephemeral and corruptible element."[114] Perhaps most injurious, given its public and repetitive use, was the incorporation of this language into his Order for Sunday Worship: "Let us raise our hearts and minds on high, where Jesus Christ is. . . . Let us not be bemused by these earthly and corruptible elements which we see with the eye and touch with the hand."[115] The language, one can only say, is regrettable.

It is virtually impossible to ascertain, simply by observing, what is happening for contemporary believers of this tradition in their cele-

---

114. Calvin, *Institutes*, 4.17.19 and 4.17.20.

115. From "The Form of Church Prayers 1542," in *Prayers of the Eucharist*, 218.

bration of the sacrament. What one can speak of more objectively is the extensively evacuated signifying power of the eucharistic elements themselves: a loaf is broken (one can indeed be thankful that, for the most part, cubes of white toast bread, of roughly the taste and consistency of tissue paper, have been discarded); fragments fall to the floor; with perfect unconcern they are later swept up and thrown out; so much, one may say, for the body of our Lord! And grape juice, insipid, saccharine, is distributed in thimble-sized individual glasses (i.e., diminished visually as well as in gustation). So to observe is not to criticize or censure those whose practices these are; as believers they are doing their best with what the tradition has bequeathed them. But if the signifying power of the sacramental elements is as direct as Calvin in his best moments said it is, one could only wish that this voice, at least in its more positive and resounding cadences, could be heard again in the churches, which bear his name. Or, from this perspective, one even wishes for the recuperation of "presence"—albeit in the circumscribed sense already mentioned.[116]

But sacramentality occupies a wider scope than the sacraments as such, even if it remains true that they are at its center. And sacramentality is broader than just public worship, but that is the frame within which I shall set these concluding reflections.

Here, interestingly enough, it is Schillebeeckx who comes to our assistance. The sacraments (or sacramentality, or gathered worship), he says, consist first and foremost in "encounter with God." Here are at least three leading ideas: the notion itself of *encounter*, that it is an encounter with *God*, and that all encounter is mediated *corporeally*.

First, then: encounter. Encounter is normally unexpected, unplanned, not predictable within the usual course of events. Encounter necessarily involves someone (or something) other than myself. It thus represents the disturbance of my self-possession, an interruption to the calm disposal of my intended or ordered life.

We have already heard the great philosopher of alterity, Levinas, on the disruptive effect, should we take it in any degree of seriousness,

---

116. The Reformed ecumenist, Leenhardt, following much the line I have taken above, even speaks of Christ "transform[ing] *the substance* of the bread" (Leenhardt, "This Is My Body," 50 [my emphasis]).

of a face—i.e., the indisputable presence to me of another. Now we must hear him on the event, which is *the encountering* of such presence: "The encounter with this other consists in the fact that despite the extent of my domination [my power in the encounter], I do not possess him. He does not enter entirely into the opening of being where I already stand. . . . It is not starting from being that he comes to meet me. . . . That which escapes comprehension in the other is *him*, a *being*."[117] In other words, to encounter another is to be reminded—since in my normal self-centeredness I will have forgotten it—of my ultimate inability to know this other person ("that which escapes comprehension") as she or he is in himself, and, no less, my inability to control or dominate him or her: he or she is an*other*! The encounter with an other thus interrupts, decenters, me. That means that to encounter someone or something is never continuous with ordinary or mundane experience. To cite another writer on the theme: "In this chronicle of solid benefits [life's normal round] the moments of the *Thou* appear as strange lyric and dramatic episodes, seductive and magical, but tearing us away to dangerous extremes, loosening the well-tried context, leaving more questions than satisfaction behind them, shattering security—in short, uncanny moments we can well dispense with."[118]

It is not conceivable, then, if we are to characterize worship or sacramentality as encounter, that a worship service will remain simply continuous with everyday experience. Encounter entails a break, a confrontation with the unexpected. Encounter means that the event, which is a worship service, will be clearly distinguishable from "the chronicle of solid benefits," which is our familiar world. This is not to countermand what was earlier said about cultural recognizability; nor does it contest the perennial imperative of hospitality.[119] If we are to persist with the notion of encounter, however, the visitor to worship, whether casual and uninitiated or of lifelong

---

117. Emmanuel Levinas, "Is Ontology Fundamental?," in *Emmanuel Levinas: Basic Philosophical Writings*, ed. Adriaan T. Peperzak, Simon Critchley, and Robert Bernasconi (Bloomington: Indiana University Press, 1996), 9 (my emphases).

118. Martin Buber, *I and Thou*, trans. Ronald Gregor Smith (Edinburgh: T&T Clark, 1937), 34 (his emphasis).

119. Lathrop, *Holy Things*, 128.

familiarity, will not be left in doubt that here something *extra*ordinary (the German *unheimlich* comes to mind) is about to eventuate. She or he will, in some degree, be "stopped in their tracks."

Second: encounter with God. Levinas very deliberately left open, ambiguous, whether the alterity of which he spoke was the mystery of another person[120] or the mystery which is God.[121] Schillebeeckx, however, allows no such ambiguity: sacramentality is the encounter with *God* (or Christ, the primordial sacrament of God). This only raises the stakes. We saw much earlier that Christian writers generally wish to avoid an absolute opposition between sacred and secular realms. At the same time there is near universal agreement that to speak of God is to speak of what is finally incomprehensible: "The language of Christian worship is speech that suffers defeat every time it tries to detain or define the divine."[122] Or Hardy says, "We must not suppose that holiness is directly cognizable. . . . [I]t has its own propriety and purity."[123] One is thus reminded of Aidan Kavanagh's widely cited saying: "[L]iturgy leads regularly to the edge of chaos, and . . . from this regular flirt with doom comes a theology different from any other."[124] We all know, of course, the depressing truth of Hardy's dictum: "[T]he occupational hazard [of churches] is to treat [praise] as a routine ritual practice of community formation."[125] But to define worship first as encounter, and then as encounter with God—and then to translate this into

120. "The relationship with the other is not an idyllic and harmonious relationship of communion or a sympathy . . . ; we recognize the other as resembling us, but exterior to us; the relationship with the other is relationship with Mystery" (Levinas, from *Time and the Other*, cited by Colin Davis, *Levinas: An Introduction* [Cambridge: Polity Press, 1996], 31).

121. See, particularly, Emmanuel Levinas, "Transcendence and Height," in Peperzak and others, *Emmanuel Levinas*, 29.

122. Mitchell, *Meeting Mystery*, 137.

123. Daniel W. Hardy, "Worship and the Formation of a Holy People," in *Holiness Past and Present*, ed. Stephen C. Barton (London and New York: T&T Clark, 2003), 481.

124. Aidan Kavanagh, *On Liturgical Theology* (New York: Pueblo, 1984), 73 (with an acknowledged indebtedness to Urban Holmes).

125. Hardy, "Worship and the Formation of a Holy People," 493.

liturgical practice!—would take us a long step in overcoming the inertia of "routinization."[126]

Finally, in line with the emphases I have made throughout this essay, Schillebeeckx avers that the encounter with God or Christ is made possible only by way of embodied experience: "[E]very human exchange . . . proceeds in and through man's bodiliness" and "Mutual human availability is possible only in and through man's bodiliness."[127] It is the sacramental *encounter*, we must insist, that contests the tendencies outlined above toward the flattening of God's alterity ("confessing to ourselves and granting ourselves absolution") and cultural assimilation. And it is the *sacramental* encounter that refutes the long suspicion of accusation against Reformed worship that it indulges simply in "spiritualization."[128] I was concerned, in the body of the essay, to show, drawing on Merleau-Ponty, that it is the senses that anchor us in reality: "Our senses question things and things reply to them," we heard him say. Carrying this over to the charge of "spiritualization," we can say that minimizing empirical experience as it does, Reformed worship is always liable to be the victim of its own introversion. Without concrete signs, it must depend heavily on subjective intuition, the "sense" of something apart from the actual senses. Calvin was always wary of those he called "fanatics"—those depending entirely on Spirit illumination, they who "no less confidently than boldly seize upon whatever they may have conceived while snoring."[129] But in deprecating physicality as he did, it remains a question as to whether he did not deliver his followers to something of a similar peril.

If one asks what form these sacramental instantiations will take, then we have already spoken of the importance of liturgical space: spatial arrangement, that is, and the proxemics of things and actions within such space, which signifies that an encounter with

126. For "routinization," see Max Weber, *Economy and Society: An Outline of Interpretive Sociology*, ed. Guenther Roth and Klaus Wittich, trans. Ephraim Fischoff and others (Berkeley: University of California Press, 1978), 246–54, 489, 492, etc.

127. Schillebeeckx, *Christ the Sacrament*, 15 and 42; see also and similarly his *The Eucharist*, 99–100.

128. Kerr, "Corpus Verum," 229.

129. Calvin, *Institutes*, 1.9.3.

transcendence is here anticipated. Related to space, obviously, are the liturgical symbols: artifacts that tell the gathered congregation both of their local identity and (as we heard) their identification within "the whole value system specific to Christianity."[130] But of singular importance too will be the presence, and manner, of a, or some, sacramental person(s). Again, this is not to deny that it is the congregation, which has gathered to worship God. It is to say that for this to happen, some*one* has to speak the people's words and, even more crucially, speak God's (or Christ's) words to the people.[131] Without this mediating figure, the worship is likely to fall back, as we have now heard often enough, into "merely hear[ing] ourselves talking."[132] Beyond such particulars, however, perhaps even more to be desired is a sacramental culture, an attitude, a form of belief which permeates and informs a church's vision of itself, of its governance, its educational programs, the disbursement of monies, and which finds its form in its public worship—the shared conviction, that is, that sacramentality is "the way the divine is manifested in the human, [the signs of] the sacred in our secular world."[133]

V

The essay has been "in search of a Reformed sacramentality." Conclusions can be fairly concisely stated. Sacramentality, I said at an early point, occupies an indeterminate space between world-affirmation and world-supersession, between physicality and spirituality, between concrete signs and a transcendent reference. We can now flesh out this preliminary statement. A Reformed sacramentality, directed by this confession's strenuous insistence on the disjunction of Creator and creation, can never allow that physical

130. Chauvet, "The Liturgy in Its Symbolic Space," 30.
131. I have said something of this in my reflections on "liturgical direction," in my *Worship as Meaning: A Liturgical Theology for Late Modernity* (Cambridge: Cambridge University Press, 2003), 160–64. See also, perhaps, my "Limping Priests: Ministry and Ordination," *Uniting Church Studies* 8, no. 1 (March 2002): 1–13.
132. Mitchell, *Meeting Mystery*, 137.
133. Irwin, "A Sacramental World," 198.

forms can be carriers of divine presence. Such a conception will always seem perilously close, for this branch of Christianity, to "idolatry," the enclosure of the divine within things of human devising, and thus available for manipulation and coercion. We need hardly reiterate this is the Calvinist's nightmare. And yet we also determined that idolatry and materiality are not the same things: though physical form can offer itself as the opportunity for idolatry (and constantly does, not just in explicitly religious senses), it need not do so. In fact, in itself, it is stuff of life, it is the medium of all human interchange, it is our point of contact with the universe. We saw in fact, in as much detail as the scope of the essay allowed, that to denigrate our physicality and sentient life generally is to run all manner of risk, precisely in terms of fidelity to Christian faith. Though material forms cannot be said to embody divinity, then, they must most certainly be allowed to direct believers to the God who has not only created the world but blesses it, finds it good, and, we confess, has visited it in fleshly form. Sacraments—and sacramentality generally—refer us beyond themselves; they are metaphors, at once consisting in and not consisting in that of which they speak. They are our pointers to transcendence. A church that disregards them is a church in danger of losing itself.

Chapter Five

Faith's Materiality, and Some Implications for Worship and Theology[1]

We do not want you to be unaware . . . of the affliction we experienced in Asia . . . so utterly, unbearably crushed that we despaired of life itself . . . so as to rely not on ourselves but on God who raises the dead. (2 Cor 1:8-9)

[A]lways carrying in the body the death of Jesus, so that the life of Jesus may also be made visible in our bodies . . . in our mortal flesh. (2 Cor 4:10-11)

We do not normally, I think, associate "faith" and "materiality." Seemingly instinctively we take faith to be a noetic or volitional human energy: an act of credence or commitment, by all means embracing certain convictions about the world but scarcely itself partaking of that world's substance. Coherently, or perhaps consequently, theology and worship (to which I turn in later sections of

1. The essay is a lightly revised version of a paper read at the conference of the British Society for the Study of Theology on 26 March 2007. The designated conference theme was: "Celebration and Accountability: Theology in the World." I was asked to address the subject of "liturgy" under this heading.

my essay) seem also to present themselves as essentially discursive matters—any material dimensions we may discover being bracketed off into "applied" disciplines, valuable in their own way but somewhat less demanding of intellectual rigor.

There are doubtless good and ancient reasons for the instinct, and in attempting to identify in faith a more corporeal dimension it will be important not to lose sight of these. On the other hand, I will contend that an attention to this often-disregarded aspect of faith brings some important constructive or corrective perspectives for contemporary worship and theology.

Faith's Materiality

"The nature of faith is given in the object to which faith is directed, the divine grace."[2] Or, faith is "taking God as God with unremitting seriousness."[3] Faith's perceived nonmateriality, then, derives directly from the fact that its reference point is no other than God: invisible, uncreated, unbounded in space and time, comprehensible only by way of negation or in images attesting their own inadequacy. Hence is biblical religion from beginning to end suspicious of physical representation. Any material likeness can never be other than a human artifact (χειροποίητον), at once a usurpation of God's uniqueness and an impermissible sequestration of power on the part of its fashioner.[4] It is from this point of view too that the Bible almost invariably favors acoustic media—preaching, the Word—over visual or tactile ones, for utterance (at any rate, prior to modern recording

2. Günther Bornkamm, *Paul*, trans. D. M. G. Stalker (London: Hodder and Stoughton, 1971), 141.

3. Rudolf Bultmann and Arthur Weiser, "Pisteuo, pistis, etc.," in *The Theological Dictionary of the New Testament*, vol. 6, ed. Gerhard Kittel and Gerhard Friedrich, trans. Geoffrey W. Bromiley (Grand Rapids, MI: William B. Eerdmans Publishing Company, 1968), 188.

4. See James D. G. Dunn, "The Image of God False and True: A Sketch," in *Der Mensch vor Gott: Forschungen zum Menschenbild in Bibel, antikem Judentum und Koran* (Festschrift für Hermann Lichtenberger zum 60. Geburtstag), ed. Ulrike Mittmann-Riehert and others (Neukirchen–Vluyn: Neukirchener Verlag, 2003), 15–23.

techniques) is the most insubstantial communicative medium we can imagine. The inner connections between "word" and "faith" are thus everywhere apparent in the Bible. It is true that Israel's faith was closely bound to the mighty acts of God by which the nation was brought into being and on which it was continually dependent.[5] Yet here too it can be argued that God's covenant relationship with Israel was faith's inner thread.[6] In the New Testament the predilection is even sharper: for here "it is not evident . . . that the crucified Jesus is the risen and ascended Lord. . . . This has to be brought to light in the Word of proclamation."[7] Paul achieves the linkage pretty succinctly: "Faith comes of what is heard" (Rom 10:17). But perhaps the most compact formulation is that of the Fourth Evangelist, for whom the Incarnate Christ is simply "Word of God" (John 1:1).[8]

The Bible, then, is at least one of the roots of our presumption about faith's nonmateriality. The intuition is massively reinforced, however, from a quite different direction; namely, the Hellenic division of reality into spiritual and material realms, each of which is read through its assigned value of worthy and good or base and misleading. Many, if not most, of us were formed within what I suppose is or was quite the most thoroughgoing version of this: the

5. Bultmann and Weiser, "Pisteuo, pistis, etc.," 198.

6. Ibid., 188, 196. See also Gerhard Ebeling, *Word and Faith*, trans. James W. Leitch (London: SCM Press, 1963), 208–10.

7. Bultmann and Weiser, "Pisteuo, pistis, etc.," 215.

8. That a report on the biblical view of faith, even so breathless as this, can reduce Paul's doctrine of "justification by faith" to a footnote is accounted for only in that Paul's achievement represents the most brilliant condensation of the tendencies already listed. The definitive treatment in chapter 4 of Romans makes clear that Abraham's faith (taken by Paul as paradigmatic) was an internal disposition, an attitude of credence and hope neither derived from nor dependent on external determinations. Characteristically (in terms of what we have already seen) Abraham responds to *God's Word*, specifically God's promise (verses 13, 16, 18, 20); he trusts God as one who brings life out of death (verses 17, 24-25); his faith is not grounded in natural or formal principles such as reward for merit (verses 4, 6, 13) or physical endowment (verse 19). The relationship with God is thus wholly a matter of grace (verse 16). As faith's first exponent—as Paul reads it—Abraham thus stands as "the ancestor of all who believe . . . and thus have righteousness reckoned to them" (verse 11; cf. verses 24-25).

Cartesian split between *res cogitans* and *res extensa*, the dualism widely taken to be the founding principle of modernity.[9] Within this paradigm too there could scarcely be doubt about which category should be faith's domicile: faith is definitely not matter.

For now upward of forty years—with some anticipations of it reaching back more than a century—we have been learning in countless ways that "there are no purities":[10] no thought, for example, abstracted from the thinker's time and place; no direct (untheorized) apprehensions of the world; no meaning, no signification apart from its material signifier(s); no text without a reader. We have been shown that consciousness is always embodied, that identity depends for its recognition on difference, that "facts" are in some significant degree constructed—and so on practically endlessly: the postmodern condition!

In a climate such as that in which we now find ourselves, a view of faith as some purely inner disposition, a more or less direct apprehension of, and response to, God's Word, must appear vulnerable to the sorts of "deconstruction" that have been practiced so extensively on similar "totalities." Deconstruction has often been regarded—not, one may say, without justification—as wholly destructive of meaning, a method in which "interpretation consists in an abyssal spiral of ironies, each ironizing the other to infinity."[11] In its more productive applications, however, deconstruction has served to bring to attention the concealed "other" in entities which—during high modernity—had been assumed to be pure or uncontaminated: rationality, to take the primary example, as rising above all local

9. For example, Stephen Toulmin, *Cosmopolis: The Hidden Agenda of Modernity* (Chicago: University of Chicago Press, 1990), 108.

10. See, for example, John McGowan, *Postmodernism and Its Critics* (Ithaca, NY: Cornell University Press, 1991), 1–12.

11. Terry Eagleton, *Ideology: An Introduction* (New York: Verso, 1991), 40.

or prejudicial views; or consciousness as a direct apperception of the self.

It is, then, with some such interrogative approach that we return to the Scriptures, specifically to St. Paul whose opposition of "faith" to "works" and whose formulation of a "righteousness by faith (alone)" are celebrated (surely correctly) as the definitive descriptions of a nonmaterialist faith.

One place in which to begin might be the discussion of antinomianism in Romans 6:1-14. At one level "faith" is not here Paul's subject; at another level, however, the passage is critically engaged with the nature of Christian embodiment and its bearing on the Christian life: the thesis offered is that *a Christian's body is the site of transition* from one life to another, from "the old humanity" (v. 6) to "walking in newness of life" (v. 4), from "dying with Christ" (v. 8) to "living before God in Jesus Christ" (v. 11). For it was the neophyte's body which was submerged in baptism, symbolizing her/ his death to the old humanity, *and* it is that same body, but now as "a new creation," as Paul will put it in another place (2 Cor 5:17), which emerges as belonging to the realm of Christ (vv. 4, 5). The temporal references attending this transition importantly require consideration. On the one hand, baptism is an action now completed in the past: "we were buried with him" (v. 4). On the other hand, it yet awaits its consummation: "we will certainly be united with him in a resurrection like his" (v. 5b). *Baptized bodies thus exist in transitional form*: the decisive moment lies in the past . . . *and* Christians await "adoption, the redemption of [their] bodies" (Rom 8:28). In this interim period it is precisely these "*mortal bodies*" with which sin must be contested (v. 12); it is their "*members*" which Christians are to "present to God as instruments of righteousness" (v. 13; cf. v. 19): "Now the horizon of his own decisions is opened for the believer: he is placed in the battle between God and sin, between the old and the new aeon. And this decision occurs again and again quite concretely in his own decision: in his body."[12]

That the body is the site of transition from baptism to perfection produces two dimensions of faith's materiality. The first is with

---

12. Günther Bornkamm, *Early Christian Experience*, trans. Paul L. Hammer (London: SCM Press, 1969), 82, with particular reference to Romans 6.

reference to Christian *praxis*, the nature or quality of Christian behavior in relation to other physical beings, notably (for Paul) one's fellow Christians; the second is with reference to the material conditions within which faith is lived.

There is, admittedly, a certain logic that would distinguish faith (in God) from good works (directed toward others): faith and love are arguably separable items. That the new life before God is embodied existence makes the one not so easily extricable from the other, however.[13] It is, then, to be noted that the famous injunction that the readers "present [their] bodies as living sacrifice[s]" (Rom 12:1) is precisely the bridge, first, to an exhortation that they honor the various gifts embodied in others in the community—which together comprise the Body of Christ (v. 5)—and, thence, to multiple enjoinments to love (12:9; 13:8-10). The injunction to a mutual respect of each person's strength or weakness of conviction (Rom 14) is anchored precisely in the fact that "we do not live to ourselves . . . we are the Lord's" (vv. 7-8). The close contiguity of faith and love finds further expression in phrases such as "faith being realized in love" (Gal 5:6) or "your work of faith, labor of love and steadfastness of hope" (1 Thess 1:3; cf. 1 Cor 13:13) or "your faith and love" (1 Thess 3:6; cf. 5:8).

But that faith is thus seated within actual (embodied) existence means, second, that the material circumstances which surround—indeed constitute—such existence are not absent from, are not even simply adjacent to, the life of faith; on the contrary, these are exactly the occasions with reference to which the believer believes in God—that God justifies the impotent, that God is a promise-keeping God, that God is able to bring life from death, and so on. It is then perhaps not coincidental that Paul can move easily from the summary sentence about being justified by faith (Rom 5:1) to the graduated scale of privations within which such faith is played

---

13. See notably Eberhard Jüngel, "Gott ist Liebe: Zur Unterscheidung von Glaube und Liebe," in *Festschrift für Ernst Fuchs*, ed. Gerhard Ebeling and others (Tübingen: J. C. B. Mohr [Paul Siebeck], 1973), 193–202. In a sophisticated argument Jüngel draws important distinctions between faith and love; he reaches the conclusion that "faith is not love's competitor. . . . But faith protects the unity of God and humans from a confusion and indistinguishability . . . , which confusion would be the death of love" (p. 200).

out (vv. 3-5). Or, more concretely (in autobiographical terms), we can come at last to the passages from 2 Corinthians, which I cited at the beginning of this section.

The apostle writes graphically of physical and mental torment: this precisely *as an apostle*! And, as now already suggested, he apprehends these hardships as constituting the stage on which he must play out his faith in God. The first passage cited (2 Cor 1:8-9) has both a backward and a forward reference: it refers back to the *berakah* of verse 3, where he praises God not simply as the Father of our Lord Jesus Christ but, pointedly, as "the Father of mercies and the God of consolation." For the facts that he has survived his ordeal, and that in its midst has found consolation in God, are exemplary: they constitute a kind of theater of faith for his converts (cf. 1 Cor 4:9). The forward reference is perhaps more politically conceived: Paul must defend himself against accusations of vacillation (1:17). The rehearsal of his affliction thus works as a witness, a testimony, to his fidelity (1:12), to his coherence with Christ who is never Yes and No but only ever Yes (1:19). (Even the fact that Paul must not infrequently act with political savvy *vis-à-vis* his converts is in its own way a statement of faith's materiality.) The second passage cited makes even more explicit connection between faith and human experience:

> We are afflicted in every way, but not crushed; perplexed, but not driven to despair; persecuted, but not forsaken; struck down, but not destroyed; always carrying in the body the death of Jesus, so that the life of Jesus may also be made visible in our bodies. For while we live, we are always being given up to death for Jesus' sake, so that the life of Jesus may be made visible in our mortal flesh. (2 Cor 4:8-11)

Here, the "disclosive" quality of Paul's humanity is even more sharply etched: in his person is to be seen both the passion and triumph of Christ. But, for our purposes, the connection of the passage with what directly follows is the crucial link: all that he has described has been "in the spirit of faith," since he knows that "the one who raised the Lord Jesus will raise us also with Jesus, and will bring us with you into his presence" (vv. 13-14). Only a little further on in the letter he will describe these actions as "walk[ing] by faith, not by sight" (2 Cor 5:7).

Faith is only ever human faith and is thus only ever embodied. The conditions in which the body finds itself are thus not somehow adjacent to, separable from, faith's exercise; on the contrary, they are exactly its material condition. It is in terms of these, or with direct reference to these, that each baptized person lives out her or his life of faith; they enter into and form a constituent element of each person's faith.

I said, however, that in exploring faith's material dimensions neither should we lose sight of the traditionally more dominant descriptions. For the human person is a marvelously complex organism. We are constituted body and soul, we say. In reality this extrapolates into a near endless, interlocking range of needs, aspirations, pleasures, and privations. It is the entire human being who believes, half-believes, or disbelieves. An expanded view of faith, attending to the more corporeal dimensions of human existence, is consequently bound not to forfeit or jettison the sorts of cognitive, emotive, and volitional attributes normally ascribed. It will rather seek to hold these within a more comprehensive vision embracing our physical as well as our spiritual constitution.

It is perhaps time, then, to notice the familiar distinction between faith as personal commitment, *fides qua creditur*, and faith as formulation requiring assent, *fides quae creditur*. Strictly, of course, these can hardly be finally separable: personal faith must find confessional form. The degree to which a one-sided preference has been accorded each within the confessional division between the Western churches over the past five centuries—and even yet, the vast strides of recent ecumenical convergence notwithstanding—is nevertheless striking.[14] On the one side, for example, Käsemann, doughty Lutheran expositor

---

14. So, Otto Hermann Pesch, "Kernpunkte der Kontroverse: Die antireformatorischen Lehrentscheidungen des Konzils von Trient (1545–1563)—und die Folgen," in *Zur Zukunft der Ökumene: Die "Gemeinsame Erklärung zur Rechtfertigungslehre*," ed. Bernd Jochen Hilberath and Wolfhart Pannenberg (Regensburg: Verlag Friedrich Pustet, 1999), 45: "When the Fathers [of the Council of Trent] hear the word 'faith,' then they think of the objective and assent-demanding

of Paul, avers: "The real point is the constantly new hearing of, and holding fast to, the divine Word. . . . We must be called to it afresh every day."[15] On the other side, the Roman Catholic Bernhard Langemeyer describes faith so: "Christ's ongoing presence in the world is not dependent on the faithfulness of individuals. Where one denies him or another falls away, he remains as present within the faith which he has elicited in others. In other words: the faith through which, and in which, he is always present in the world is the faith of the community, the faith of the church."[16] There is a strong sense in which what we here observe are divergent estimations of faith's materiality. The Protestant view zealously holds faith to be a moment-by-moment encounter with God's ineluctable Word; the other virtually equates the church's consolidated faith with Christ's presence in the world. In their isolation each seems to me to generate a legacy of problems, some of which we shall touch on subsequently. Over against both I hope that a more nuanced understanding of faith's material dimensions can go some distance toward their—the problems'—resolution.

Celebration

"The tastes of the Kingdom are bread and wine"[17]

A sense for the materiality embedded within our most abstract expressive forms has entered postmodern consciousness through

---

revelation of God in the church's teaching. When Luther utters the word 'faith,' he is asking after that on which his troubled conscience may depend."

15. Ernst Käsemann, *Perspectives on Paul*, trans. Margaret Kohl (London: SCM Press, 1971), 84, 101.

16. Bernhard Langemeyer, "Die Weisen der Gegenwart Christi im liturgischen Geschehen," in *Martyria, Leiturgia, Diakonia* (Festschrift für Hermann Volk, Bischof von Mainz, zum 65. Geburtstag), ed. Otto Semmelroth (Mainz: Matthias–Grünewald–Verlag, 1968), 291.

17. The sentence is derived from, not an exact citation of, Geoffrey Wainwright, *Eucharist and Eschatology* (London: Epworth, 1971), 171–72. Wainwright's actual sentences are: "The eucharist is a taste of the kingdom. The word 'taste' has lost some of its evocative power through being used as a practically dead metaphor (something is in 'good taste' or 'bad taste'). But the Lord's Supper, in which bread is eaten and wine is drunk, should keep the word, as far as the church is concerned, firmly rooted in an elementary physiological sensation."

various channels. One quickly thinks of Jacques Derrida's insistence on the inscripted character ("grammatology") of language as against what he saw as modernity's "phonocentrism."[18] Or reference might be made to Julia Kristeva's analysis of the "semiotic" and "symbolic" dimensions of poetic diction: its creative energy compressed into manageable forms.[19] Arguably the most prolific source of the notion, however, has been Marxist theory. It was already foundational to Marx's and Engels's denunciation of the then-regnant Idealism:

> He [Feuerbach] never manages to conceive the sensuous world as the total living sensuous *activity* of the individuals composing it; and therefore when, for example, he sees instead of healthy men a crowd of scrofulous, overworked and consumptive starvelings, he is compelled to take refuge in the "higher perceptions" and in the ideal "compensation in the species," and thus to relapse into idealism at the very point where the communist materialist sees the necessity . . . of a transformation . . . of social structures.[20]

We now understand that the reforming zeal was itself impossibly one-sided, that the human condition consists in material circumstance and ideas.[21] Subsequent Marxist thought has thus moved to

18. Jacques Derrida, *Of Grammatology*, trans. Gayatri Chakravorty Spivak (Baltimore: Johns Hopkins University Press, 1974).

19. See Julia Kristeva, *Revolution in Poetic Language*, with an introduction by Leon S. Roudiez, trans. Margaret Waller (New York: Columbia University Press, 1984), esp. 28, 63. John Lechte, *Julia Kristeva* (London: Routledge, 1990), 129, observes: "What Kristeva intends is that we should see a link between the *significance* and the materiality of language . . . the sound and rhythm of words, and . . . the graphic disposition of the text on the page." Some decades earlier, the philosopher of language Ernst Cassirer had put the point succinctly: "The sensuous character of expression and the logical factor of signification cannot be separated in the actual reality of language" (Ernst Cassirer, *The Philosophy of Symbolic Forms*, vol. 3, *The Phenomenology of Knowledge*, trans. Ralph Manheim [New Haven, CT: Yale University Press, 1957], 111).

20. Karl Marx and Friedrich Engels, *The German Ideology*, ed. with an introduction by C. J. Arthur (London: Lawrence and Wishart, 1970), 64 (their emphasis).

21. Eagleton, *Ideology*, 73–80.

secure the reflexivity of thought and praxis: "I shall therefore say that . . . [an individual's] ideas are his actions inserted into material practices governed by material rituals which are themselves defined by the material ideological apparatus from which derive the ideas of that subject."[22]

That Christian liturgy encompasses both ideas (theology) and concrete things and practices has become something of a commonplace among liturgical theologians:[23] "The Sunday meeting of Christians . . . [is] focussed around certain things: primarily a book, a water pool, bread and wine on a table; and secondarily fire, oil, clothing, a chair, images, musical instruments. These things are not static, but take on meaning in action as they are used."[24] This sensitivity to worship's "thingness," together with a similarly expanding attention to its ritual qualities, is much to be welcomed as reflecting a (relatively recent) awareness of Christian faith's material dimensions, at least in its most visible form, the Sunday assembly of believers.

Yet one may be permitted some reservations. First, the enumeration of worship's "things" by liturgical writers generally remains at an elementary level. In other words, the things are listed *as* objects but, usually, without further inspection of their particular materiality. A book, for example—but seldom in terms of its size and appearance or the nature and quality of its binding; or bread and wine apart from their texture and taste. Second, perhaps even less frequently is recognized the interpenetration of sense and significance—the critical importance, that is, of the things' and actions' sentient values in the construction and conveying of theological meaning.[25]

22. Louis Althusser, *Lenin and Philosophy and Other Essays* (London: NLB, 1971), 158.

23. Perhaps the most extensive statement of this is to be found in Gordon W. Lathrop's trilogy: *Holy Things: A Liturgical Theology* (Minneapolis: Augsburg Fortress, 1993), *Holy People: A Liturgical Ecclesiology* (Minneapolis: Augsburg Fortress, 1999), and *Holy Ground: A Liturgical Cosmology* (Minneapolis: Augsburg Fortress, 2003).

24. Lathrop, *Holy Things*, 10.

25. But, exceptionally, see Mary Collins, "Critical Questions for Liturgical Theology," *Worship* 53, no. 4 (July 1979): 303–4: "The classic statement of

A couple of anecdotes might help to make the point.

The congregation of the Presbyterian Church of New Zealand into which I was ordained and inducted had been accustomed only ever to celebrate the Lord's Supper quarterly—not according to any liturgical calendar but on the first Sunday of each third month. I had been the people's minister for perhaps two years when I began to sense the sad inadequacy of an Easter celebration apart from the Holy Supper—though this had always been understood among us as the reenactment of the Last Supper. The elders rather bemusedly assented to a celebration of Communion on Easter Day; and, in all innocence, I resolved that since this would not be a "regular" communion service, I would break the bread, not, as usually, a slice of sandwich loaf shorn of its crusts and with a density approximating tissue paper, but with a loaf: it would be a *breaking* of *bread*. I had never in my life done this nor seen it done; and, in my naiveté, it did not occur to me to experiment before the service. It remained for me then to discover in the celebration itself just how much effort is required to tear apart a loaf of bread. The people watched—in horror or fascination, or possibly a mixture of both—for the several seconds it required for the loaf to be rent. Afterward, one of the worshipers, a strapping farmer (and player of rugby football) pleaded that I never do it again (he subsequently revised his opinion): he had not hitherto been so confronted with the declaration "broken for you."

We know, of course, that "broken" is a late textual addition to 1 Corinthians 11:24 (though the man whose story I tell had never heard it otherwise) and that the "breaking of the bread" has everything to do with sharing one loaf (1 Cor 10:17) and nothing at all to do with Jesus' crucifixion, where it is specifically said that the body was not broken (John 19:36). And I now better understand the problem of fragments from the loaf falling to the table or floor. All this notwithstanding: the action, indissolubly bound as it was to the material composition of the loaf, imprinted itself on this man's

---

liturgical objectivity . . . seems to leave little room or none at all for affirming and interpreting particularity and subjectivity as essential components of the faith of the Church." She goes on, pp. 306–7, to highlight the signifying power of various styles and textures of eucharistic bread.

Christian awareness—his faith, dare we say—more deeply than a hundred other celebrations of the sacrament.

In a second example, I was the recipient rather than the agent of material signification. In the tradition to which I have just referred, the eucharistic cup (if indeed it can be so called) was offered only ever in the form of individual glasses containing a sip of (unfermented) grape juice. This was distributed in the pews where we sat—admittedly dressed in "houseling cloths" for the Lord's Supper. The impact on me of the first occasion on which I rose from my seat and went forward to be served with a silver chalice containing wine is then hardly to be wondered at. I recall, perhaps forty years later, the effect of wine in my gullet as I turned and made my way back to my place. Somewhat analogously to the person of my previous account, I grasped—through physical sensation—the Eucharist as Christ's passion and victory in a way never previously imagined.

In drawing the first section of the essay to a close, I suggested that insight might be gained at certain contested points in contemporary church life in contemplating the degree to which, and perhaps the manner in which, faith is recognized as having a material dimension. The status and role of an ordained worship leader appears to me to be one such case.

Materiality appertains not just to things. As we saw well enough in our observations on embodiment in Paul, it applies to people and relationships: to the *manner* in which things are said and done no less than the things themselves, and to the *material conditions* within which they are transacted (who has, and who lacks, power; whether authority is recognized or not; and any number of other relational facets). When it is reckoned that this web of physicality constitutes at least part of people's apprehension of the divine, it is scarcely surprising that the minister's role—as prominent and strategic as it is—should have generated such extensive debate in the churches over the past several decades. At the same time, our considerations thus far strongly suggest that in the event—in an actual service of worship, that is—the role cannot be disentangled from the personhood or personality of him or her who occupies it.

At its heart the sixteenth-century Reformation was a struggle over the nature of faith—explicitly over faith's materiality or immateriality. Unquestionably there were differences among the Reformers on precisely this point, so that a graduated scale can be drawn from Luther's comfort with the "adiaphora" of ritual embellishment to Zwingli's iconoclasm. At base, however, faith was held unambiguously to be a nonmaterial principle. "Justifying faith" means personal, noninstitutionalized faith. Even those who held the sacraments in high regard (Luther and Calvin) were in no doubt about the priority of Word to Sacrament—so that it is essentially God's promise that we apprehend in the sacraments. For Luther especially, but for the others too, ministry was grounded in baptism, so that ordination was essentially a practical necessity for the sake of order; that, or for Calvin a teaching office. All the mainline Reformers saw the need for a designated ministry.[26] But the deeply iconoclastic tendencies embedded within Protestantism,[27] the massive priority it ascribes to an evanescent Word,[28] and its insistence

26. For a concise overview of the Reformers' theology of ministry against the background of their times, see Bernard Cooke, *Ministry to Word and Sacraments: History and Theology* (Philadelphia: Fortress Press, 1976), 133–59.

27. The standard work is Carlos M. N. Eire, *War Against the Idols: The Reformation of Worship from Erasmus to Calvin* (Cambridge: Cambridge University Press, 1986); but see also Margaret Aston, "Iconoclasm in England: Official and Clandestine," in *The Impact of the English Reformation 1500–1640*, ed. Peter Marshall (London: Arnold, 1997), 167–92. William A. Dyrness in his excellent *Reformed Theology and Visual Culture: The Protestant Imagination from Calvin to Edwards* (New York: Cambridge University Press, 2004) makes the point that Protestant iconoclasm was in considerable measure a social response to abuses of inequality in the Catholic hierarchy. He also shows how a Calvinist stress on ordinariness as the theater of God's action had, by the middle of the eighteenth century, left it seriously exposed to secularist revisionism.

28. One of the most far-reaching misapprehensions of the Reformers and of subsequent Protestantism is that language has no material content. We now reckon otherwise. See, for example, Terry Eagleton, *Criticism and Ideology: A Study in Marxist Literary Theory* (London: NLB, 1976), 54–55. "Language, that most innocent and spontaneous of common currencies, is in reality a ter-

on personalistic faith[29] have contributed cumulatively to a general uncertainty or indifference about the need, or value, or moment of ordained leaders, so that in our time the question can seriously be put as to whether we need them at all.[30]

A material view of faith insists otherwise.

There is, admittedly, no agreed definition as to what a service of worship is.[31] One important construal, however, well-established in the literature, and offering significant gains over others as I see it, is that worship is essentially a dialogue, the shared exchange between God and an assembly of people gathered for just this purpose. "Dialogue" here is not restricted to purely verbal exchange: things are done as well as said. It does mean, first, that worship is not a monologue: each partner has something to contribute. Second, it is a speaking in turn; both do not speak at once—in Luther's limpid sentence, "Our dear Lord himself speaks with us through his holy Word and in response we speak with him through praise and prayer."[32]

---

rain scarred, fissured and divided by the cataclysms of political history. . . . Language is first of all a physical, material reality, and as such is part of the forces of material production."

29. Werner Führer, *Das Amt der Kirche: Das reformatorische Verständnis des geistlichen Amtes im ökumenischen Kontext* (Neuendettelsau: Freimund Verlag, 2001), 25–74, draws a line directly from the theology of justification by faith to a Lutheran doctrine of ordination.

30. For example, Val Webb, "Is It Permissible to Ask Why We Ordain at All?," *Uniting Church Studies* 3, no. 1 (1997): 13–38.

31. Mary Collins, for example ("Critical Questions," 303), proceeds from a characteristically Roman Catholic perspective: "The liturgy of the Church sets out the mystery of Christ as the paschal mystery—his *transitus* to the Father 'for us and for our salvation.'" David Stancliffe, "The Making of the Church of England's *Common Worship*," *Studia Liturgica* 31, no. 1 (2001): 16, offers an Anglican view: "In general terms every act of worship should be a vehicle by which each worshiper in each community is caught up into the one, perfect sacrificial self-offering of Christ to the Father."

32. The sentence comes from Luther's "Sermon at the Dedication of the Castle Church in Torgau, Luke 14:1-11, October 5, 1544," in *Luther's Works*, ed. Jaroslav Pelikan and Helmut T. Lehmann, vol. 51, *Sermons, I*, ed. and trans. John W. Doberstein (Philadelphia: Muhlenberg Press, 1959), 333. Karl-Heinrich Bieritz draws attention to the striking similarities of the Constitution on the Liturgy's statement (par. 33): "[I]n the liturgy God speaks to his people

In this exchange between God and people some*one* must speak for God, and at certain representative moments, someone must speak on the people's behalf. The second movement is of course not confined to one person: at several places the people make their own acclamation; and, in all our newer orders of service, leadership is shared among readers, musicians, and prayer leaders, to name only those most apparent. But even here, on this side of the exchange, that is, the people's speaking is entrusted at critical moments—notably but not only in the Great Prayer of Thanksgiving—to the presiding minister. For this speaking is one of the central actions of the entire liturgy: it is the people's "sacrifice of praise."

"Worthy and right" as is this song of praise, it pales in comparison with the words which come *to* the people: the initial word of greeting that creates these gathered individuals into a congregation; the words of assurance and pardon; the Word of consolation, correction, and encouragement in Scripture and its exposition; the greeting of peace; and, by no means least, God's blessing in departure. Without these words, everything said from the people's side remains groundless: wishful projection rather than assured response.

And herein lies the deepest paradox of our subject: God's words require a human spokesperson. Faith depends on materiality.

But particular materiality! The eminent ritual theorist Catherine Bell, in addressing a meeting of Societas Liturgica a year or two ago, made reference to a Buddhist leader who had said that to be effective in a secularist society, Japanese Buddhism would need to look to the religious personhood of its priests: their honesty, simplicity, conviction, human empathy. Bell said that as an anthro-

---

. . . and the people respond . . . in song and prayer" (*Vatican Council II: The Basic Sixteen Documents*, ed. Austin Flannery [Northport, NY: Costello Publishing Company, 1996], 129). See Karl-Heinrich Bieritz, *Liturgik* (Berlin and New York: Walter de Gruyter, 2004), 258. Subsequently to the council the idea of worship's dialogical structure found favor among numerous Roman Catholic writers. See, for example, Aimé Georges Martimort, "Structure and Laws of the Liturgical Celebration," in *The Church at Prayer: Principles of the Liturgy*, ed. Aimé Georges Martimort (Collegeville, MN: Liturgical Press, 1987), 85–223, esp. 131–71: "The Dialogue between God and His People." See also James Empereur, *Worship: Exploring the Sacred* (Washington, DC: Pastoral Press, 1987), 131–32.

pologist of ritual she would never have come to this conclusion: "Ritualists like to look at the structure of the rite. Certainly, I know of no formal studies that ask if the humanity and sincerity of the celebrant matter *more than anything else* in making a ritual into a strong experience for lay participants."[33] Professor Bell clearly supposed that this point of view might, or should, gain the interest of liturgical specialists.

That the humanity of one who presides in worship becomes, as it were, an icon, a material representation of God's presence,[34] confounds some of Protestantism's deepest instincts, but it challenges Catholic theory too, at one point at least. On its Protestant side, the assertion counters directly a confessional hermeneutical prejudice: the conviction, that is, that everything written subsequently to Paul represents devolution into "early Catholicism" and that everything the Old Testament (though received within the Christian canon!) might say about priesthood is of less than no account.[35]

33. Catherine Bell, "Ritual Tensions: Tribal and Catholic," *Studia Liturgica* 32, no. 1 (2002): 22 (my emphasis).

34. A reviewer of the essay, in its preparation for publication, advised against the use of the word "icon" in this sentence: "this is a rather Western take on a deeply sacramental and sacred concept. I think it is probably inappropriate here." Against this better judgment I have retained the word; I respect the point being made but would want to say that is just this sort of sacramentality which is so severely absent in Protestant sensibilities. Iconicity is not *just* an Orthodox idea; it is one central thread in Charles S. Peirce's semiotic theory and one on which I have drawn, with reference to liturgical leadership, in my *Worship as Meaning: A Liturgical Theology for Late Modernity* (Cambridge: Cambridge University Press, 2003); see, for example, 148–70.

35. Käsemann, whom I cited earlier on faith in Paul, is damning of the Pastoral Letters and the Lukan writings for allowing a more materialist view of ministry than Paul's apocalyptic, charismatic ideas had encompassed: "[P]rimitive Jewish Christianity . . . appears before us in a new guise in the early Catholic conception of the Church as an institution purveying salvation" (*Essays on New Testament Themes*, trans. W. J. Montague [London: SCM Press, 1964], 92). Samuel E. Balentine, in his *The Torah's Vision of Worship* (Minneapolis: Fortress Press, 1999), several times makes the point that scholarly interpretation of the Pentateuch has, until very recently, been undertaken almost singularly by Protestants and that, beginning with Julius Wellhausen, one can now trace a decidedly "Protestant bias" (p. 16) against the priestly

To acknowledge faith's materiality must push Protestants several degrees closer to a theology of "Catholic substance."[36] But a view ascribing importance to this minister's humanity also works against the Catholic notion *ex opere operato*, according to which "the effectiveness of a minister . . . comes most basically from his [*sic*] office, from the fact that he is speaking officially, as one ordained to speak in this recognized position."[37] Here, "Catholic substance" is critiqued precisely by "Protestant principle," which insists—whatever else—that faith shall at least be *personal*, that is, that the minister's personal conviction counts. A consideration of faith's materiality, applied to ministers of worship, thus seems to me to affect a crossover point between the two.

Theology

"As we pray so we believe."

Is any of this yet theology? Contrary to the tendency to which I alluded much earlier of separating the practical disciplines from theology proper,[38] an acceptance of faith's materiality urges that

---

tradition in favor of its prophetic critics. Balentine, conversely, believes that it was precisely the priestly vision, which was able to sustain Israel through the time of Persian suzerainty (539–333 BCE). A similarly revisionist assessment of the priestly tradition may be found in Richard D. Nelson, *Raising Up a Faithful Priest: Community and Priesthood in Biblical Theology* (Louisville, KY: Westminster John Knox, 1993).

36. I encountered Paul Tillich's highly suggestive pairing of "Protestant Principle and Catholic Substance" only as I was well into my reflections on faith's materiality. I find myself encouraged by what seems to me a close contiguity between Tillich's notions and my own. See, for example, several of the essays in *Paul Tillich: A New Catholic Assessment*, ed. Raymond F. Bulman and Frederick J. Parrella (Collegeville, MN: Liturgical Press, 1994); or Gabriel Daly, "Protestant Principle and Catholic Substance," *Uniting Church Studies* 3, no. 2 (1997): 1–11.

37. Cooke, *Ministry*, 258. See further Karl Rahner, *The Church and the Sacraments*, trans. W. J. O'Hara (Freiburg and London: Herder and Nelson, 1963), 25–33, 98–102.

38. One recalls Aidan Kavanagh's acerbic remonstrance: "Sacramental discourse . . . is often thought of as theological adiaphora best practiced by

people's sentient experience is at least partly, but irreducibly, constitutive of their view of God. Practical theology is theology!

Confirmation of this seems to be coming from the widespread contemporary agreement among liturgical theologians that the worship in which people engage both brings to expression and powerfully forms or consolidates their convictions about God and the nature of the divine-human relationship. One will refer perhaps to Bridget Nichols's hermeneutical analyses of Anglican worship, where she argues that liturgy "proposes" or "presents the possibility of the Kingdom."[39] Lathrop rather similarly speaks of the liturgy "proposing a world larger than we had imagined" and goes on to ask, "*What* world does the liturgy propose? How is it . . . a sanctuary of meaning?"[40] Or Don Saliers speaks of "liturgy as revelatory art."[41] From these writers' points of view, the question is not whether theology happens in the thousands of worshiping congregations on any Sunday morning but of what kind is that theology.

There is similar agreement that, given its formative power, some substantial degree of responsibility redounds—as critically placed practical theologians!—to those who design and implement Christian public worship. Unquestionably, worshipers must feel themselves "at home" in the language and ritual forms that are constructed. But liturgical planners are not there only to reflect to people prevalent or popular styles:[42] "[T]here must be some room for theological *prescription* as well."[43]

In which respects? Or in which directions? What is the theological prerogative for our time?

---

those with a taste for banners, ceremonials and arts and craft" (in his *On Liturgical Theology* [Collegeville, MN: Liturgical Press, 1984], 46).

39. Bridget Nichols, *Liturgical Hermeneutics: Interpreting Liturgical Rites in Performance* (Frankfurt: Peter Lang, 1994), 53, 74, 83–84, and frequently.

40. Lathrop, *Holy Things*, 135 (my emphasis).

41. Don E. Saliers, *Worship as Theology: Foretaste of Divine Glory* (Nashville: Abingdon Press, 1994), 197–202.

42. See Maxwell E. Johnson, "Can We Avoid Relativism in Worship? Liturgical Norms in the Light of Contemporary Liturgical Scholarship," *Worship* 74, no. 2 (March 2000): 135–55; or Alan Barthel, "The United Church of Canada Celebrates God's Presence," *Studia Liturgica* 31, no. 1 (2001): 75.

43. Johnson, "Can We Avoid Relativism in Worship?," 154.

My judgment about this, implied perhaps in what has gone before but now only here made explicit, is that this (preeminent theological requirement of our time) consists in the assertion and defense of God's radical otherness. "Difference" does not mean "distance"; for no evangelical account of God can or will compromise God's immediacy to the created order. But: an uncompromising alterity. Evidence abounds of a wistfulness in postmodern people for some kind of transcendence; the same evidence suggests, however, that it is an undemanding deity—one making no claim on themselves or the disbursement of their time, energies, and goods—that they seek.[44] At least some of the examples (of worship practices), which I have yet to introduce, suggest that worshiping Christians are by no means immune to such cultural inclinations. Dietrich Bonhoeffer warned of the ever-lurking danger of "confessing our sins to ourselves and also granting ourselves absolution."[45] By extension, without a strong liturgical conviction about—and expression of—God's difference from ourselves, we run the constant risk of speaking to no one other than ourselves.

I spoke earlier of worship's dialogical character and of the presiding minister's pivotal role in this. Now we must stress that it is exactly this dialogical structure which—when allowed its proper weight—delivers worship from the kind of solipsism Bonhoeffer feared; for of course any genuine dialogue can only be with an other. Materiality is again of central importance: certainly, in terms of the presider's actions and attitudes, but perhaps now even more critically in terms of the physical structure—temporal progression, that is—of worship. The leader speaks at some points on God's behalf

44. In a survey of religious dispositions in Germany, the monthly journal *Geo* found that 66% of Germans believe in a personal guardian angel (47% believe in God as an ultimate reality; 30% believe that their life's purpose is to live a life pleasing to God). Guardian angels seem to be "in": the Provinzial insurance company regularly runs primetime TV advertisements featuring an angel just one pace behind people in various everyday circumstances, intervening to ward off potential hazards or unperceived dangers. See also Nathan Mitchell, "Negotiating Rapture," *Worship* 71, no. 4 (July 1997): 350–57, on the popularity of a US television series depicting benign, ever-helpful angelic beings.

45. Dietrich Bonhoeffer, *Life Together*, trans. and with an introduction by John W. Doberstein (London: SCM Press, 1954), 91.

and at others for the people, but not for both at once! Otherwise said, in distinguishing the roles she or he must occupy and (hopefully) in allowing this variation to be apparent, the minister makes clear that people have gathered not only, and not even primarily, to greet one another, nor to be entertained, not as recipients of helpful advice, but before their Creator, their Judge and bountiful Redeemer; in the presence, that is, of a God who speaks and awaits our response.

There are numerous points in modern liturgy where this cardinal principle seems to me to be compromised.

A Catholic version—by no means as problematic, I judge, as the Protestant instances which I will note—is the now widespread idea that Christ worships with or in or through the church: "Liturgy is the 'action' of the *whole Christ (Christus totus)*. . . . It is the whole *community*, the Body of Christ united with its Head, that celebrates."[46] This point of view is regularly anchored to the Second Vatican Council's Constitution on the Liturgy: "In [the liturgy], complete and definitive public worship is performed by the mystical body of Jesus Christ, that is, by the Head and his members."[47] The idea, and the term *totus Christus*, can be traced as far back as Augustine.[48] The Constitution thus speaks of Christ's presence in all of worship's dimensions: in the sacraments, in the Word, and "when the church prays and sings."

Pope John XXIII's vision of *aggiornamento* ("updating") in calling the council centrally included, among other things, an overcoming of the centuries-old rigid distinction of priests and people and its accompanying assumptions that the church consisted essentially in its ordained members and that, accordingly, baptized Christians and any ministries they might bring were of negligible worth. (A similar intention was informing other Christian deliberations at the time, notably the WCC Faith and Order Commission's *Baptism,*

---

46. *The Catechism of the Catholic Church* (London: Geoffrey Chapman, 1994), 260–61 (their emphases).

47. The Constitution on the Sacred Liturgy, par. 7 (Flannery, *Basic Documents*, 121).

48. David N. Power, "Representing Christ in Community and Sacrament," in *Being a Priest Today*, ed. Donald J. Goergan (Collegeville, MN: Liturgical Press, 1992), 115.

Eucharist and Ministry and, not least, what would be the Uniting Church's *Basis of Union*.) In the conciliar documents, accordingly, baptism becomes the chief identifying mark of Christians,[49] within which classification ordination finds its place.[50] And "participation" becomes the chief desideratum in worship.[51] Coming back, then, to the conception of worship in which Christ prays in and with and through the prayer of the people, which perception has gained such widespread favor in Catholic circles, as I noted, there can be no disputing the depth of the tradition which identifies Christ with his people: to be "in Christ" and that "Christ is in me" are favorite Pauline expressions, as is "abiding in Christ" and "Christ abiding in us" in John, to say nothing of "the Body of Christ" as a description of the church. Yet these terms can on no account be reckoned as exhaustive: Christ is always infinitely more than the church; as creatures we do not, and never will, partake of God's holy Trinity; if Christ shares in the life of the church, intercedes for it, gives himself for it, equally he stands over against it as its Lord and Redeemer. This means that there must be a place—theologically and liturgically—for Christ to address his people as well as share his life with them. This dialectic, however, is not always, or not often, recognized in the literature to which I refer.[52] In the end one cannot resist the

49. The Dogmatic Constitution on the Church, par. 7 (Flannery, *Basic Documents*, 6–7).

50. Ibid., par. 11 (Flannery, *Basic Documents*, 16).

51. The Constitution on the Sacred Liturgy, par. 41 (Flannery, *Basic Documents*, 133).

52. The conciliar and postconciliar recognition that a priest in the liturgy speaks *in persona Christi* and also *in persona Ecclesia* has, as was to be expected, generated voluminous discussion. Representatively, see Sara Butler, "Priestly Identity: 'Sacrament' of Christ the Head," *Worship* 70, no. 4 (July 1996): 290–306; David Coffey, "The Common and Ordained Priesthood," *Theological Studies* 58, no. 2 (June 1997): 209–36; Edward J. Kilmartin, "Apostolic Office: Sacrament of Christ," *Theological Studies* 36, no. 2 (June 1975): 243–64; David N. Power, "Church Order: The Need for Redress," *Worship* 71, no. 4 (July 1997): 296–309; Lawrence J. Welch, "Priestly Identity Reconsidered: A Reply to Susan Wood," *Worship* 70, no. 4 (July 1996): 307–19; Susan K. Wood, "Priestly Identity: Sacrament of the Ecclesial Community," *Worship* 69, no. 2 (March 1995): 109–27. What seems seldom, if ever, to be recognized

question as to whether this (mostly) unqualified identification of Christ and church is not unwittingly influenced by the desire for immanence so characteristic of our age.

The two Protestant cases stand to each other antithetically even though in both the outcome is the same: the vitiation of any dialogical sense of worship. In so-called seeker services, the entire operation is a speaking to the audience/congregation: "By the repeated emphasis on communicating a message . . . seeker service churches build an image that the saving activity of Christ is solely proclamation."[53] This worship can scarcely be regarded as trinitarian; it exemplifies rather "a unitarianism of the Second Person of the Trinity."[54] No "answering praise and prayer" here!

Oppositely, E. Byron Anderson describes an ostensibly Methodist group in the United States (ostensible in that it nowhere publicly displays its affiliation) where the participants gather "'for coffee around tables, sharing ancient and new stories and talking about issues that affect [their] lives and [their] relationship with God and one another.'"[55] At a certain point, an invitation to one of the tables, which "has been prepared as a 'liturgical center' with candles, bread, grape juice, baskets, and other items [for the reception of prayer requests] . . . is offered to all. Some individuals come to the table serving themselves bread and wine. Others . . . [place] prayer

---

in these discussions is the *temporal oscillation* of a presiding minister's roles; as I have now stated repeatedly, *at certain points* in the liturgy the presiding minister speaks and acts on God's behalf (*in persona Christi*, we might say, at any rate in the older sense of the term) and at other points on behalf of the people (*in persona Ecclesiae*). The roles are thus distinguished and distinguishable by way of their temporal juxtaposition. They need not, and definitely ought not, to be fused or confused. It is precisely this temporal oscillation in roles, which seems to me to be the key, which is somehow missing in so much Catholic discussion.

53. Lester Ruth, "Lex Agendi, Lex Orandi: Toward an Understanding of Seeker Services as a New Kind of Liturgy," *Worship* 70, no. 5 (September 1996): 403.

54. Frank C. Senn, "'Worship Alive': An Analysis and Critique of 'Alternative Worship Services,'" *Worship* 69, no. 3 (May 1995): 217.

55. E. Byron Anderson, "Worship and Belief: Liturgical Practice as a Contextual Theology," *Worship* 75, no. 5 (September 2001): 442.

requests in one of the baskets. . . . Others remain quietly at their tables."[56] In this "worship," everything is contained within: there is no Word, no eucharistic gift, no blessing. Accordingly, neither in this case can there be answering praise or prayer.

No one, I am sure, can seriously wish a return to the times in which—effectively for Protestants no less than for Catholics—ordained ministers were somehow seen as being the church. The recognition of baptism as the primary sign of Christian identification has released untold energies in both forms of Western Christianity. Can the pendulum swing too far in an opposite direction? Where (in Catholicism) the worshiping congregation is practically identified with Christ and (among Protestants) no clear distinction can be found between what God will say to us and we say to God, then, the essay has attempted to say, Christian identity and Christian theology are seriously endangered. A strong recognition of the importance of the visible, of physical signification, of embodied being—both with reference to the responsibilities resting on ordained members of the community as spokespersons for God and in a distinguishing of the moments in the liturgy as to which come from God to us and which are offered by worshipers to God—can importantly help safeguard the ultimate and inalienable difference between the Creator and his creatures. Materiality, I have tried to say, is a critical dimension of theology.

56. Anderson, "Worship and Belief," 443.

Chapter Six

The Last Interview

With William Emilsen

EMILSEN: So let's go back to the beginning. You had finished your big book on *Worship and Meaning* and then you were looking around for a new project.[1] Tell me the background to this project.

HUGHES: It is hard to say exactly where were the headwaters. There was a good deal of acuity and unclarity when I had finished the book on meaning about where to jump after that. I suppose that it had to do with the question of ordination. If the role of the ordained person is as important to the implementation of this meaning project as seems to be implied in the *Meaning* book, then what do we have to say about ordination and its meaning? What is the meaning of meanings—an old, hoary old question, of course. Differently put, what do we think we are doing when we ordain a person, set someone aside as a person who facilitates this meaning project?

It took me longer than I foresaw, in fact, to realize that I was in the wrong place in time. I did actually realize that it would have to be, whatever it was, a project in Reformed theology. The trigger for

---

1. See Graham Hughes, *Worship as Meaning: A Liturgical Theology for Late Modernity* (Cambridge: Cambridge University Press, 2003).

that was work that Stephen Pickard was sending me at the time, which eventually became part of his book.[2] He was sending me chapters on episcopacy. It was quite clear that Stephen was able to proceed as confidently and with as clear a goal as he was doing, because he knew very clearly for which confession he was writing. So that became the catalyst, so to speak, or the trigger. I realized that if I was to do anything further along these lines it would need to be founded in a Reformed frame of reference, so to speak. But it still remains somewhat puzzling to me that it took me as long as it did even recognizing that. I was in the wrong place at the wrong time. In other words, I was in Germany and all the stuff that I could turn up on ordination was keyed into Lutheran questions of ordination. There were plenty of questions the Lutherans were walking around—questions not dissimilar to the ones that, I supposed, would be a part of the Reformed agenda. But the real point I am trying to make is that it took me a surprisingly long time to realize that they were doing it from a Lutheran background and with Lutheran presuppositions, a Lutheran history of doctrine.

E: So, is this what you mean by you were not in the right place?

H: Yes, that is pretty much exactly what I mean. I'm surprised in retrospect that it took me as long as it did to recognize [that] this is not going to go ahead as long as I'm still in Germany. I've got to work in a Reformed context. The questions [about ordination] were running right across the various synods of the Lutheran Confession, but they were not our questions, I came to see in the end.

So the thing, for longer than I care to remember, fell into some sort of abeyance. I didn't know just what to do and where to go. It may well have been the Calvin Quincentenary, which was the

2. According to Stephen Pickard (personal correspondence with William Emilsen), he and Graham spent many hours discussing the matter of holy orders and ministry when Pickard was preparing the manuscript for his book, *Theological Foundations for Collaborative Ministry* (Farnham, UK, and Burlington, VT: Ashgate, 2009). The chapters on ministry and their subsequent conversations on the matter of a relational ontology and the nature of promise and vow persuaded Graham to set off on his own inquiry into sacrament and ministry within Reformed Christianity.

catalyst for me to be able to see that it's actually not a question of ordination.[3] Ordination is certainly of central importance, but the question is to be conceived much more comprehensively. And that is to say, what do we think we are doing when we nominate and ritually declare some people as sacramental persons in the larger church and in local congregations? And then, the thing began to open up into the question of our Reformed sacramentality, embedded in which is by all means the question of ordination and ordained ministry.

Rather coincidently, I think, I had got to see that it's a question of sacramentality, not just of the sacraments, and not just of ordination, and not just of the other various intensely sacramental actions and moments, persons and things, which we nominate in our Christian life. Maybe coincidently, I was asked to write this paper for the Theological Studies Society in England. I think that was in 2007. I was invited to present a paper on materiality and that was a way into seeing that the problem for Reformed Christianity has to do with the materiality side of the sacraments, that is to say, the physicality.[4]

And then I started on several essays, exploring the history of that concept and the difficulty that it has had in the Reformed churches. It gradually emerged for me that the difficulty that we have is actually being able to bring together this collectivity or fusion of spiritual, intellectual, and, I suppose you might include in there, didactic doctrinal dimensions of the Christian faith, with physical forms. We know how that works out. We know, for example, that the actual physical dimension of baptism in Reformed Christianity—we're not now talking just about doctrine, theology, we are actually talking about practice—the physical dimension of baptism in our neck of the woods has to do with the sprinkling of

3. Graham gave a paper at the Calvin Quincentenary, which William Emilsen organized at United Theological College in Sydney, Australia, in 2009. The paper was subsequently published. See Graham Hughes, "The Uncertain Place of Materiality in the Reformed Tradition," *Uniting Church Studies* 17, no. 1 (June 2011): 97–109. The paper is included in this volume as chap. 3.

4. William Emilsen suggests that this paper, which Graham had given in 2007, was identical to the one that he gave in 2009 at United Theological College at the Calvin Quincentenary. See the previous footnote.

a few drops of water on a baby's forehead. The actual physicality of the action is reduced almost to invisibility.

I have also come to the conclusion that our problem with infant baptism is not, in the end, a doctrinal question. I think the New Testament is perfectly open in either direction about the admission of infants to the church as it is to the admission only of adults. I don't think that it rules on that. The Greeks and the Russians have caught this point infinitely more clearly than we have, which is why they are not so deeply threatened as we are in a modern and postmodern age, because the child is actually immersed into the water. In some versions of Roman Catholic Christianity, churches and cathedrals are being built with fonts actually sunk into the floor of the cathedral.

Now, I can pretty well believe that for a person in midlife to be converted to Christianity and to offer him- or herself for baptism is a pretty life-affecting moment, that it certainly will change things very powerfully for them. But I am also convinced that we need to recover the actual materiality of the sign. If we can just recall for a moment that the sign has two references (if we can use that language): it references washing, and it references the death and burial of the believer with Christ. Now, I can believe that for a person to become a Christian in midlife and to be baptized in the normal models that we have—that is, in the normal forms of a person turning up and being admitted to a Christian congregation with the marking of the cross three times with water with the forefinger or the thumb of the presiding minister in the middle of the congregation—the joy of that for the congregation and the baptismal candidate will be pretty moving. But I think it would be many times more moving, it would capture infinitely more graphically, so to say, the meaning of dying and rising with Christ to actually go down and be submersed in water and come back up out of water.

Let's now bring that across to infant baptism. It is an almost impossible idea for Reformed Christians to think of our having baptismal fonts, which were of sufficient capacity for parents actually to see their child dunked, submersed in water, and brought up out of water. But if we had such fonts, I don't think we would have anything like the same problems that we have. I don't think we'd have anything like the same doctrinal problems that we have over baptism and whether baptism is for adults only or for infants only.

[Day 2]

E: Yesterday, Graham, you finished by talking about baptism and, in particular, a diminished form of baptism in Reformed Christianity. You were talking about the sprinkling and how within the Reformed traditions we diminished the symbol.

H: That's right, and of course that is either anchored in or arises from the low level of attention that we seem to have learned to give to the material aspect of the sacrament in our tradition. Baptism becc· in a way a case study, I suppose you might say, in the physica

First of all, there is the serious inadequacy of sprinkling or ev, thankfully, in more recent times—the threefold marking of the crc by the presiding minister on the candidate for baptism. There is the serious inadequacy of that from the material side of the sacrament in terms of expressing the meaning of this Christian sacrament, which actually from very early in the tradition has this twofold reference point or dimension: It is first a ritual of washing—but, I mean, one is hardly washed with the finger or thumb of the presiding minister—and even more disappointing, the signification of death, burial, and rising to new life, which was for centuries expressed in the immersion of the candidate. And in both cases, whether we are talking about a symbolic act of washing or a symbolic act of death, burial, and resurrection—even if we grasp the newer sacramental forms, in which one can indeed rejoice, which are an improvement over the sprinkling of a few drops of water—even there, there is a serious inadequacy.

E: I was just trying to work out whether at some time you should put the five papers that you've written into some sort of context.

H: Just on that note: When you say I should put them into context, I really think my time is now passed. If somebody else can see why I'm doing it, I would be very thankful for that. I mean, part of the problem in this whole assignment is that the five papers walk around the topic without ever actually in one single monograph pushing it forward or making it into a comprehensive study of sacramentality and of the seriously disappointing inadequacies of sacramentality in our particular tradition, and even more important, the consequences that flow from it in terms of church governance and matters of liturgical reform. And, I'm not alone in this, but those of us who are attempting to grasp that nettle, if that's the right way to put it, are very solitary voices and my—or our—anxiety is that really quite anxious-making consequences flow from this in terms of the future of the church's life in the face of modern and, in some places, militant secularism. Our church—that is to say, the Reformed churches—seems to have been especially prone to invasion by assumptions that are not at all Christian ones.

E: So your hope for the book was that it would be a comprehensive study of sacramentality?

H: Yes, but I know I have a tendency to wander off into the scrub of academic exploration and I probably really needed to discipline my thoughts as well as I should, as well as I could, so that it didn't become a historical or academic or even theoretical study of sacramentality and go right over the heads of the people whom I really do have in mind, which is to say, senior church leaders, people in places of political decision making.

But if I can just pick up where we were yesterday. I was attempting to make the point that the way in which we think about baptism in our Reformed churches, whether we're talking about adult baptism or infant baptism, is seriously, seriously impaired by the low level of what—following earlier trains in my thought—I have been inclined to call the semiosis of baptism or the service of baptism itself, the act of baptism. And I said that I could see that from the point of view of an adult person who has found conversion to Christian life in adulthood and comes seeking the sacrament for himself or herself, that it will be a very meaningful moment, even if that is an act of sprinkling, or rather better, an act of the sign of the cross, but it would be infinitely more powerful for someone if they are invited actually to be submersed in a body of water and to rise up out of that water with the proclamation that we are now the baptized members of Christ's body.

Now, because of the history of things, I think that will be even more challenging but carry even more weight if we were to get to the point—which I can barely imagine—where an infant were actually submersed in a baptismal font, not unlike the way in which the Orthodox tradition has preserved. And I think it's because [baptism] has become such a trivial thing from its material point of view. That is to say, the cognitive side of the ritual, the actual meaning is so seriously impaired by the very low level of semiosis of sprinkling or even the sign of the cross—and we've tried to bolster that with the giving of a candle and so on—as compared with submersion. I think that becomes even more sharply etched and a much more major consideration for parents who are then asked whether they really do want this sacrament of death and burial and resurrection for their newly born baby. Is this what they want?

E: Because it's quite challenging, isn't it?

H: Well, I think it's supposed to be challenging. And part of the point is that it has become a dogmatic problem because the physicality of the administration of the sacrament has become so diluted.

Now, if we can traverse from there to the sacrament of Holy Communion, the thing becomes—I suppose unfortunately, but anyway it does—a good deal more complicated. The issue applies to baptism as well as Eucharist, but the issue here is, as the Greek Fathers saw, and even earlier, about in the eighth century, that an image has to bear a perceptible likeness. There has to be a perceptible likeness between the prototype and the ectype. The prototype being this belief that I am buried and raised, and the ectype the act, the physicality of being submerged and emerging as a member of Christ's body on earth.

Now, if one carries these ideas across to [the] Eucharist, the fact again remains that the ectype—in this case the sacrament of Holy Communion—is seriously diminished in face of what in fact is the celebration of the holy meal, the eschatological joining of Christ with his church in festal banquet—however we want to state all of those things. Now at the outset, that is to say, in Jesus' own ministry, the prototype was entirely clear. The distance between the prototype and the ectype was barely to be seen. Jesus actually sat around a table and the order in which people sat, that is to say, any notion of the head of the table and the foot of the table, all of those things were simply slashed through and there was no difference for the people who gathered with Jesus around a table and celebrated with wine and bread and every other kind of festivity. So here the meaning in Jesus' ministry is present in the actions. There is barely any distance. You don't have to say what is the meaning of this. The kingdom is actually breaking into people's lives. In this proclamation God celebrates the eschatological—here "eschatological" in inverted commas—banquet with the people of his faith, meaning in fact all people, because there were no distinctions, there were no gradations, there were no exclusions and inclusions, which of course was very serious, which was one of the factors that led to his demise.

But now, very early in the church's history, that immediacy between prototype and ectype was beginning to be set aside. Already we hear in the Pauline accounts of the Eucharist that the ritual moment was distinguished from its meaning. The meaning is the celebration of the presence of Christ and therefore the presence of the kingdom of God. And Paul is already saying that this will not be celebrated in an actual meal in which people simply have a jolly good time and that is understood and recognized to be the celebration of God's inbreaking upon us. Already the ritual, which is to say the eucharistic service, is separated from, is distinguished from, its meaning.

Now, the meaning still has to come across—that is also Paul's point, namely, that you cannot have gradations, distinctions, between slave people and slave owners, between rich people and poor people, and so on. This really does have to be an ectypical celebration of the inbreaking of the kingdom, of the presence of Christ, here in the midst of his disciples. And today it's not. I don't think there is any serious expectation that we will have a meal, though I certainly think that there are some people who would want to push it through to that. But I don't think that's what a sacrament is. A sacrament is in a way—there's nothing new in this either—a metaphor. This ritual action and the repetition of certain words and the distribution of certain foods is a metaphor, saying that it both is and is not the thing that it is pointing to. And the pointing to is of great importance, because we in this post-Easter church, of which we are now speaking, have no real possibility of the direct apprehension of Christ. We apprehend Christ always through or via this sacramental meal.

And this is always a problem: Catholics are actually prone to this in their endless disputations over real presence, and even Catholic writers nowadays are no longer wanting to push the point that there is a real presence of Christ in the sacramental celebration. I don't think I myself have actually truly understood what is meant by the paschal exchange, and even if I did, it's not something that we as Protestants could subscribe to, because we do not subscribe to the offering of sacrifice. We subscribe to the reception of Christ's presence and his benefits to us. That is to say, in receiving this fragment of bread and this sip of wine I'm actually receiving the very presence of Christ himself. So it's a critical distinction between whether the most central action of the sacrament of Eucharist is reception, as a Protestant point of view would have it, or of offering, which is the Catholic point of view.

Of course, Calvin himself and the Protestant tradition in a sense have forever said: Of course, there is an offering, but it is the offering of praise. It is not, it cannot ever be, the offering of Christ again, the offering of Christ's sacrifice again. And even if that is now conceived in terms of offering, that is, the offering of Christ's paschal victory, it is still an act of offering, which stands seriously over against the basic lines of approach of the Protestant or Reformed understanding of Eucharist.

Now that comes back to the question—and I really do not have the answer to this, but it comes back to the integrity or the intimacy or the proximity of prototype and ectype. That is to say, if we stay within Reformed frames of reference, how closely can we bring the actual experience, the semiosis of the sacramental action of the celebration of the sacrament, how closely can we bring that back, in its now ritual form, to the kinds of immediacy between actual and metaphorical that were experienced in Jesus' own ministry. And then he left to the church the ritual forms, the sacramental forms, in which we receive his presence. We receive Christ's presence in and with and behind—I probably need to think about each of those prepositions—these sacramental forms. I can't think of any more powerful way in which Christ week by week enters my body or enters my life than by receiving this fragment and this sip of wine, than through the celebration of Holy Communion.

But I am pretty confident that the symbols or significations that we do have—just as in the case of baptism—are seriously diminished in the forms. Of course, I'm referring to little glasses of grape juice, the power of which, both in taste and actually in sight, is so diminished. I mean, how can this tiny glass of grape juice compare with a handsome silver cup of port wine? There can hardly be a comparison. So there is a great deal still to be done in bringing the physicality, the actual taste of the element into coherence, into some kind of semiotic conformity with what we are saying is the meaning of this sign, and similarly with the fragment of bread. I made the point in one of the papers somewhere that mercifully we no longer put into people's hands a tiny cube of white bread that feels and tastes more like damp cardboard and a tiny glass of grape juice and suppose that that can mean anything to the people who receive them, precisely because of the inadequacy of the semiotic power.

Now, what this means, circling back, both in baptism and in the celebration of the Eucharist, is that people actually have to do 90 percent of the work in their heads. They have to imagine that here I am participating in Christ's festal banquet or that I have here communion with Jesus and the forgiveness of my sins. All of that has to be a kind of emotional response, an intellectual response. We have to imagine, as Calvin wanted to put it, that we are lifted up out of this earthly life and that we eat and drink of Christ, that we eat of Christ and drink of his blood, but as he was forced immediately to say, of course, this is a spiritual eating and drinking, which is to say, it all has to happen in my imagination, it all has to happen in the things I am thinking about. And you actually see people receive the fragment, the cube of bread and the glass of wine—well it's not wine, that's a large part of the point—and they have to think about it and feel by some kind of act of imagination that they are here joined with Christ or that Christ is giving himself to them.

Now, in the long and complicated essay on "What Is a Sacrament? What Is Sacramentality?"[5] I was saying that the sacraments themselves are images. Sacraments have their own image quality. An image is a fusion, an inextricable confusion of physicality and intellectuality—one can hang different words around that—but it

---

5. See above, chap. 2.

has this doubled polarity: feeling or emotion and physicality. All of those words can be hung around this single idea.

Now, the fact that, I suspect, is often lost sight of is that at ground level the sacraments themselves are images. In other words, the sacrament of baptism has a double-headed image. It is an image of washing, and it is an image of death and resurrection. And I have now already said a good deal of length that in the church's life, and especially very markedly in the Reformed tradition, the physical side of the sacraments was overtaken by its meaning, by this cognitive reference. That is to say: Because any meaning, any signification that is going to come out of the physicality of sprinkling is almost invisible, I have to think about it, I have to feel, I have to imagine myself dying and rising with Christ. Because, heaven help us, there is little enough meaning coming out of the actual experience of going down into water and coming up out of water.

So, the sacraments themselves are images. The sacrament of baptism is an image of dying to Christ and rising with him and, secondary, of washing. And the sacrament of Eucharist also has a double-headed meaning: it is an image of eating and drinking, so it is a meal—it images a meal in which I actually consume the body and blood of the one for whom I now live and die—and, second, it is an image of union. One loaf is broken and one cup is poured out and that was not least important for Paul in his dealing with the Corinthian conundrum. So we have to regrasp the fact that the sacraments themselves are images, but that leads us back to the thought that the sacraments—that is to say the sacrament of baptism, the sacrament of Holy Communion—are themselves profoundly embedded in this much, much larger broadly conceived idea of sacramentality, which is to say, the fusion of meaning and physicality.

E: Sometimes you use form and spirit.

H: Yes, it can wander around between any of those. I don't think I want to use the word polarity, but a sacrament has a spiritual dimension and a physical form, each of which is utterly dependent on the other. In our case, this dependency is so seriously damaged by the diminution of the sacrament's physicality, its actual materiality, both for baptism and for Eucharist. Now, if it's true, as Christians want to say, that the sacraments of baptism and Eucharist are embedded in this large and comprehensive field of sacramentality, then they give us a kind of canonicity as to what sacramentality is. The essay "What Is a Sacrament? What Is Sacramentality?" starts from the point of view that sacramentality is present almost in the very act of breathing. In the very act of utterance, we are putting form and spirit together. We are finding sacramentality in the act of utterance, in the act of putting words on paper or forming sounds on the ear, which are intended for someone else's eardrum. The very fact of being human is the ground and origin of sacramentality.

But then the question becomes: Can you actually distinguish anything anywhere? For Christianity, the sacraments actually are able to make this distinction, because they lie at the heart of this faith, which joins us to Christ, which enables his mercy and ministry to come into our lives week by week in one case and, finally and without return in the other case, in Eucharist and baptism. They give us a kind of reference point, I suppose, or a canon in all of this vast and diffused presence of God in ordinary life. The two sacraments are to us a kind of canon of what sacramentality is, without which we just simply drift into a kind of universality.

There's one little example in one of the papers somewhere about a woman—obviously a very lovely woman—insisting that the act of putting out the rubbish and of feeding her dog is the act of celebrating God's presence. Well then, everything and nothing is God's presence. There are no distinctions. So, the reason for moving from this indiscriminate generalization to the specific reception of Christ and the taking of Christ into my body in eating and drinking week by week gives us a kind of canonical standard in very similar ways to the ways in which the church had to figure out which would be its canonical writings. There were any number of writings to choose from. But they [the early Christians] could also see that many of them were very misleading. And they had to draw up a canon that would guide us and keep us from the dangers of this universality or universalization, which would otherwise simply mean that the church would just sink into the sands of syncretism.

So this method, I suppose it is, of moving from the sacramentality of life in general to what Dan Hardy calls the bright mystery of faith in the two sacraments themselves is what offers some kind of sacramental center, some kind of sacramental reference point that we can say: Well yes, this is a sacramental appropriation of God's presence in the world and this is just suiting myself. I mean, in the secular Christianity of the 1980s everything and therefore in the end nothing could be a manifestation of God's presence.

So that's the point of securing the two sacraments as a kind of canonical reference point for this larger sacramental presence of God, which is not to be despised. I failed to say something about the primordiality of Christ as sacrament. It's a commonplace now, and I apprehend and rejoice in speaking of Christ as the primal sacrament. It is Christ, in the vastness and in the vagueness of God's presence in the universe, which actually allows us to say who God is and even to say who is God for us. But without those two sacraments we could not speak with any kind of confidence about that.

E: I don't want to stop your flow of consciousness there but it does raise the question of, say, the Orthodox person kissing the icon, the other so-called sacraments in the Catholic tradition, and, say, a Hindu putting a marigold on a statue of Shiva. Is there some sort of gradation in your understanding of sacramentality?

H: There is certainly a gradation. I'm not inclined to argue the toss with this young woman—I can't help feeling she was a young woman—for whom putting out the rubbish on Wednesday night is an act of worshiping God. But the question is, how would she know about God? And why is it that millions and millions and millions of other people in putting out the rubbish on Wednesday night don't also apprehend God's presence in this act on a Wednesday night? And the answer to that is: She is able to celebrate putting out the rubbish as an act of sacramentality because she knows about Christ's sacramental presence in the world and because she has undergone this ritual moment of joining herself in death and baptism and because she receives, perhaps not as frequently as some might like, the body and blood of Christ week by week. It is for these very reasons that she is able to see all these other vast and vague and indiscriminate actions of her life as sacramental actions. I can just say that again: without the church's sacraments she would not know this.

Now, I am not inclined to be troubled by other people's religious experience in the great world religions of which you speak. Yet, for me there is a certain centrality to the Abrahamic religions, given that we all share at least part of the Scriptures, which the church names as its holy canon. Still, even so, in the end, one has to say: well, what we are talking about is God as Christians have learned to name God. And that comes to us in its most concrete and vivid and unmistakable form in the life and in the consequent death—because there is a consequence—and in the resurrection of Jesus of Nazareth. And the sacraments are in some sense or another—this is a very delicate thing—the sacraments of baptism and Holy Communion are the way in which Christ left us to know his presence as believers and followers, disciples.

E: Graham, we've been going now for almost an hour, so I think we'll pause. I had wondered if we can do this again. One thing I'd like you to reflect a little bit upon is sacred space, and how that connects with your thoughts on sacramentality, because that fits in again with this de-emphasizing the physicality in some ways.

H: Well, yes, that leads on pretty swiftly.

E: So, do you mind, if we pause now?

H: I think so.

E: I think that would be good.

Bibliography

Allen, Ronald J. "Preaching and the Other." *Worship* 76, no. 3 (May 2002): 211–25.

———. *Preaching and the Other: Studies of Postmodern Insights*. St. Louis, MO: Chalice Press, 2009.

Althusser, Louis. *Lenin and Philosophy and Other Essays*. Translated by Ben Brewster. London: NLB, 1971.

Anderson, E. Byron. "Worship and Belief: Liturgical Practice as a Contextual Theology." *Worship* 75, no. 5 (September 2001): 432–52.

Ashcroft, Bill. "The Sacred in Australian Culture." In *Sacred Australia: Post-Secular Considerations*, edited by Makarand Paranjape, 21–43. Melbourne: Clouds of Magellan, 2009.

Aston, Margaret. *England's Iconoclasts*. Oxford: Clarendon, 1988.

———. "Iconoclasm in England: Official and Clandestine." In *The Impact of the English Reformation 1500–1640*, edited by Peter Marshall, 167–92. London: Arnold, 1997.

Baillie, Donald Macpherson. *The Theology of the Sacraments: And Other Papers*. London: Faber and Faber, 1957.

Balentine, Samuel E. *The Torah's Vision of Worship*. Minneapolis: Fortress Press, 1999.

Banks, Robert. *And Man Created God: Is God a Human Invention?* Oxford: Lion Hudson, 2011.

Barthel, Alan. "The United Church of Canada Celebrates God's Presence." *Studia Liturgica* 31, no. 1 (2001): 70–82.

Barthes, Roland. "The Grain of the Voice." In *Image Music Text*, essays selected and translated by Stephen Heath, 179–189. London: Fontana Press, 1977.

Barton, Stephen C. "Dislocating and Relocating Holiness: A New Testament Study." In *Holiness Past and Present*, edited by Stephen C. Barton, 193–216. London and New York: T&T Clark, 2003.

Bell, Catherine. *Ritual: Perspectives and Dimensions*. New York: Oxford University Press, 1997.

———. "Ritual Tensions: Tribal and Catholic." *Studia Liturgica* 32, no. 1 (2002): 15–28.

———. *Ritual Theory, Ritual Practice*. New York: Oxford University Press, 1992.

Benedict, Philip. "Calvinism as a Culture: Preliminary Remarks on Calvinism and the Visual Arts." In *Seeing Beyond the Word: Visual Arts and the Calvinist Tradition*, edited by Paul Corby Finney, 19–48. Grand Rapids, MI: William B. Eerdmans Publishing Company, 1999.

Berkouwer, Gerrit Cornelis. *Man: The Image of God*. Grand Rapids, MI: William B. Eerdmans Publishing Company, 1962.

Bieritz, Karl-Heinrich. *Liturgik*. New York: Walter de Gruyter, 2004.

Boersma, Hans. *Heavenly Participation: The Weaving of a Sacramental Tapestry*. Grand Rapids, MI: William B. Eerdmans Publishing Company, 2011.

Bonhoeffer, Dietrich. *Life Together*. Translated and with an introduction by John W. Doberstein. London: SCM Press, 1954.

Bornkamm, Günther. *Early Christian Experience*. Translated by Paul L. Hammer. London: SCM Press, 1969.

———. *Paul*. Translated by D. M. G. Stalker. London: Hodder and Stoughton, 1971.

Bossy, John. *Christianity in the West 1400–1700*. Oxford: Oxford University Press, 1988.

Bowker, John. "Religionless Christianity." In *The Concise Oxford Dictionary of World Religions*, edited by John Bowker, 482. Oxford: Oxford University Press, 2000.

Buber, Martin. *I and Thou*. Translated by Ronald Gregor Smith. Edinburgh: T&T Clark, 1937.

Bulman, Raymond F., and Frederick J. Parrella, eds. *Paul Tillich: A New Catholic Assessment*. Collegeville, MN: Liturgical Press, 1994.

Bultmann, Rudolf. *Theology of the New Testament*. Vol. 1. Translated by Kendrick Grobel. London: SCM Press, 1965.

Bultmann, Rudolf, and Arthur Weiser. "Pisteuo, pistis, etc." In *The Theo logical Dictionary of the New Testament*, vol. 6, edited by Gerhard Kittel and Gerhard Friedrich. Translated by Geoffrey W. Bromiley, 174–228. Grand Rapids, MI: William B. Eerdmans Publishing Company, 1968.

Burnet, George B. *The Holy Communion in the Reformed Church of Scotland: 1560–1960*. Edinburgh: Oliver and Boyd, 1960.

Butler, Sara. "Priestly Identity: 'Sacrament' of Christ the Head." *Worship* 70, no. 4 (July 1996): 290–306.

Calvin, John. "The Form of Church Prayers." In *Prayers of the Eucharist: Early and Reformed*, edited by Ronald Claud Dudley Jasper and Geoffrey J. Cuming, 250–57. Collegeville, MN: Liturgical Press, 1992.

———. *Institutes of the Christian Religion*. Edited by John T. McNeill. Translated by Ford Lewis Battles. Philadelphia: Westminster Press, 1960.

Calvin, Jean [John]. "Ordinances for the Supervision of Churches in the Country." In *Calvin: Theological Treatises*, edited and translated by John Kelman Sutherland Reid, 76–82. Library of Christian Classics. Vol. 22. Philadelphia: Westminster Press, 1954.

———. "Short Treatise on the Holy Supper of Our Lord and Only Saviour Jesus Christ." In *Calvin: Theological Treatises*, edited and translated by John Kelman Sutherland Reid, 140–66. Library of Christian Classics. Vol. 22. Philadelphia: Westminster Press, 1954.

Caputo, John D. *The Tears and Prayers of Jacques Derrida: Religion without Religion*. Bloomington: Indiana State University, 1997.

Cassirer, Ernst. *The Philosophy of Symbolic Forms*. Vol. 3. *The Phenomenology of Knowledge*. Translated by Ralph Manheim. New Haven, CT: Yale University Press, 1957.

The Catechism of the Catholic Church. London: Geoffrey Chapman, 1994.

Chauvet, Louis-Marie. "The Liturgy in Its Symbolic Space." In *Concilium*. Vol. 3. *Liturgy and the Body*, edited by Louis-Marie Chauvet and François Kabasele Lumbala, 29–39. London: SCM Press, 1995.

———. *The Sacraments: The Word of God at the Mercy of the Body*. Collegeville, MN: Liturgical Press, 2001.

———. *Symbol and Sacrament: A Sacramental Reinterpretation of Christian Existence*. Translated by Patrick Madigan and Madeleine E. Beaumont. Collegeville, MN: Liturgical Press, 1995.

Cheong, Geoff. "Sports Loving Australians: A Sacred Obsession." In *Sacred Australia: Post-Secular Considerations*, edited by Makarand Paranjape, 238–52. Melbourne: Clouds of Magellan, 2009.

Coffey, David. "The Common and Ordained Priesthood." *Theological Studies* 58, no. 2 (June 1997): 209–36.

Collins, Mary. "Critical Questions for Liturgical Theology." *Worship* 53, no. 4 (July 1979): 302–17.

Confession of Faith: The Larger Catechism, The Shorter Catechism, The Directory for Public Worship, and the Form of Presbyteral Church Government. Edinburgh and London: William Blackwood and Sons, 1955.

Cooke, Bernard J. "Body and Mystical Body: The Church as *Communio*." In *Bodies of Worship: Explorations in Theory and Practice*, edited by Bruce T. Morrill, 39–50. Collegeville, MN: Liturgical Press, 1999.

Cooke, Bernard J. *The Distancing of God: The Ambiguity of Symbol in History and Theology*. Minneapolis: Fortress Press, 1990.

———. *Ministry to Word and Sacraments: History and Theology*. Philadelphia: Fortress Press, 1976.

Cornford, Francis M. *Before and After Socrates*. Cambridge: Cambridge University Press, 1960.

Cox, Harvey. *The Secular City: Secularization and Urbanization in Theological Perspective*. London: SCM Press, 1965.

Crossan, John Dominic. *The Birth of Christianity*. San Francisco: HarperCollins, 1998.

Daly, Gabriel. "Protestant Principle and Catholic Substance." *Uniting Church Studies* 3, no. 2 (August 1997): 1–10.

Davies, Horton. *The Worship of the American Puritans, 1629–1730*. New York: Peter Lang, 1990.

Davies, John Gordon. *Every Day God: Encountering the Holy in World and Worship*. London: SCM Press, 1973.

Davis, Colin. *Levinas: An Introduction*. Cambridge: Polity Press, 1996.

Derrida, Jacques. *Margins of Philosophy*. Translated, with notes, by Alan Bass. Chicago: University of Chicago Press, 1982.

———. *Of Grammatology*. Translated by Gayatri Chakravorty Spivak. Baltimore and London: Johns Hopkins University Press, 1974.

Deverell, Gary. "Uniting in Worship? Proposals toward a Liturgical Ecumenics." *Uniting Church Studies* 11, no. 1 (March 2005): 21–36.

DeVries, Dawn. "Calvin's Preaching." In *The Cambridge Companion to John Calvin*, edited by Donald K. McKim, 106–24. New York: Cambridge University Press, 2004.

Dews, Peter. *The Limits of Disenchantment: Essays on Contemporary European Philosophy*. London and New York: Verso, 1995.

Dillard, Annie. *Holy the Firm*. New York: Bantam Books, 1979.

Douglas, Mary. *Natural Symbols: Explorations in Cosmology*. New York: Penguin Books, 1978.

Dowey, Edward A. *The Knowledge of God in Calvin's Theology*. New York: Columbia University Press, 1965.

Dunn, James D. G. "The Image of God False and True: A Sketch." In *Der Mensch vor Gott: Forschungen zum Menschenbild in Bibel, antikem Judentum und Koran* (Festschrift für Hermann Lichtenberger zum 60. Geburtstag), edited by Ulrike Mittmann–Riehert and others, 15–23. Neukirchen–Vluyn: Neukirchener Verlag, 2003.

———. "Jesus and Holiness: The Challenge of Purity." In *Holiness Past and Present*, edited by Stephen C. Barton, 168–192. London and New York: T&T Clark, 2003.

Dyrness, William A. *Reformed Theology and Visual Culture: The Protestant Imagination from Calvin to Edwards*. New York: Cambridge University Press, 2004.

Eagleton, Terry. *Criticism and Ideology: A Study in Marxist Literary Theory*. London: NLB, 1976.

———. *Ideology: An Introduction*. New York: Verso, 1991.

Ebeling, Gerhard. *Word and Faith*. Translated by James W. Leitch. London: SCM Press, 1963.

Edie, James M., ed. *The Primacy of Perception*. Evanston, IL: Northwestern University Press, 1964.

Eire, Carlos M. N. *War Against the Idols: The Reformation of Worship from Erasmus to Calvin*. Cambridge: Cambridge University Press, 1986.

Emilsen, William W., ed. *An Informed Faith: The Uniting Church at the Beginning of the Twenty-First Century*. Melbourne: Morning Star Publishing, 2014.

Emilsen, William W., and John T. Squires, eds. *Prayer and Thanksgiving: Essays in Honour of Rev. Dr. Graham Hughes*. Sydney: UTC Publications, 2003.

Empereur, James L. *Worship: Exploring the Sacred*. Washington, DC: Pastoral Press, 1987.

Flannery, Austin, ed. *The Basic Sixteen Documents of Vatican Council II: Constitutions and Declarations*. Northport, NY: Costello Publishing Company, 1996.

Ford, David F. *Self and Salvation: Being Transformed*. Cambridge: Cambridge University Press, 1999.

Freedberg, David. *The Power of Images: Studies in the History and Theory of Response*. Chicago: University of Chicago Press, 1991.

Frijhoff, Willem. "Witnesses to the Other: Incarnate Longings—Saints and Heroes, Idols and Models." *Studia Liturgica* 34, no.1 (2004): 1–25.

Führer, Werner. *Das Amt der Kirche: Das reformatorische Verständnis des geistlichen Amtes im ökumenischen Kontext*. Neuendettelsau: Freimund-Verlag, 2001.

Gallie, Walter Bryce. *Philosophy and the Historical Understanding*. New York: Schocken Books, 1968.

Gerrish, Brian A. *Grace and Gratitude: The Eucharistic Theology of John Calvin*. Eugene, OR: Wipf and Stock Publishers, 2002.

Gerth, Hans H., and C. Wright Mills, eds. *From Max Weber: Essays in Sociology*. London: Routledge & Kegan Paul, 1974.

Gribben, Robert. "The Future of Christianity?" *Uniting Church Studies* 18, no. 1 (June 2012): 1–12.

Griffith, Colleen M. "Spirituality and the Body." In *Bodies of Worship: Explorations in Theory and Practice*, edited by Bruce T. Morrill, 67–83. Collegeville, MN: Liturgical Press, 1999.

Habermas, Jürgen. *The Philosophical Discourse of Modernity: Twelve Lectures*. Translated by Frederick G. Lawrence. Cambridge, MA: MIT Press, 1995.

———. *Postmetaphysical Thinking*. Translated by William Mark Hohengarten. Cambridge, MA: MIT Press, 1992.

———. *The Theory of Communicative Action*. Vol. 2. *Lifeworld and System: A Critique of Functionalist Reason*. Translated by Thomas McCarthy. Cambridge: Polity Press, 1987.

Hardy, Daniel W. "Calvinism and the Visual Arts: A Theological Introduction." In *Seeing Beyond the Word: Visual Arts and the Calvinist Tradition*, edited by Paul Corby Finney, 1–18. Grand Rapids, MI: William B. Eerdmans Publishing Company, 1999.

———. *Finding the Church: The Dynamic Truth of Anglicanism*. London: SCM Press, 2001.

———. *God's Ways with the World: Thinking and Practising Christian Faith*. Edinburgh: T&T Clark, 1996.

———. "Worship and the Formation of a Holy People." In *Holiness Past and Present*, edited by Stephen C. Barton, 477–98. London and New York: T&T Clark, 2003.

———. "Worship as the Orientation of Life to God." *Ex Auditu* 8 (1992): 55–71.

Hardy, Daniel W., and David Ford. *Jubilate: Theology in Praise*. London: Darton, Longman & Todd, 1984.

Hare, Douglas R. A. *Matthew: Interpretation Bible Commentary for Teaching and Preaching*. Louisville, KY: John Knox Press, 1993.

Haskell, Dennis. "The Sardonic and the Sacred: Australian Identity and Australian Poetic Language." In *Sacred Australia: Post-Secular Considerations*, edited by Makarand Paranjape, 199–236. Melbourne: Clouds of Magellan, 2009.

Hauerwas, Stanley. "Facing Nothingness—Facing God." Chap. 7 in *Without Apology: Sermons for Christ's Church*. New York: Seabury Books, 2013.

Hefner, Philip. "*Imago Dei*: The Possibility and Necessity of the Human Person." In *The Human Person in Science and Theology*, edited by Niels Henrik Gregersen and others. Edinburgh: T&T Clark, 2000.

Heidegger, Martin. *Being and Time*. Translated by John Macquarrie and Edward Robinson. Oxford: Blackwell, 1962.

Herbert, George. "Praise (II)." In *The Complete English Poems*, edited by John Tobin, 137–38. New York: Penguin Books, 1991.

Heron, Alasdair. *Table and Tradition: Towards an Ecumenical Under-standing of the Eucharist.* Edinburgh: The Handsel Press, 1983.

Herzfeld, Noreen. *In Our Image: Artificial Intelligence and the Human Spirit.* Minneapolis: Augsburg Fortress, 2002.

Holifield, E. Brooks. *The Covenant Sealed: The Development of Puritan Sacramental Theology in Old and New England 1570–1720.* New Haven, CT: Yale University Press, 1974.

Horton, Michael A. "Participation and Covenant." In *Radical Orthodoxy and the Reformed Tradition: Creation, Covenant and Participation,* edited by James K. A. Smith and James H. Olthuis, 107–32. Grand Rapids, MI: Baker Academic, 2005.

Howard-Brook, Wes, and Anthony Gwyther. *Unveiling Empire: Reading Revelation Then and Now.* Maryknoll, NY: Orbis Books, 1999.

Hughes, Graham. "Limping Priests: Ministry and Ordination." *Uniting Church Studies* 8, no. 1 (March 2002): 1–13.

———. "The Uncertain Place of Materiality in the Reformed Tradition." *Uniting Church Studies* 17, no. 1 (June 2011): 97–109.

———. *Worship as Meaning: A Liturgical Theology for Late Modernity.* Cambridge: Cambridge University Press, 2003.

Husserl, Edmund. *Cartesian Meditations.* Translated by Dorion Cairns. Boston: Kluwer Academic Publishers, 1993.

Hutchison, William R. *The Modernist Impulse in American Protestantism.* Oxford: Oxford University Press, 1976.

Huyssteen, J. Wentzel van. *Are We Alone? Human Uniqueness in Science and Theology.* Grand Rapids, MI: William B. Eerdmans Publishing Company, 2006.

Irwin, Kevin W. "A Sacramental World—Sacramentality as the Primary Language for Sacraments." *Worship* 76, no. 3 (May 2002): 197–211.

Jameson, Frederic. "The Silence of the Real: Theology at the End of the Century." In *Theology at the End of the Century: A Dialogue on the Postmodern,* edited by Robert P. Scharlemann, 14–40. Charlottesville: University of Virginia Press, 1990.

Jenson, Robert W. *Systematic Theology.* Vol. 2. New York: Oxford University Press, 1999.

Johnson, Mark. *The Body in the Mind: The Bodily Basis of Meaning, Imagination and Reason.* Chicago: University of Chicago Press, 1987.

———. *The Meaning of the Body: Aesthetics of Human Understanding.* Chicago: University of Chicago Press, 2007.

Johnson, Maxwell E. "Can We Avoid Relativism in Worship? Liturgical Norms in the Light of Contemporary Liturgical Scholarship." *Worship* 74, no. 2 (March 2000): 135–55.

Jüngel, Eberhard. "Gott ist Liebe: Zur Unterscheidung von Glaube und Liebe." In *Festschrift für Ernst Fuchs*, edited by Gerhard Ebeling and others, 193–202. Tübingen: J. C. B. Mohr (Paul Siebeck), 1973.

Käsemann, Ernst. *Commentary on Romans*. Translated by Geoffrey William Bromiley. London: SCM Press, 1980.

———. *Essays on New Testament Themes*. Translated by W. J. Montague. London: SCM Press, 1964.

———. *Perspectives on Paul*. Translated by Margaret Kohl. London: SCM Press, 1971.

Kavanagh, Aidan. *On Liturgical Theology*. New York: Pueblo, 1984.

Keenan, James F. "Current Theology Note: Christian Perspectives on the Human Body." *Theological Studies* 55, no. 2 (June 1994): 330–46.

Kerr, Nathan R. "*Corpus Verum*: On the Ecclesial Recovery of Real Presence in John Calvin's Doctrine of the Eucharist." In *Radical Orthodoxy and the Reformed Tradition: Creation, Covenant and Participation*, edited by James K. A. Smith and James H. Olthuis, 229–242. Grand Rapids, MI: Baker Academic, 2005.

Kilmartin, Edward J. "Apostolic Office: Sacrament of Christ." *Theological Studies* 36, no. 2 (June 1975): 243–64.

Kristeva, Julia. *Revolution in Poetic Language*, with an introduction by Leon S. Roudiez. Translated by Margaret Waller. New York: Columbia University Press, 1984.

Kümmel, Werner Georg. *Introduction to the New Testament*. Translated by Howard Clark Kee (revised and updated translation of *Einleitung in das Neue Testament* by P. Feine and J. Behm). London: SCM Press, 1975.

Langemeyer, Bernhard. "Die Weisen der Gegenwart Christi im liturgischen Geschehen." In *Martyria, Leiturgia, Diakonia* (Festschrift für Hermann Volk, Bischof von Mainz, zum 65. Geburtstag), edited by Otto Semmelroth, 286–307. Mainz: Matthias–Grünewald–Verlag, 1968.

Lathrop, Gordon W. *The Four Gospels on Sunday: The New Testament and the Reform of Christian Worship*. Minneapolis: Augsburg Fortress, 2012.

———. *Holy Ground: A Liturgical Cosmology*. Minneapolis: Augsburg Fortress, 2003.

———. *Holy People: A Liturgical Ecclesiology*. Minneapolis: Augsburg Fortress, 1999.

———. *Holy Things: A Liturgical Theology*. Minneapolis: Augsburg Fortress, 1993.

Lechte, John. *Julia Kristeva*. London: Routledge, 1990.

Leenhardt, F. J. "This Is My Body." Chap. 2 in *Essays on the Lord's Supper*, edited by Oscar Cullmann and F. J. Leenhardt. London: Lutterworth Press, 1958.

Leeuw, Geradus van der. *Sakramentales Denken: Erscheinungsformen und Wesen der außerchristlichen und christlichen Sakramente*. Kassel: Johannes Stauda Verlag, 1959.

Lessing, Gotthold Ephraim. "On the Proof of the Spirit and of Power." In *Lessing: Philosophical and Theological Writings*, edited by Hugh Barr Nisbet, 83–88. Cambridge: Cambridge University Press, 2005.

Levinas, Emmanuel. *In the Time of the Nations*. Translated by Michael B. Smith. Bloomington: Indiana University Press, 1994.

———. "Is Ontology Fundamental?" In *Emmanuel Levinas: Basic Philosophical Writings*, edited by Adriaan T. Peperzak, Simon Critchley, and Robert Bernasconi, 1–10. Bloomington: Indiana University Press, 1996.

———. "Meaning and Sense." In *Emmanuel Levinas: Basic Philosophical Writings*, edited by Adriaan T. Peperzak, Simon Critchley, and Robert Bernasconi, 33–64. Bloomington: Indiana University Press, 1996.

———. *Totality and Infinity: An Essay of Exteriority*. Translated by Alphonso Lingis. Pittsburgh: Duquesne University Press, 1969.

———. "The Trace of the Other." In *Deconstruction in Context: Literature and Philosophy*, edited by Mark C. Taylor, 345–59. Chicago: University of Chicago Press, 1986.

———. "Transcendence and Height." In *Emmanuel Levinas: Basic Philosophical Writings*, edited by Adriaan T. Peperzak, Simon Critchley, and Robert Bernasconi, 11–32. Bloomington: Indiana University Press, 1996.

Living Stones—Theological Guidelines for Uniting Church Worship Buildings. Melbourne: The UCA Synod of Victoria Office of the General Secretary, Property, Insurance Services, 1997.

Louth, Andrew. "The Body in Western Catholic Christianity." In *Religion and the Body*, edited by Sarah Coakley, 111–30. Cambridge: Cambridge University Press, 1997.

Luther, Martin. "Sermon at the Dedication of the Castle Church in Torgau, Luke 14:1-11, October 5, 1544." In *Luther's Works*, edited by Jaroslav Pelikan and Helmut T. Lehmann, vol. 51, *Sermons, I*, edited and translated by John W. Doberstein, 331–54. Philadelphia: Muhlenberg Press, 1959.

———. "The Blessed and Holy Sacrament of Baptism, 1519." In Hans J. Hillerbrand, Kirsi I. Stjerna, and Timothy J. Wengert, general eds., *The Annotated Luther*, vol. 1, *The Roots of Reform*, edited by Timothy J. Wengert, 207–23. Minneapolis: Fortress Press, 2015.

Lyotard, Jean-François. *The Postmodern Condition: A Report on Knowledge*. Translated by Geoff Bennington and Brian Massumi. Foreword by Fredric Jameson. Minneapolis: University of Minnesota Press, 1984.

Marion, Jean-Luc. "The Idol and the Icon." Chap. 1 in *God without Being*, translated by Thomas A. Carlson, with a foreword by David Tracy. Chicago: University of Chicago Press, 1991.

Martimort, Aimé Georges. "Structure and Laws of the Liturgical Celebration." Section 2 in *The Church at Prayer: Principles of the Liturgy*, edited by Aimé Georges Martimort. Collegeville, MN: Liturgical Press, 1987.

Marx, Karl, and Friedrich Engels. *The German Ideology*. Edited with an introduction by C. J. Arthur. London: Lawrence and Wishart, 1970.

Mays, James L. "The Self in the Psalms and the Image of God." In *Preaching and Teaching the Psalms*, edited by Patrick D. Miller and Gene M. Tucker, 51–67. Louisville, KY: Westminster John Knox Press, 2006.

McAuley, James. *Collected Poems 1936–1970*. Sydney: Angus and Robertson Publishers, 1971.

McDonald, Lee M. *The Formation of the Christian Biblical Canon*. Peabody, MA: Hendrickson Publishers, 1995.

McGowan, John. *Postmodernism and Its Critics*. Ithaca, NY: Cornell University Press, 1991.

McGrath, Alister. *Evangelicalism and the Future of Christianity*. Downers Grove, IL: Intervarsity, 1996.

———. *The Future of Christianity*. Oxford: Blackwell Manifestos, 2002.

Mehl, Roger. *The Sociology of Protestantism*. London: SCM Press, 1970.

Menke, Karl-Heinz. *Sakramentalität: Wesen und Wunde des Katholizismus*. 2nd ed. Regensburg: Verlag Friedrich Pustet, 2012.

Mentzer, Raymond A., Jr. "The Reformed Churches of France and the Visual Arts." In *Seeing Beyond the Word: Visual Arts and the Calvinist Tradition*, edited by Paul Corby Finney, 200–210. Grand Rapids, MI: William B. Eerdmans Publishing Company, 1999.

Merleau-Ponty, Maurice. *Phenomenology of Perception*. Translated by Colin Smith. London: Routledge, 1962.

———. *The Primacy of Perception: And Other Essays on Phenomenology Psychology, the Philosophy of Art, History, and Politics*. Edited with an introduction by James E. Edie. Evanston, IL: Northwestern University Press, 1964.

Middleton, J. Richard. *The Liberating Image: The* Imago Dei *in Genesis 1*. Grand Rapids, MI: Brazos Press, 2005.

Mitchell, Nathan D. *Meeting Mystery: Liturgy, Worship, Sacraments*. Maryknoll, NY: Orbis Books, 2006.

———. "Negotiating Rapture." *Worship* 71, no. 4 (July 1997): 350–57.

Moore, Gerard. "Sacramentality: An Australian Perspective." In *Christian Worship in Australia: Inculturating the Liturgical Tradition*, edited by Stephen Burns and Anita Monro, 139–53. Strathfield: St Pauls Publications, 2009.

Moule, Charles Francis Digby. *The Phenomenon of the New Testament: An Inquiry into the Implications of Certain Features of the New Testament*. London: SCM Press, 1967.

Murphy, Nancey. *Bodies and Souls, or Spirited Bodies?* Cambridge: Cambridge University Press, 2006.

Murphy, Peter. "Sacred Icon: Jørn Utzon's Sydney Opera House." In *Sacred Australia: Post-Secular Considerations*, edited by Makarand Paranjape, 287–305. Melbourne: Clouds of Magellan, 2009.

Naphy, William G. "Calvin's Geneva." In *The Cambridge Companion to John Calvin*, edited by Donald K. McKim, 25–38. Cambridge: Cambridge University Press, 2004.

Nelson, Richard D. *Raising Up a Faithful Priest: Community and Priesthood in Biblical Theology*. Louisville, KY: Westminster John Knox Press, 1993.

Nichols, Bridget. *Liturgical Hermeneutics: Interpreting Liturgical Rites in Performance*. Frankfurt: Peter Lang, 1994.

Noll, Ray R. *Sacraments: A New Understanding for a New Generation*. Mystic, CT: Twenty-Third Publications, 2003.

Osborne, Kenan B. *Christian Sacraments in a Postmodern World: A Theology for the Third Millennium*. New York: Paulist Press, 1999.

Pannenberg, Wolfhart. *Jesus—God and Man*. Translated by Lewis L. Wilkins and Duane A. Priebe. London: SCM Press, 1969.

———. *Systematic Theology*. Vol. 1. Grand Rapids, MI: William B. Eerdmans Publishing Company, 1991.

Paranjape, Makarand. "Preface." In *Sacred Australia: Post-Secular Considerations*, edited by Makarand Paranjape, ix–xiii. Melbourne: Clouds of Magellan, 2009.

———. "A Passage to Uluru: Rethinking Sacred Australia." In *Sacred Australia: Post-Secular Considerations*, edited by Makarand Paranjape, 1–20. Melbourne: Clouds of Magellan, 2009.

———, ed. *Sacred Australia: Post-Secular Considerations*. Melbourne: Clouds of Magellan, 2009.

Pelikan, Jaroslav. *The Spirit of Eastern Christendom (600–1700)*. Chicago: University of Chicago Press, 1974.

Pesch, Otto Hermann. "Kernpunkte der Kontroverse: Die antireformatorischen Lehrentscheidungen des Konzils von Trient (1545–1563)—und die Folgen." In *Zur Zukunft der Ökumene: Die "Gemeinsame Erklä-rung zur Rechtfertigungslehre,"* edited by Bernd Jochen Hilberath and Wolfhart Pannenberg, 24–57. Regensburg: Verlag Friedrich Pustet, 1999.

Pettegree, Andrew. "The Spread of Calvin's Thought." In *The Cambridge Companion to John Calvin*, edited by Donald K. McKim, 207–24. Cambridge: Cambridge University Press, 2004.

Pickard, Stephen. *Theological Foundations for Collaborative Ministry.* Farnham, UK, and Burlington, VT: Ashgate, 2009.

Pilcher, Carmel. "Poinsettia: Christmas or Pentecost—Celebrating Liturgy in the Great South Land That Is Australia." *Worship* 81, no. 6 (November 2007): 508–20.

Polanyi, Michael, and Harry Prosch. *Meaning.* Chicago: University of Chicago Press, 1975.

Polkinghorne, John. *Science and Theology: An Introduction.* London and Minneapolis: SPCK and Fortress Press, 1998.

Power, David N. "Church Order: The Need for Redress." *Worship* 71, no. 4 (July 1997): 296–309.

———. "Representing Christ in Community and Sacrament." In *Being a Priest Today*, edited by Donald J. Goergan, 97–123. Collegeville, MN: Liturgical Press, 1992.

———. *Sacrament: The Language of God's Giving.* New York: Crossroad, 1999.

Putnam, Hilary. *Realism with a Human Face.* Cambridge, MA: Harvard University Press, 1990.

Rad, Gerhard von. *Genesis: A Commentary.* Translated by John H. Marks. London: SCM Press, 1972.

———. "εἰκών." In *Theological Dictionary of the New Testament*, edited by Gerhard Kittel, vol. 2, translated and edited by Geoffrey W. Bromiley, 390–92. Grand Rapids, MI: William B. Eerdmans Publishing Company, 1964.

———. *Old Testament Theology.* Vol. 1. Translated by D. M. G. Stalker. London: SCM Press, 1975.

Rahner, Karl. *The Church and the Sacraments.* Translated by W. J. O'Hara. New York: Herder and Herder, 1964.

———. "Considerations on the Active Role of the Person in the Sacramental Event." Chap. 10 in *Theological Investigations*, vol. 14, translated by David Bourke. London: Darton, Longman & Todd, 1976.

———. "On the Theology of Worship." Chap 10 in *Theological Investigations*, vol. 19, translated by Edward Quinn. New York: Crossroad, 1983.

Ricoeur, Paul. *The Conflict of Interpretations: Essays in Hermeneutics.* Evanston, IL: Northwestern University Press, 1974.

————. *History and Truth*. Translated and with an introduction by Charles A. Kelbley. Evanston, IL: Northwestern University Press, 1965.

————. *Husserl: An Analysis of His Phenomenology*. Translated by Edward G. Ballard and Lester E. Embree. Evanston, IL: Northwestern University Press, 1967.

————. *Lectures on Ideology and Utopia*. Edited by George H. Taylor. New York: Columbia University Press, 1986.

————. *Oneself as Another*. Translated by Kathleen Blamey. Chicago: University of Chicago Press, 1992.

————. "The Symbol: Food for Thought." *Philosophy Today* 4, nos. 3–4 (Fall 1960): 196–207.

Rogerson, John. "What Is Holiness?" In *Holiness Past and Present*, edited by Stephen C. Barton, 3–21. London and New York: T&T Clark, 2003.

Ruben, Miri. *Corpus Christi: The Eucharist in Late Medieval Culture*. Cambridge: Cambridge University Press, 1991.

Ruth, Lester. "Lex Agendi, Lex Orandi: Toward an Understanding of Seeker Services as a New Kind of Liturgy." *Worship* 70, no. 5 (September 1996): 386–405.

————. "Reconsidering the Emergence of the Second Great Awakening and Camp Meetings Among Early Methodists." *Worship* 75, no. 4 (July 2001): 334–55.

Saliers, Don E. *Worship as Theology: Foretaste of Divine Glory*. Nashville: Abingdon Press, 1994.

Schillebeeckx, Edward. *Jesus: An Experiment in Christology*. Translated by Hubert Hoskins. New York: Crossroad, 1981.

————. *Christ the Sacrament of the Encounter with God*. Translated by Paul Barrett and N. D. Smith. English text revised by Mark Schoof and Laurence Bright. Kansas City, MO: Sheed and Ward, 1963.

————. *The Eucharist*. Translated by N. D. Smith. London: Sheed and Ward, 1968.

Schmemann, Alexander. *The Eucharist: Sacrament of the Kingdom*. Crestwood, NY: St Vladimir's Seminary Press, 1988.

————. "Theology and Liturgical Tradition." In *Worship in Scripture and Tradition*, edited by Massey H. Shepherd, 165–78. New York: Oxford University Press, 1963. Reprinted in *Liturgy and Tradition: Theological Reflections of Alexander Schmemann*, edited by Thomas Fisch, 1–20. Crestwood, NY: St Vladimir's Seminary Press, 1990.

Schweizer, Eduard. *Church Order in the New Testament*. London: SCM Press, 1961.

Senn, Frank C. "'Worship Alive': An Analysis and Critique of 'Alternative Worship Services.'" *Worship* 69, no. 3 (May 1995): 194–224.

Seubert, Xavier John. "The Trivialization of Matter: Development of Ritual Incapacity." *Worship* 67, no. 1 (January 1993): 38–53.

Shagan, Ethan H. *Popular Politics and the English Reformation.* Cambridge: Cambridge University Press, 2003.

Shults, F. LeRon. *Reforming Theological Anthropology: After the Philosophical Turn to Relationality.* Grand Rapids, MI: William B. Eerdmans Publishing Company, 2003.

Skelley, Michael. "The Liturgy of the World and the Liturgy of the Church: Karl Rahner's Idea of Worship." *Worship* 63, no. 2 (March 1989): 112–32.

Skudlarek, William. *The Word in Worship: Preaching in Liturgical Context.* Nashville: Abingdon Press, 1981.

Smart, Ninian. *The Concept of Worship.* London: Macmillan Press, 1972.

Smit, Laura. "'The Depth Behind Things': Toward a Calvinist Sacramental Theology." In *Radical Orthodoxy and the Reformed Tradition: Creation, Covenant and Participation,* edited by James K. A. Smith and James H. Olthuis, 205–27. Grand Rapids, MI: Baker Academic, 2005.

Smith, James K. A. *Desiring the Kingdom: Worship, Worldview, and Cultural Formation.* Grand Rapids, MI: Baker Academic, 2009.

———. *Imagining the Kingdom: How Worship Works.* Cultural Liturgies Series. Vol. 2. Grand Rapids, MI: Baker Academic, 2013.

Smith, James K. A., and James H. Olthuis, eds. *Radical Orthodoxy and the Reformed Tradition: Creation, Covenant and Participation.* Grand Rapids, MI: Baker Academic, 2005.

Stancliffe, David. "The Making of the Church of England's *Common Worship.*" *Studia Liturgica* 31, no. 1 (2001): 14–25.

Starr, George. "Art and Architecture in the Hungarian Reformed Church." In *Seeing Beyond the Word: Visual Arts and the Calvinist Tradition,* edited by Paul Corby Finney, 200–210. Grand Rapids, MI: William B. Eerdmans Publishing Company, 1999.

Stephens, W. Peter. *The Theology of Huldrych Zwingli.* Oxford: Clarendon, 1986.

Tacey, David. "Spirituality in Australia Today." In *Sacred Australia: Post-Secular Considerations,* edited by Makarand Paranjape, 44–64. Melbourne: Clouds of Magellan, 2009.

Tamburello, Dennis E. "Calvin and Sacramentality: A Catholic Perspective." In *John Calvin and Roman Catholicism: Critique and Engagement, Then and Now,* edited by Randall C. Zachman, 193–215. Grand Rapids, MI: Baker Academic, 2008.

Taylor, Charles. *A Secular Age.* Cambridge, MA: Belknap Press of Harvard University Press, 2007.

————. *Sources of the Self: The Making of the Modern Identity*. Cambridge: Cambridge University Press, 1989.

Tillich, Paul. "Dynamics of Faith." In *Paul Tillich: Main Works*, edited by Carl Heinz Ratschow, vol. 5, *Writings on Religion*, edited by Robert P. Scharlemann, 231–90. Berlin and New York: Walter de Gruyter, 1988.

————. "The Permanent Significance of the Catholic Church for Protestantism." In *Paul Tillich: Main Works*, edited by Carl Heinz Ratschow, vol. 6. *Theological Writings*, edited by Gert Hummel, 235–45. Berlin and New York: Walter de Gruyter, 1992.

————. *The Protestant Era*. Abridged edition. Translated by James Luther Adams. Chicago: University of Chicago Press, 1957.

————. *The Protestant Era*. Translated and with a concluding essay by James Luther Adams. Chicago: University of Chicago Press, 1948.

————. "The Recovery of the Prophetic Tradition in the Reformation." In *Paul Tillich: Main Works*, edited by Carl Heinz Ratschow, vol. 6, *Theological Writings*, edited by Gert Hummel, 319–61. Berlin and New York: Walter de Gruyter, 1992.

————. *Systematic Theology*. Vol. 3. London: James Nisbet and Co., 1964.

Toulmin, Stephen. *Cosmopolis: The Hidden Agenda of Modernity*. Chicago: University of Chicago Press, 1992.

Tripp, David. "The Image of the Body in the Formative Phases of the Protestant Reformation." In *Religion and the Body*, edited by Sarah Coakley, 131–52. Cambridge: Cambridge University Press, 1997.

Troeger, Thomas H. *The Parable of Ten Preachers*. Nashville: Abingdon Press, 1992.

————. Unpublished lecture: "The Landscape of the Heart: The Function of the Conventional Imagination in Worship." Given at United Theological College, North Parramatta, Sydney, on 15 August 1995.

Turner, Bryan S. "The Body in Western Society: Social Theory and Its Perspectives." In *Religion and the Body*, edited by Sarah Coakley, 15–41. Cambridge: Cambridge University Press, 1997.

Vorgrimler, Herbert. *Sacramental Theology*. Translated by Linda M. Maloney. Collegeville, MN: Liturgical Press, 1992.

Wainwright, Geoffrey. *Eucharist and Eschatology*. London: Epworth, 1971.

Wardlaw, Don M. "Realigning the Three Languages in Worship." *Reformed Liturgy and Music* 21, no. 1 (Winter 1987): 21–24.

Ware, Kallistos. "'My Helper and My Enemy': The Body in Greek Christianity." In *Religion and the Body*, edited by Sarah Coakley, 90–110. Cambridge: Cambridge University Press, 1997.

Webb, Val. "Is It Permissible to Ask Why We Ordain at All?" *Uniting Church Studies* 3, no. 1 (March 1997): 13–38.

Weber, Max. *Economy and Society: An Outline of Interpretive Sociology.* Edited by Guenther Roth and Klaus Wittich. Translated by Ephraim Fischoff and others. Berkeley: University of California Press, 1978.

———. *The Protestant Ethic and the Spirit of Capitalism.* Translated by Talcott Parsons, with an introduction by Anthony Giddens. New York: Routledge, 1992.

Welch, Lawrence J. "Priestly Identity Reconsidered: A Reply to Susan Wood." *Worship* 70, no. 4 (July 1996): 307–19.

White, James F. "From Protestant to Catholic Plain Style." In *Seeing Beyond the Word: Visual Arts and the Calvinist Tradition*, edited by Paul Corby Finney, 457–76. Grand Rapids, MI: William B. Eerdmans Publishing Company, 1999.

———. "How Do We Know It Is Us?" In *Liturgy and the Moral Self: Humanity at Full Stretch before God; Essays in Honor of Don E. Saliers*, edited by E. Byron Anderson and Bruce T. Morrill, 55–65. Collegeville, MN: Liturgical Press, 1998.

———. *The Sacraments in Protestant Practice and Faith.* Nashville: Abingdon Press, 1999.

White, Susan J. *Christian Worship and Technological Change.* Nashville: Abingdon Press, 1994.

Willey, Basil. *The Seventeenth Century Background.* Harmondsworth: Penguin Books, 1962.

Wood, Susan K. "Priestly Identity: Sacrament of the Ecclesial Community." *Worship* 69, no. 2 (March 1995): 109–27.

Wordsworth, William. *The Poetical Works of William Wordsworth.* London and Edinburgh: William P. Nimmo, 1878.

Wright, David E. "Calvin's Role in Church History." In *The Cambridge Companion to John Calvin*, edited by Donald K. McKim, 277–88. Cambridge: Cambridge University Press, 2004.

Zachman, Randall C. "Jesus Christ as the Image of God in Calvin's Theology." *Calvin Theological Journal* 25, no. 1 (April 1990): 45–62.

Index

accommodation, xxiv, 98, 126, 128, 132 n. 71

alterity, xxv, xxviii–xxx, xxxiii, xxxiv, xxxvii, xl, xli, xlviii–li, 17, 19, 22, 25, 68–71, 129, 134, 136, 142, 147, 149, 150, 172

Anglican, 46, 167 n. 3, 171

Anglicanism, xiii, 146

aniconic, 2, 3, 6, 7, 20, 116, 136

Anderson, E. Byron, 175

antimaterialism, 95

antimaterialist, xl, 117, 125

Aston, Margaret, 58

autonomy, 28, 29, 73, 76

baptism, viii, ix, xxxviii, xlii–xliv, xlvi, xlvii, 1, 12, 88, 89, 127, 135, 157, 173, 174, 176, 179–83, 185–90

Bell, Catherine, 24, 168, 169

Berkouwer, Gerrit Cornelis, 71, 73 n. 144

Best Account, xvi, xx, xxxii, xxxiii, xxxvi

Boersma, Hans, 2

Bonhoeffer, Dietrich, 22, 134, 172

Bucer, Martin, 122

Bullinger, Heinrich, 122

Calvin, John, ix, xxxi, xxxviii, xl, xlv, xlix, l, 17, 21 n. 60, 26, 44 n. 32, 58, 61, 72 n. 144, 77 n. 169, 84, 86, 91–103, 108–11, 117–28, 130, 136, 140, 141, 145–47, 150, 166, 178, 185, 186

Calvinism, 18, 26, 91, 103, 104, 115 n. 8

Calvinist, 92, 115, 152, 166 n. 27

Calvinists, xxxi, 59

Cassirer, Ernst, 125 n. 51, 162 n. 19

catechism, 77, 173

catholic, 4, 22, 145

Catholic, viii, ix, xiii, xliv n. 152, 13, 18, 33, 52, 93, 97, 102, 103, 145 n. 113, 166 n. 27, 169, 170, 173, 174, 175 n. 52, 185, 189

early, 9, 14, 23

Roman, xxii, xxix, xxxviii, 2, 21 n. 60, 88 n. 198, 121 n. 25, 142, 143, 161, 167 n. 31, 168 n. 32, 180

substance, 117, 170

Catholicism, 88 n. 198, 94, 113, 176

early, xlvii, 6, 8, 11, 169

medieval, 93 n. 6

Roman, 114 n. 6, 146, 204

Catholics, 110, 113, 115, 117, 124 n. 41, 144, 176, 185

Roman, xxii, xxix, xxxviii, 21 n. 60

charismatic, 6, 7, 8, 169 n. 35

Chauvet, Louis-Marie, xlv, 13, 14, 18–22, 34, 52, 133, 138

Cheong, Geoff, 105